DATE DUE

~~DE 3 '97~~		
~~DE 19 '97~~		
~~DE 1 0 '00~~		
~~AP 18 '02~~		
~~AP 8 '02~~		
~~NO 1 9 '03~~		
~~AG 1 2 '09~~		

DEMCO 38-296

A Gathering of Voices on
The Asian American Experience

A Gathering of Voices on The Asian American Experience

Edited by

Annette White-Parks
Deborah D. Buffton
Ursula Chiu
Catherine M. Currier
Cecilia G. Manrique
Marsha Momoi Piehl

Highsmith PRESS
Fort Atkinson, Wisconsin

Published by Highsmith Press
W5527 Highway 106
P.O. Box 800
Fort Atkinson, Wisconsin 53538-0800

1-800-558-2110

Library of Congress Cataloging in Publication
A Gathering of voices on the Asian American experience / edited by
　Annette White-Parks ... [et al.].

　　　p.　　cm.

　　Includes bibliographical references (p.) and index.

　　ISBN 0-917846-26-5

　　1. Asian Americans--Congresses.　I. White Parks, Annette.

E184.06G38 1994
973' .0495--dc20　　　　　　　　　　　　　　　94-28517

Contents

Contents

Introduction

On March 23-25, 1993, the University of Wisconsin - La Crosse hosted a most successful National Asian American conference on our campus, a conference sponsored by the University of Wisconsin System as part of their Design for Diversity program. This publication is an outgrowth of that conference. All conference participants had the opportunity to submit their papers for consideration, and, from those submitted, an editorial board selected the twenty-six papers that compose this book's contents.

The selections you will find here represent the variety of subjects and ideas, interests and perspectives, generated by the conference. To clarify to readers the sense of an overall theme, some background is helpful. In the early stages of planning, our first task—at that time, as a program committee—was to establish a conference focus. This focus is voiced in the conference title, "Asian Americans: Probing the Past, Living the Present, Shaping the Future" and reflects dominant themes of both the conference and this book. We were unanimous in our commitment to the following goals: representation of diverse Asian American ethnic populations and class situations, equitable inclusion by gender, concentration on community as well as academic issues, participation from broad geographic regions and varied subject interests.

The program that resulted was especially strong, with a dynamic variety of paper and session topics. That the conference was successful from the views of its participants was obvious in the tremendous energy of the sessions, the enthusiastic networking that continued among participants on their planes going home, and the positive comments we received on post-conference evaluations.

One major reason for the excitement among both those who planned and those who attended was the great diversity among keynote speakers, panelists, and audience. This diversity is reflected in the broadly national and international nature of conference registrants, who came from most states in the nation as well as from other countries. Moreover, a wide range of different Asian American groups attended—Hmong, Filipino, Chinese, Indian, Japanese, etc.—as well as non-Asian Americans. Presentations from high school, and college students, community leaders and members, as well as academics, allowed the conference to enjoy the inclusiveness that had been a major goal of the planning committee from the beginning.

The outcome was a gathering of voices which inspired the title of this volume. While we do not presume to cover all issues affecting Asian Americans, we believe the conference was in touch with many of the issues facing Asian Americans today. Some of these issues are represented in the six sections that follow: Between Tradition and Change; Self-identity; Insider/Outsider Perspectives; Educational Challenges; Popular Culture; and Clash of Cultures. Our editorial policy throughout this volume is to spell Asian American without the hyphen.

Acknowledgments

We wish to thank the Asian Americans of Wisconsin Organization for providing the idea and impetus for a National Asian American Conference, the University of Wisconsin System for sponsoring it, and our Chancellor Judith L. Kuipers for bringing it to the University of Wisconsin-La Crosse campus. We would also like to acknowledge Tom Gushiken, Conference Coordinator; Penny Tiedt, who has handled all our correspondence and material arrangements with an efficiency and sensitivity that is still bringing in compliments from conference registrants, and Mary Lynum, student assistant. Finally, we want to express our appreciation to everyone who participated in the conference, both on our home campus and from other places, with a special thanks to presenters. While not all presentations could be included in this anthology, it is our intent to capture the spirit and enthusiasm to which all contributed, within these pages.

Between Tradition and Change

This section concerns the challenges and tensions that result from being a part of two different cultures, each with different values and customs. In particular, second generation Asian Americans often find themselves torn between the costs and the benefits of adopting the new "American" culture and giving up or altering their old "Asian" ways. While changing to fit a dominant white U.S. culture may earn Asian Americans acceptance within that society, it also can cause conflict with fellow Asian Americans, and undermine the values of the "Asian" side of their identity. In the process of adapting to new values, old cultural values can be lost. The difficulties affect, among other things, child-rearing practices, education, language use, political participation, social mobility, and one's sense of patriotic duty, as reflected in the five papers included in this section.

Michael Ferris studied one aspect of the degree to which Hmong residents of La Crosse, Wisconsin, had assimilated into U.S. culture: their political participation. His paper suggests that despite their low socioeconomic status and educational levels, the Hmong are relatively active in local, if not national, politics. In that sense, they are atypical of the majority of eligible voters in the U.S. who choose not to vote or to become involved in politics.

Ray Hutchinson studies a group of Hmong people living in Green Bay, Wisconsin, to determine the degree to which they are literate in English, and how literacy cuts across generational lines. He concludes that, while the next generation of Hmong children will most likely use

English as its main language, giving up the original language may not necessarily translate into improvements in social status, since other factors, including discrimination, may limit opportunities to move up the social ladder.

Christian Ghasarian reveals how Hindu immigrants in the San Francisco Bay area attempt to reconcile the concept of hierarchy that is characteristic of their Indian culture with the idea of equality found in the U.S. Accommodation to U.S. culture requires them to revise their perceptions of cultural values in both societies.

Susan Adler's study of Japanese American child-rearing and education practices reveals the questions and problems that arise from trying to combine two different cultural backgrounds. How are race, ethnicity, and gender perceived in each culture, and how do those perceptions affect the ways children are raised? When the two cultural backgrounds conflict, how does one choose which takes precedence? And finally, in a nation of immigrants, what does it mean to be "American?" Can there be, necessarily, one definition of the term?

Finally, Yufeng Wang's examination of Chinese American servicemen during World War II reveals yet another way some Asian American groups have sought to assimilate and gain acceptance in the U.S. While their experience may have improved their social and legal status in the U.S., it was not without its costs, as the decision to fight for a country that discriminated against them was an agonizing one.

1

A Study of Political Participation in a Hmong Community

Michael Ferris

Introduction

The community of La Crosse, Wisconsin, is home to approximately 2,500 Hmong immigrants. These refugees, imbued with a sense of independence and self-reliance, have fled the relatively simple society of Laos and emigrated to a technologically modern society whose language and customs differ radically from their own. Like the many immigrant groups before them, the Hmong are slowly assimilating into American society as they increasingly learn and understand the language, laws, and customs of this nation. While the difficulties that the Hmong have faced during assimilation have been thoroughly documented, little research has been done in the field of Hmong political awareness and participation in the United States.[1] This paper will examine the extent of political participation among the Hmong in La Crosse and determine some of the variables which facilitate their active involvement in the political process.

Methodology

The author prepared a questionnaire based on Verba and Nie's survey[2] and distributed it to forty Hmong aged 19–54 over a six week period from early November to mid December, 1992. These participants included college students, members of English classes held at the local technical college, and a local church friendship center.

Unaware of whether the extent of Hmong political activity would be less than, or more than, that of Americans in general, I took an uncommon approach to my research design and formed two political participation hypotheses to test. These hypotheses were formulated by using two sets

3

of assumptions based on results of American political participation studies and my own knowledge of the Hmong.[3]

These studies found a positive relationship between political participation and the independent variables education[4] and socioeconomic status.[5] Since many of the Hmong are unemployed and dependent on government assistance while learning English and/or job skills, their socioeconomic status is low. In addition, many have little or no formal education, few have graduated from high school and even fewer have attended college. These two factors formed the basis of the first hypothesis: Hmong political participation would be relatively low when compared to our reference study.

On the other hand, the Hmong are relatively untainted by the cynicism and apathy that have engendered a weak sense of political efficacy[6] among many Americans. According to Verba and Nie, most Americans feel that the return (i.e., perceived benefits) on time invested does not warrant their active participation with the exception of voting.[7] Another study reported that individuals are more likely to have confidence in their capacity to affect change at a local level than at a national level.[8] Campbell, et.al., have noted the positive relationship between one's sense of political efficacy and participation.[9] The Hmong's strong sense of self-determination and independence, as reflected in the tremendous progress that they have made adjusting to U.S. society, would seem to indicate a strong sense of personal efficacy. Would this carry over into the political arena? As members of a low socioeconomic class, they would also have more to gain from active involvement. Based on this set of factors, my second hypothesis states Hmong political participation would be relatively high.

I quantified average political activity by adding the percentages of affirmative responses from Verba and Nie's survey (upon which my survey is based) to form a reference point of 287 with which to compare the results of my study. Any total from the survey of the Hmong within five percentage points of this reference was considered average political activity, while totals outside this range indicated either high or low activity.

Findings

The sum of my survey results was 397, thus indicating a relatively high level of political participation by the Hmong community in La Crosse. All of the Hmong participants in my study[10] who are U.S. citizens (seven of 40 respondents) are not only registered to vote, but do so in both local and national elections. This 100 percent voter turnout contrasts sharply with our reference which indicates 47 percent of Americans vote in local elections and 52 percent vote in national elections. This would seem to indicate that our newest citizens place a high value on their civil rights and probably reflect the Hmong community's sense of self-determination.

Overall, most Hmong do not have a high level of interest in national and local politics. Of those respondents who indicated 'high' and 'very high' interest in politics, it appears they have a greater interest in local politics than in national politics. This local interest is evidenced by the high participation of Hmong who work to solve community problems. I will examine this participation in greater detail shortly.

Similarly, most Hmong are not highly knowledgeable about American politics and government. There appears to be a direct relation between the Hmong's self-described knowledge of American politics, with 55 percent describing their knowledge as 'low' or 'very low' and self-described fluency in English, again 55 percent saying that their fluency is low. This would appear to correlate with the fact that 62.5 percent have not completed high school. The Hmong seem to realize the importance of formal education which accounts for their determination to learn English and the emphasis that Hmong parents place upon their children's education.[12]

The sources of their political knowledge therefore provide little surprise with 75 percent citing school as the most common source, followed by electronic media (47.5 percent), family and friends (42.5 percent) and, lastly, print media and books tied at 37.5 percent. I was somewhat surprised to see that 70 percent indicated that they watched less than ten hours of television per week as compared to the average weekly television viewing time of over 27 hours for the rest of American society.[13]

Examining political affiliation, I found that 92.5 percent did not belong to any political party and 47.5 percent did not identify with any party. Of the 21 individuals who did identify with a political party, 80 percent identified with the Democratic party, 14 percent identified with an unspecified party and only 4 percent identified with the Republican party. This probably can be attributed to the perception that Democrats are less likely to cut spending on social programs that affect the Hmong. In addition, the Democratic party typically attracts those of lower income and the survey indicates that half of the respondents have an annual income of less than $10,000. Very few of the respondents have attended party rallies or worked or donated money to a party or candidate.[14]

Despite the low knowledge and interest in American government and politics, a large number of Hmong are involved in dealing with community problems. Forty-five percent (45 percent) of the respondents said they belong to organizations that deal with community problems. Even more work with others in solving community problems (52.5 percent). Forty percent (40 percent) have attended a government meeting within the last three years. Historically, many immigrant groups have been actively involved in solving problems concerning their community as they struggled to survive in their new home. It will be interesting to see how these levels of participation change as the Hmong are further integrated into American mainstream society.

Conclusions

Based upon the findings, my first hypothesis is disconfirmed, for despite low socioeconomic status and a lack of education, the Hmong are relatively active in politics.

My second hypothesis is confirmed. The Hmong's sense of political efficacy is reflected in the percentage of eligible voters who vote in both local and national elections. This contrasts sharply with the typical attitude among many Americans that their vote "doesn't count." The high percentage of Hmong who participate in community activities, which usually demand more time and effort, indicates the value they place on political activity relative to other activities. This may also reflect the fact that political efficacy is higher at local levels.

Acknowledgments

First and foremost, my thanks goes out to Dr. Cecilia Manrique whose guidance, encouragement and insight proved to be invaluable. In addition, I am very grateful to Denis Tucker of the Hmong Mutual Assistance Association, Nhia Vang of Western Wisconsin Technical College and Lisbeth Reynertson of the La Crosse Friendship Program for giving directions and opening doors that gave this project a greater scope than would have otherwise been possible. Clinton Bast deserves my gratitude for survey distribution and word processing help as does Dr. Deborah Buffton for last second editorial guidance. Finally I would like to thank all of the respondents to the survey for taking the time to fill them out.

Notes

1. Glenn Hendricks, ed., *The Hmong in Transition* (Staten Island, New York: Center for Migration Studies, 1986).

2. Sidney Verba and Norman Nie, *Participation in America* (New York: Harper and Row, 1972), p. 31. If you would like a copy of the questionnaire, please contact the author c/o Cecilia Manrique, Political Science Department, University of Wisconsin - La Crosse.

3. Verba and Nie, *Participation*.

4. Angus Campbell, Philip E. Converse and Donald E. Stokes, *The American Voter* (New York: John Wiley and Sons, 1960), pp. 475-81.

5. Verba and Nie, *Participation*, pp. 129-33.

6. According to Campbell, et. al., political efficacy is an individual's feeling "...that his vote counts in the operation of government and feels furthermore that there are other reasonable ways in which he can influence the progress of the system beyond going to the polls."

7. Verba and Nie, *Participation*, pp. 49-51.

8. Robert A. Dahl and Edward R. Tufte, *Size and Democracy* (Stanford, California: Stanford University Press, 1973) pp. 53-65.

9. Campbell, Converse and Stokes, *American Voter*, pp. 515-19.

10. The results of this survey are based on 40 responses to approximately 65 surveys distributed or a 61percent response rate to the survey.

11. Verba and Nie, *Participation*, pp. 30-31.

12. Vang Pobzeb, *Hmong Culture Related to Law and Education* (Denver, Colorado: Hmong Council Education Committee, 1992), "Five Unwritten Codes of Discipline in Education," p. 41.

13. Robert T. Bower, *The Changing Television Audience in America* (New York: Columbia Press, 1985), p. 40.

14. Yen Le Espiritu, *Asian American Panethnicity* (Philadelphia: Temple University Press, 1992) Comparatively, a survey of California's registered Asian Americans revealed that party identity was evenly split between the Democrats and Republicans, 42 percent and 41 percent respectively. Nearly one in five consider themselves mild or non-partisan, a higher percentage than other ethnic or racial groups. In the area of campaign finance, Asian Americans are believed to be the most generous after Jewish Americans.

2

English Language Use in the Hmong Community

Ray Hutchison

Introduction

Patterns of language use indicate behavioral differences between public and private domains, and may also reflect the degree of acculturation among minority-language groups. Because many studies show a positive association between English language use and educational outcomes, advancement to higher income occupations, and overall assimilation to American culture,[1] the analysis of language patterns has become an important area of research in the social sciences. A number of factors appear to increase the likelihood that immigrants will shift from their native language to English. These include age at time of migration, length of residence in the United States, and intermarriage: the earlier one migrates to the United States and the longer one lives continuously in the country, the more likely one is to speak English.[2]

Much of the recent research on language use and language shift in the United States has focused on the Hispanic population, the largest of the "new immigrant groups." A much smaller body of literature concerns language use and language shift among Asian immigrants, even though many of the issues important for the social and cultural integration of Asian immigrants are similar to those of the Hispanic population—including especially the acquisition of English language ability to ensure participation in the economy and to provide opportunities for social integration. This paper examines language patterns and language shift within the Hmong community in Green Bay, Wisconsin.

Previous Research

Although the first Hmong refugees arrived in the United States barely 15 years ago, there is an extensive body of research on Southeast Asian refugee groups including the Hmong. The Hmong are often described as a pre-literate, hill-tribe people from the mountains of Laos with no occupational experience beyond small-scale swidden agriculture and little exposure to the outside world. According to the usual narrative, little is known of the history of the Hmong people until they were recruited by the French military in the 1950s to fight against the communist Pathet Lao. Following the defeat of French forces at the battle of Dien Bien Phu in 1954, the Hmong were recruited by the CIA to assist in secret operations during the Vietnam war. Beginning in the late 1970s, Hmong refugees were resettled in France, Australia, and the United States.

Most research on the Hmong notes that they did not develop a written alphabet until sometime in this century. Indeed, Tapp[3] indicates that an important aspect of ethnic identity for the Hmong is derived from the various myths that the Chinese either stole their language or prevented them from developing a written alphabet. The first alphabet was in fact developed by a French missionary in 1951-53; since then at least fourteen different writing systems have been developed. The development of indigenous Hmong writing systems, often by messianic spiritual leaders, began around this time and continues to the present.[4]

While several studies focus on the issue of language acquisition,[5] there is little information on patterns of language use and the extent of language shift in the Hmong population. Some studies which include general information on English language proficiency do not report detailed information on the measure or measures used (Westermeyer's research, for example, mentions that mental health is positively associated with speaking English, but does not provide further information about the language measures).[6] Robson's study[7] of Hmong participants in an English-as-a-Second-Language (ESL) class at the Ban Vinai refugee camp in Thailand reported that 36 percent were literate in Hmong or Laotian, and that native language literacy was more important for learning the English language than was prior formal education. A more recent study, also from the Ban Vinai camp, indicated that nearly half (49 percent) of the adult population was literate in one or more languages. In the Minneapolis–St. Paul Hmong Community Study, 31.2 percent of the adults indicated that they spoke English "not at all," 42.6 percent "very little," and 25.0 percent "well;" only 1.2 percent said they spoke English "very well."[8] Reder's study of 335 households in the Hmong community in Portland, Oregon indicated that males have greater language proficiency than females, but that only a third of the sample was literate in Hmong. Nearly forty percent indicated that they had no English language proficiency; 23.5 percent reported "a bit;" 27.8 "a little," and 19.5 percent reported "fair." Only two percent reported that they could speak English well.[9] Green and Reder's longitudinal research on the acquisition of English found that the individual's age, proficiency in reading Hmong, and extent of formal education prior to migration were the most important influences on learning English.[10]

Social isolation as a consequence of the inability to learn English figures predominantly in studies pointing to mental health problems in the adult and elderly population. And just as English-language proficiency is related to employment and earnings for other immigrant groups, Haines notes that English language competence is an "essential element" in successful employment for Southeast Asian refugees: a 1980 study showed that only a fifth of the adults who could not speak English were in the labor force, while three-fifths of those who spoke English well were employed.[11]

Methodology

In 1990 the Hmong population in Green Bay–Brown County included nearly 300 households and numbered approximately 2,000 persons. To obtain a probability sample of the Hmong population we first compiled a list of all households living in the Green Bay–Brown County area from information supplied by the Hmong Association. Our final sampling frame included the names, addresses, and phone numbers for 280 Hmong households living in Green Bay–Brown County, from which we drew a systematic sample of 200 households. We completed 125 interviews, making a contact rate of 71 percent. The final response rate for the households actually contacted by the interview staff was approximately 88 percent.

Our questionnaire made extensive use of material from the Indochinese Health and Adaptation Research Project (IHARP) conducted by Ruben G. Rumbaut and John P. Anderson in San Diego. We appended a series of questions on language patterns, leisure and recreation activity, and personal experiences in Green Bay. Staff members from the Hmong Association also suggested questions on housing quality and satisfaction which were included in the final version of the questionnaire.

Results of the Green Bay research

Our questionnaire included two groups of questions focusing on language and literacy. The first series of questions asked what languages the respondent was able to speak, read, and write. These questions are a simple self-report on basic literacy; they do not indicate how well individual respondents are able to read or write a particular language. The results may be surprising given the familiar statement that the Hmong come from a pre-literate culture which had little contact with the outside world:

> More than sixty percent of the adult Hmong respondents reported that they are fully literate (ability to read, write, and speak) in Hmong.

> Sixty-five percent indicated that they spoke a second language (usually Laotian). Of this group, fifty percent could speak, read, and write in the second language.

> Twenty-five percent reported that they speak a third language (usually Thai). Thirty-five percent of this group indicate that they could speak, read, and write in a third language.

> Sixty-five percent reported that they are able to speak English. Fully half of this group (approximately a third of the total sample) indicated that they can speak, read, and write in English.

A second group of questions asked which language was usually spoken (Hmong, mostly Hmong, both Hmong and English, mostly English, or English) by the respondent and other family members in six different situations: with their spouse, with relatives, with adult friends, with children, when children answered parents, and when children spoke with one another. Responses to these questions indicate only the respondent's subjective evaluation of which language is most often used in each situation; it does not provide more detailed information on code-switching (the use of various combinations of English and Hmong in different interaction settings) and other language behavior.

Language used when...	Hmong	Mostly Hmong	Both	Mostly English	English
Speaking with spouse	52.8	36.8	8.0	--	--
Speaking with relatives	64.0	33.6	2.4	--	--
Speaking with friends	44.0	27.0	28.0	1.0	--
Speaking with children	31.0	35.0	27.0	6.0	1.0
Children with one another	19.0	20.0	37.0	18.0	7.0
Children with friends	16.0	17.0	33.0	21.0	13.0

Table 1: English Language Use in Green Bay Hmong Households. Note: Figures represent percent of responses to individual questions as indicated. Total N=125.

Descriptive information concerning language use in Hmong households is shown in table 1. These results indicate that a sizeable minority of respondents (approximately thirty percent) are mono-lingual in Hmong (where Hmong is used in each of the language interactions involving adults in the household; note that this figure corresponds very closely with the sixty-five percent of respondents who indicated that they were able to speak some English). Although Hmong is used almost exclusively among adults, there are significant levels of English language use among children. We anticipate that English language use by Hmong children would be even greater were it not for the large number of pre-school children who speak only Hmong at home.

A bivariate analysis (not shown here) indicates that English language use is positively correlated with the three intervening measures of cultural integration (such as number of American friends, participation in the labor force, and participation in ESL programs). It is not, however, correlated with several demographic variables (such as respondent's age and Hmong language literacy) as might be expected. The strongest correlation between English language use and the variables examined is with length of residence in the United States. In other words, increased length of residence in the United States, participation in the labor force, in ESL programs, and in social networks which include persons outside of the Hmong community are associated with English language use. The respondent's age and literacy in the Hmong language do not have a direct association with language use.

Responses to the six language questions were also combined to form an index measure of English language use, which was then used in multivariate analyses which included background variables such as the respondent's age and length of residence in the United States (two measures used in other studies of language use and language shift), Hmong language literacy (indicating if the respondent could speak, read, or write in their home language); intervening variables such as the extent of Anglo friendship networks and the length of time spent in ESL classes has been incorporated. In addition, a dummy variable indicating participation in the labor force replaces the more usual measures of occupation and income, and is placed as an intervening (rather than background) variable. The results of the multivariate analyses (not shown here) indicate that length of residence and participation in the work force have the strongest positive influence on English language use (increased residence in the United States and employment in the labor market is related to the use of English rather than Hmong). Participation in ESL programs also has a statistically significant positive influence on English language use in two of the three models for Hmong adults, and on the final index measure.

One of the most significant results of the research presented here is the influence of ESL programs for the adult Hmong; in the overall model this is the second most important variable predicting English language use, and the only factor over which individuals in the outside society have any significant degree of influence. The policy implication is clear: to facilitate the development of English language use in the Hmong community, and thus facilitate employment of Hmong adults and the social integration of Hmong households, more extensive ESL programs need to be developed for the adult population.

Discussion and conclusions

The level of language literacy revealed in these results is substantially greater than that suggested in some earlier studies. It is important to note, however, that much of our information about the Hmong community has come from social service providers who have contact with those households which have most recently arrived in the community; by definition, families where parents are employed and children are in mainstream classes ordinarily will not have contact with caseworkers, ESL instructors, and other service providers. In other words, our understanding of language issues in the Hmong community—including especially the studies of language acquisition—are derived from those groups which have sought services in the local community or are enrolled in special programs (ESL courses for adults, ESL programs for elementary and high school students). Trueba, Jacobs, & Kirton comment on this phenomenon in their study of a Hmong community in California.[12]

Many Americans working with Hmong children are unaware of the individual differences in the community. They rely, instead, on the tried and true generalizations perpetuated by the press. While teachers spread the word that the Hmong have no written language, Hmong children see adults writing Hmong in three different scripts—one using the Romanized Popular Alphabet, one using Lao script, and the third developed and perpetuated by the Hmong. While children hear in the larger community that Hmong did not go to school before they came to the United States, they hear Hmong adults describe the family sacrifices made for access to the limited educational opportunities in Laos.

The results also indicate significant differences in the preferred language and evolving language patterns of Hmong adults and Hmong children. Lopez notes that the "pivotal shift" to English occurs in the second generation. While Hmong is used by adults in the household and with other relatives, nearly a third of the children use English when speaking with one another and with their friends. Many households have developed bilingual communication patterns, where both English and Hmong are used when speaking with adult friends and with children.[13]

The rapid shift in language use in Hmong households was also noted by our respondents. Parents understand very well that speaking English is necessary for their children to do well in school and to obtain good jobs, and several persons commented that their lack of English language proficiency limited their activities and social contacts. At the same time, speaking the Hmong language was one characteristic of Hmong culture which parents wanted their children to continue in the next generation. For many of respondents, speaking Hmong is associated with the more general issue of respect for Hmong culture and traditions, as the following comments from our personal interviews indicate:

"Hmong children should learn Hmong language, Hmong culture and customs such as religion, folk music, crafts, learn how to perform Hmong marriage ceremony and funeral ceremony. Teach children to respect parents and elderly."

"I would like to have a Hmong language class [so that] Hmong language, Hmong culture and customs are taught to the children. This is the only way we can preserve the culture. The program must be taught to children at the age of six. If we wait until they become teenagers, they will not listen and they will not learn."

The degree to which changes in language patterns have taken place within Hmong households is part of a larger question focusing on the more general process of cultural and structural assimilation among immigrant groups. This research suggests a high degree of language literacy in the adult Hmong generation, and a substantive shift to English language use in the first generation. But the relationship between language use and social and economic mobility may be hindered by other factors. Although 80 to 90 percent of Hmong students graduate from high school,[14] relatively few Hmong students work during the high school years, and thus have little work experience or references to draw upon when looking for employment when they graduate from high school. Discrimination in local labor markets may limit opportunities for mobility. While English will likely become the dominant language for the next generation of Hmong children in Green Bay and other communities across the country, it remains to be seen if this will translate into status gains in the dominant society.

Notes

1. R.M. Fernandez, "Bilingualism & Hispanic Scholarship Achievement: Some Baseline Results," *Social Science Research* 65:537-550; M. Tienda & L.J. Neidert, "Language, Education and Socio-economic Achievement of Hispanic Men," *Social Science Quarterly*, 65 (1984):519-536; E.L. Olmedo & A.M. Padilla, "Empirical and Construct Validity of a Measure of Acculturation for Mexican Americans," *Journal of Social Psychology*, 105 (1978): 179-187.

2. G.R. Hawkes, J. Smith, & T. Acredolo, "English Language Use Among Mexican Immigrants: A Causative Analysis," *Hispanic Journal of Behavioral Sciences*, 2(1980): 161-176.

3. N. Tapp, *Sovereignty and Rebellion: The White Hmong of Northern Thailand* (New York: Oxford University Press, 1989).

4. See, for example, the recent volume by W. Smalley, C.K. Vang, & G.Y. Yang, *Mother of Writing: The Origin Development of a Hmong Messianic Script* (Chicago: University of Chicago Press, 1990).

5. S. Reder, "A Hmong Community's Acquisition of English." In B.T. Downing & D.P. Olney (eds.), *The Hmong in the West: Observations and Reports* (New York: Center for Migration Studies, 1982): 268-303; B. Robson, "Hmong Literacy, Formal Education, and Their Effects on Performance in an ESL Class." In B.T. Downing & D.P. Olney (eds.), *The Hmong in the West: Observations and Reports* (New York: Center for Migration Studies, 1982): 201-226)

6. J. Westermeyer, J. Neider, & T.F. Vang. "Acculturation and Mental Health: A Study of Hmong Refugees at 1.5 and 3.5 Years Postmigration," *Social Science Medicine* (19884), 18: 87-93.

7. S. Reder, *Ibid.*

8. B.T. Downing, "Language Issues." In *The Hmong in Transition,* G.L. Hendricks, B.T. Downing, & A.S. Deinard (eds.) (New York: Center for Migration Studies, 1986): 187-193.

9. S. Reder, *Ibid.*

10. K.R. Green & S. Reder, "Factors in Individual Acquisition of English: A Longitudinal Study of Hmong Adults." In *The Hmong in Transition,* G.L. Hendricks, B.T. Downing, & A.S. Deinard (eds.) (New York: Center for Migration Studies, 1986): 229-329.

11. D.W. Haines, *Refugees in the United States: A Reference Handbook* (Westport, Connecticut: Greenwood Press 1985): 28-29.

12. H.T. Trueba, L. Jacobs & E. Kirton. *Cultural Conflict and Adaptation: The Case of Hmong Children in American Society* (New York: The Falmer Press, 1990).

13. D.E. Lopez, "Chicano Language Loyalty In An Urban Setting." *Sociology and Social Research.* 62(1978): 267-278.

14. M. McNall &K. Call. "Poverty, Ethnicity, and Youth Adjustment: A Comparison of Poor Hmong and Non-Hmong Adolescents." In *Adolescence, Careers, and Cultures*, W. Meeus, M. de Goede, W. Kox and K. Hurrelmann (eds.) (Berlin: De Gruyter, 1993).

3

Dharma and Social Mobility

The Value of Hierarchy Among Asian Indians in the United States

Christian Ghasarian

Multicultural societies constitute an interesting place where one can observe particularly vividly the disjunctures between cultural values. On the basis of data I have collected in California (notably in the San Francisco Bay Area),[1] I present here the way Hindu immigrants manage the positive value of hierarchy they brought from India in relation to a strongly contrastive notion of equality they are confronted with in the United States. This opposition of values requires that immigrants reconsider some of their former attitudes to avoid cultural misunderstandings. After a brief presentation of the social and cultural context of the immigration of South Asians to this country, I will describe the complex of values in which hierarchy and equality are ideologically emphasized in India and in the United States. I will then point out the new experience Asian Indians have of these two values in the family, in the community and in the society at large.

Although Indian immigrants are perceived as a single ethnic group in the multicultural mosaic of American society, their internal diversity is important (regional and linguistic background, caste, religion, age of immigration, etc.). Indeed, the heterogeneous nature of India is reflected in the wide variety of Asian Indians in the United States. Indian immigrants living in this country are not at all representative of the general economic population in India. An important number of them have a high level of education and come from upper classes and castes in India. In addition, numerous Asian Indians come from countries other than India. Nevertheless, despite many internal distinctions, members of the ethnic category "Asian Indians" in the United States share some fundamental values found in India, among them, the concept of hierarchy.

The United States is a society of tremendous cultural diversity. It is currently engaged in a political and ethical discourse about flexibility, tolerance and openness towards its minorities. In a context of political correctness, ethnicity is officially valued. This ideological context allows immigrants to conserve their distinct way of life without meeting overt disapproval. However, the explicit permissiveness of the society at large does not necessarily imply a special interest in others' differences. In the standard situations of everyday life and at the work place, when cross-cultural interactions occur, things are a little more complex: Anglo-Saxon values, institutions and ways of life still implicitly constitute the mainstream model of the society.

The main concept of Indian culture, providing the foundation for the sense of hierarchy, is probably that of *dharma*, whose basis is traced to the Veda[2] as ultimate authority. Among its many definitions, *dharma* expresses "the natural order of things." No one arrives on earth without a *dharma*. The individual *dharma* is a reflection of the cosmic *dharma*, responsible for maintaining the universe as it is. *Dharma* is thus strongly connected with the notions of duty, virtue and law. It involves different status, privileges and obligations. People are not equal to each other. The righteous way to fulfill one's *dharma* is to conform to others' expectations in any situation. Norms and precepts of *dharma* are notably expressed by the division of the society. The main injunction of *dharma* is "better one's duty ill performed than that of another, to perfection."[3] Total acceptance of *dharma* does not really leave room for amelioration or improvement. This is *dharma* as a moral concept of the textual tradition, and one may suspect that it is far removed from everyday life in India. Fieldwork I have conducted in South India, though, has convinced me that while the concept of *dharma* is rarely mentioned by people, it does underlie their frequent reference to a fate one can hardly change (the Tamil expression *talai eluttu*, "fate is written on one's forehead," is in this respect quite explicit). God being supposed to have decided the way things are, the devotional attitude favors the acceptance of one's situation. Indian society is thus more duty- and other-oriented than rights- and individual-oriented. This conception of life is evidently at work in the arranged marriages numerous young people still have to comply with.

This acceptance of things is directly connected with hierarchy. Hierarchical differences are expressed in many ways in India (including caste, gender and age). The most salient expression of hierarchy, which has led to an enormous anthropological discourse on India—and a growing counter discourse—is the caste status, ascribed at birth. Whether hierarchy is a central problem or not in Indian society, this idea is, with separation and division, one of the characteristics of the caste system.[4] Though economic pressure and foreign stimulus lead to a certain social mobility within the structure, hierarchy is still a striking feature of this society. In contemporary India more and more people (especially those who have a good position in the hierarchy) reemphasize the loyalties and the endogamy of caste. Another expression of well-established hierarchy connected with *dharma* can be found in gender relations. Men's rights over their spouses and respect for elders and their privileges are other important aspects of hierarchy in India. The positive value of hierarchy is overtly signaled in the everyday interactions by the proper pronouns of address used towards a superior or an inferior. Almost all relationships in India, especially at work, are characterized either by paying or receiving respect.

If authoritarian and subordinate transactions are prevalent and explicit, that does not mean that hierarchy is not contested. Moreover, ideal hierarchical views do not always fit with the facts. Concerning caste in India, for instance, people from low backgrounds generally do not accept their place in the hierarchy without questioning it; most notably they may claim high caste origins. Remaining in an inferior position does not imply that nothing would tempt one to change it, if the opportunity occurred. However, one must keep in mind that contesting of one's position in the system does not necessarily threaten the hierarchical system at large. Actually, by referring to a fault, a mistake of an ancestor, or simply an injustice, the rationalization used to explain one's present situation just reinforces the oppression of the system.[5]

If duty and *dharma* underlie the idea of hierarchy in India, freedom and social mobility underlie that of equality of opportunities in the United States. Even if U.S. behavior is not quite homogeneous, one cannot deny that there are nevertheless some general cultural models of behavior which are recognized as such by everybody living in the country. These general models are predominantly carried on by the middle class population originally from western Europe. The Declaration of Independence, with its proclamation that "all men are created equal," gives the foundation to the American ideal according to which the birth status should not reduce the equality of opportunity. Inequality should only result from differences in levels of achievement; otherwise it is considered bad or "unfair." One accedes to a class, or occupation (the two notions being almost equivalent), not because of one's family but because of one's merits. This explains why competition and the desire to win are everywhere, and why success is constantly rewarded. Status differences are principally based on achievement in occupation, education and wealth. Achievement being much more valued than inheritance in determining an individual's position, the worthwhile person is the one who "goes ahead" and "gets results." Equality of rights and the quest for success through achievement place a high value on individuality and self-reliance, which is the core value of American culture.[6] Everyone is thought to be in control of his/her own destiny and is considered responsible for advancing or regressing in society.

The problem with this ideal view is that it naturally leads to an inequality in results: some succeed more than others because of their skills, their merits and their luck. With the chance of success, there is the risk of failure. Like success, failure is thought to be one's responsibility. Dreams of upward mobility and nightmares of downward mobility are therefore inevitably linked. The success and superiority of some are necessarily based on the failure and inferiority of others. In a society rewarding effort, competition and individual achievement, the majority must inevitably be in lower positions. Despite the focus on egalitarianism and individual freedom, these notions constitute more a moral imperative than a fact of life in the United States. Some categories of the population operate within a larger structure of material and cultural inequality. The discourse on social mobility forgets ascribed handicaps linked to sexual and ethnic differences. On the basis of ethnicity and gender, a considerable proportion of the population has not been—and is still not—given the same opportunities as others. Class is a real structure of the social life in the United States, but it is rarely spoken of in its own right and its discourse is almost under a "taboo."[7] Instead, it is considered that all people have, or should have, equal opportunities for achievement. The ideological point is that, if hierarchy exists, it is only as an unavoidable result of the egalitarian conception. The egalitarian nature of the society is re-emphasized in the US Supreme Court's legal resolutions for equal treatment of minority groups.

Their unavoidable involvement in the host society allows Indian immigrants to adopt some attitudes that were not valued in India. Some spheres of their life have a more egalitarian nature; others are still marked by hierarchy. Sometimes a clash occurs between Indian and American expectations. Let us examine how Asian Indians in the United States experience hierarchy and equality in three social contexts: the family, the ethnic community and the larger society.

Inside the family, Asian Indians are confronted with new patterns of behavior associated with gender and seniority. The longer the family has been living in the United States, the more it has been subject to a certain erosion of traditional authority. The family, inevitably under the influence of the host society, can hardly ignore the woman's position there which, even if it is far from ideal, is incomparably better than that of the woman in India. The widespread Indian presentation of the urbanized woman as the "bad," sexually suspect woman can no longer prevail in the cultural context of the United States. The Asian Indian woman, exposed to American influences (in television, movies, magazines, social interactions, etc.) displaying women's rights and individual autonomy, has the possibility to develop and to legitimize a feeling of independence. In this western context, the Asian Indian girl can contest her parents' point of view more freely than in India, and can reject their eventual decision concerning her marriage. The Asian Indian woman has more opportunities to make decisions for herself. She can also more easily divorce. The numerous divorces among Indian couples in the United States appear to be the result of the woman's affirmation of herself. In this new context, South Asian women have the possibility of being more independent and thus getting rid of the burden of ascribed gender hierarchical status they were used to in India.

The other domain where family authority is threatened is seniority. There is an unavoidable gap between parents born in India and children raised in the United States. In India, the traditional family is patriarchal. The Indian childhood is a disciplined apprenticeship to the role of adult by learning the implicit rules and by imitating models. Child rearing practices construct a special image of authority that will later characterize the valorized subordinate relationship of the employee to the employer. On the American side, strict authoritarian-disciplinarian parents do not characterize the family. Obedience is a strong pattern in Indian families where children must respect their parents' wishes and, above all, must not ask questions. Conversely, verbal dissent is common for American children who are taught that their own opinions are important and worth expressing. Childhood in the United States is generally a period of great freedom. Children are respected as persons and may express their feelings. They usually have the right to ask "why?" and to expect an answer. In school with their mates, Asian Indian children learn an alternative way of life that they naturally bring back home. They learn that childhood in the United States does not silence the self, and learns that, in this non-lineal society, generation differences are not stressed. Asian Indian children of the second generation are inevitably Americanized, particularly boys, and tend to argue freely and give advice to their parents, as American children would do. If the parents keep referring to the Indian point of view, according to which the worst sin is disrespect for one's parents, they may regard their child as abusing them. By the same American logic, Asian Indians' children generally do not envisage later treating their parents in old age as dependent persons. This is why many immigrants of the first generation frequently criticize the permissiveness of their host society with its lack of respect for the elderly.

Among peers of Indian background, there is a continuity and a change in the experience of hierarchy. Among the new expressions of hierarchy, we find the maintenance and the display of Indian traditions in the alien American cultural context. This attitude, typical of those in situations of diaspora, appears for instance in the expression "Indian values," or even "strong Indian values," that one can find in matrimonial ads in Indian magazines throughout the United States.[8] To keep to Indian ways in the western context appears to be a difficult challenge, but success procures a valued status among the peers. Concerning caste distinctions, there is a continuity in the sense of hierarchy. In India, most people do not know all the categories of the caste hierarchy (especially in urban settings), and the main distinction is the opposition Brahmins/non-Brahmins. Once in the United States, many Indians begin to forget the caste differences, but this basic separation remains. In this new context, the caste status is primarily considered as relevant by those who have an advantageous position in the hierarchy. The significant change is that, in the American cultural context, the advantageous caste status is only relevant inside the community and cannot be overly emphasized without entailing the risk of signaling a futile pride. Caste distinctions emerge particularly when dealing with the marriage of children. The ascribed caste status is the main cause of conflict, notably when the two partners are not from Brahmin background. Whatever the financial situation of the non-Brahmin partner, he/she is a non-Brahmin and cannot do anything to change this fact (contrary to the economic situation). The continuous arrival of new immigrants from India, with a traditional system of reference, and the traditional views always surfacing when it is question of marriage, explain why the caste criterion is still alive in the United States. It is important to remark that non-Brahmin Indians are the ones who tend to forget caste distinctions the fastest. The compensations for not being of high caste-status come only with a valued economic and wealth status that places the person or the family on another scale of hierarchy, in another system of value and reference (that prevailing in the United States). Because of the colonial history of India some external western patterns of behavior are also valued among Indians. People who have adopted these behavioral patterns are notably those who define themselves as "open minded" in matrimonial ads, in opposition to those having "strong Indian values."

It is in the societal sphere that the Indian sense of hierarchy is experienced in the most different manner since Brahmin/non-Brahmin patterns and perception of dominance and subordination are nonexistent in the United States, non-Brahmins often cite individual freedom as a very important value in their new lives. Nevertheless, for Indians of Brahmin and non-Brahmin background, appropriate behavior in the host society demands some psychological adjustments. Numerous aspects of life in the United States stress equality of everyone. Another example of ideological difference can be found in the student/teacher relationship. Indian students are a bit surprised to see that teachers in the United States may have an informal chat with their students, each of them calling the other by their first names. They are also often amazed to see their American counterparts saying to the teacher: "I think you're mistaken..." when the relation student/teacher in India is one of the most hierarchical. The explicit dominant/subordinate transactions as they occur in India are not expected here: people in the United States are more likely to behave in a casual manner, even if there are important age and status differences between them. This is why Asian Indians often refer to American familiarity and openness. An Indian teacher or supervisor for whom it would be appropriate to remain aloof from his students or co-workers in his culture, can be criticized for the same attitude in the United States. Another cultural clash can be found in verbal interaction. Americans become sometimes appalled at the intensity with which Indians generally present their views in social settings. The frequent desire to take over a conversation contrasts with the typical interchange in the United States where nobody should attempt to take down others' views. The common pattern in this society is instead to give and take as equals, without anyone having too much influence. The Indian hierarchical relationship, where it is accepted that one person clearly has influence over others is, in this cultural context, considered pushy and childish. On the other side, the Indian need for the active support and involvement of authority figures in the hierarchy in order to work productively, and the tendency to avoid a competitive mode of behavior, can lead to another misunderstanding. In the United States, the desire to be co-operative and in accord is often mistaken as being too passive and compliant. An absence of questioning or disagreement may be considered as an absence of motivation or self-assertiveness.

Despite these occasional misunderstandings, it is quite clear that the structural assimilation of Indian immigrants is one of the most successful among the ethnic groups in the United States. Numerous Asian Indians are still concentrated in the "white collar" occupational category. Like the American middle class, they are primarily concerned with economic prosperity and the acquisition of material goods. As they mainly come from the upper strata of Indian society, where a great emphasis is placed on educational achievement, Asian Indians experience practically no conflict with norms in the United States stressing the importance of education. Whether or not parents were student migrants, they put a strong emphasis upon educational achievement and social mobility. Like people in the United States, Asian Indians prize upward mobility for themselves as well as for their children who regularly do very well at school. The incorporation of the desire for upward social mobility does not pose a problem, because it can still be predicated on a value of hierarchy.

Their successful structural assimilation to their host society does not imply that Indian immigrants adopt the total scale of values of the first immigrants (the Anglo-group). Still, it is important to distinguish their structural assimilation from their cultural assimilation. In such areas as education and occupation, Asian Indians have apparently assimilated the existing American models. Their definitive inclusion into the culture of the United States, however, demands other form of assimilation as well. These include the reconsideration of original hierarchical patterns and the adoption of the egalitarian values of the host society. Among peers in the community, many traditional ways are considered "pure," and, because of the positive value given to Indianness, can endure without bringing any conflict. Within the family and in society at large, behavioral adjustments are necessary to avoid some generational and gender conflicts here and some cultural misunderstandings or clashes there. The current official valuation of cultural pluralism in the United States works principally with ideal images (one of which is ethnic diversity) and does not really fit the facts. In daily American working life, the split between the respectable ("like us") and non respectable ("others") people is still implicitly central. It is noteworthy that Asian Indians generally do not say that they have been discriminated against in their jobs, but they do sometimes feel that, as Indians, they have some "disadvantages." While it is possible to manifest or maintain some native patterns when interacting with members of their own culture, non-adaptation to the principal norms of the dominant society (among those, the egalitarian view) can work against one's interests and be a source of stress.

It should be pointed out that the disinclination some Asian Indians feel to enter the mainstream of their host society also results from their cultural background; namely, the relative marginalization they can experience as new immigrants, and that of others they can observe around them, is not very far from what they were used to in India, where people are distinguished and even discriminated against on the basis of numerous ascribed features (among them, gender, caste, language, religion, etc.). This cultural habit prevents a great number of Indian immigrants from deciding to involve themselves culturally in the host country. Nevertheless, their accommodation to their new cultural environment entails the revision of some presumed cultural truths (like hierarchy and its discriminations of rank). It also requires processes of learning and re-learning which are tied both to the duration of the stay in the United States and to the desire for change itself.

Notes

1. Research for this study has involved reading numerous anthropological texts on Indian and American cultures, and by interviewing both first and second generation immigrants from India and some U.S. citizens. My main goal was to understand their perceptions of differences during social interactions. Each time I tried to enter the inner world of value of people I was talking with.

2. The Veda is the entire body of Hindu sacred writings. For the orthodox, these authoritative scriptures are eternal, and not the product of human minds.

3. Arnold Kunst, "Use & Misuse of Dharma," in *The Concept of Duty in South Asia,* Wendy Doniger O'Flaherty and J. Duncan M. Derret (eds.) (New Delhi: Vikas, 1978).

4. Louis Dumont, *Homo Hierarchicus: Essai sur le systme des castes* (Paris: Gallimard, 1966).

5. Gerald Berreman, "Caste in India and the United States," in *The Nacirema. Readings on American Culture*, James A. Spradley and Michael A. Rynkievich (eds.) (Boston: Little, Brown & Company, 1975).

6. F.L.K. Hsu, "American Core Value and National Character, " in *The Nacirema. Readings on American Culture*, James A. Spradley & Michael A. Rynkievich (eds), (Boston: Little, Brown & Company, 1975).

7. Sherry B. Ortner. "Reading America: Preliminary notes on class and culture," in *Recapturing Anthropology. Working in the Present,* Richard G. Fox (ed.) (New Mexico: School of American Research Press, 1991.)

8. Notably *India Abroad* in the entire country and *India Currents* and *India West* in California.

4

A Pilot Study of Midwestern Japanese American Women

Perspectives on Child-rearing and Education

Susan Matoba Adler

Japanese American *nisei* (second generation) who settled in the Midwest after leaving World War II internment camps, initiated a course of acculturation that has produced mainstream *sansei* (third generation) and biracial *yonsei* (fourth generation). Darrel Montero[1] predicted that the geographic dispersal of *nisei* would contribute to rapid assimilation. Kitano and Daniels further explain that the "*sansei* are more apt to reflect the ambience of their surrounding communities, rather than a strictly ethnic one. A Japanese American growing up in St. Louis will be more Missourian than Japanese...." My pilot study on this population helped focus my research on the following questions: How does the racial/ethnic identity of Midwestern Japanese American women influence their perspectives on child-rearing and education? and Have Japanese cultural beliefs about child-rearing and education been transformed or reconstructed by Midwestern Japanese American mothers?

This qualitative study included three *nisei* women, three *sansei* women and one *yonsei* woman, all of whom are mothers or grandmothers. Each woman was interviewed in her or my home using an open-ended ethnographic interview style. I observed the *yonsei* mother with her two young daughters. I was curious about the women's awareness of two Japanese concepts, *amae*,[2] described by Takeo Doi and *gambare*.[3] Multiple issues of race, ethnicity and gender emerged from the domain analysis of interview data.

One of the first questions asked of the women was, "How and from whom did you learn about raising children?" Many of the women had working mothers rather than full-time homemaker mothers so parenting models included grandparents, siblings, friends and even self-education.

Kitano's study on Japanese American child-rearing indicated that *nisei* parenting methods were based on literature from experts, using more of a scientific approach, rather than on traditional models passed down from their *issei* (first generation) parents.[4]

For the immigrant *issei*, the cultural tradition of valuing education originated during the Japanese Meiji period (1867-1912) which emphasized scholarly goodness, and Confucian beliefs of the malleability of human behavior. Research comparing Japanese family influence and mainstream American influence on student achievement indicates that Japanese parents stress the importance of effort over ability.[5] This legacy of hard work and perseverance seems to have led to high academic achievement for Japanese Americans. Has this legacy of achievement continued for Japanese Americans who grew up in areas where they were forced to become quickly acculturated? Montero predicted that there would be a decline in success rates as Japanese Americans became geographically removed from their ethnic communities.[6]

The women in my pilot study shared their interpretation of their racial/ethnic identities. As one *nisei* informant put it, "I'm quite Japanese-sey" but, she lamented that her daughters' *sansei* generation was entirely different. "I didn't really feel I was an Asian as a teenager," noted one *sansei* woman. Two *sansei* informants shared their shock and discomfort at being with so many Japanese people at an ethnic picnic, while visiting relatives in California. "I was floored because everybody there was Asian... and I just felt that I didn't belong," said one woman. The other recalled "being surprised, frightened and feeling out of place, at the sight of so many Japanese people, especially children."[7]

De Vos & Romanucci-Ross' research reminds us that "Ethnicity is determined by what a person feels about himself, not by how he is observed to behave." Yanagisako expands this perspective: "What makes a person racially Japanese is substance rather than conduct. Hence, even the *sansei*... whom the *nisei* view as 'very Americanized' and as exhibiting almost no 'Japanese' social conduct and interactional styles, are considered fundamentally, and in essence, 'Japanese.'" For the *sansei* in my study, seeing themselves through the reflection of other Japanese Americans was a novel experience. Maria Root, in her study of biracial women, examines ethnic identity in different contexts. She writes: "...we can have a different contextual identity in different situations though our sense of self can remain stable... The labels Asian, Asian American, Amerasian, or *sansei* can refer to a single person at different points in time and in different settings."

Other issues illustrating the intersection between race and gender also emerged from my interviews with these women. One *sansei* woman, who had been employed as a computer programmer in the 1970s shared her sensitivity to gender issues first, before considering race and ethnicity. For her, the Women's Movement had more impact than the Civil Rights Movement. Another *sansei* teacher called herself the "token minority" in her school where she was the only teacher of color. She mentioned the insensitivity of an administrator who told her that he was pleased that she helped the school district attain their minority quota.

The identity formation and future of the *yonsei* generation is of great concern. A recent article, in the public press, noted that "For every 100 children now born to two parents of Japanese ancestry, 139 are born to one Japanese parent and one white parent." In response to this rapid assimilation, ethnic studies professor Ron Takaki, pointed out that in the future there may no longer be a viable Japanese-American community and that the races would essentially be "blended in."[8]

I am *sansei* too

What motivated me to study Japanese American mothers? Was it a new found awareness of my own mother's child-rearing perspectives or reflection on my own ethnicity? Let me reach back into my personal history for a glimpse of the development of my own ethnic identity.

My father tells the story of how I came home from grade school in the early 1950s, here in Wisconsin, and announced to the family that I no longer wanted to be Japanese. Derogatory name calling probably caused this response, but at any rate, it was obvious that I was acutely aware of my racial/ethnic difference. Studies in child development indicate that children as young as three and four years old are aware of racial differences.[9]

I grew up with a small group of eight or nine Japanese American families, who came together primarily so that the *issei*, who spoke only Japanese, could have some companionship. I remember gatherings where my grandmother played the Japanese card game, "hana," with her friends, while the *nisei* gathered to chat and the *sansei* children spent time getting to know each other. Occasionally the elders would dress us little girls in kimonos and attempt to have a *Bon Odori*.[10] We had no idea what it meant, but enjoyed "dressing up" in the silk kimonos.

At the elementary school level my experiences were typical of the 1950s (spelling bees, violin, girl scouts) except that my sister and I were the only Asians (or even children of color) in our school. This "all American" pattern (cheerleading, honor society, science fair) continued throughout my junior high and high school years in upstate New York, where we had moved. My contact with Japanese Americans, except my immediate family which included my grandmother, during that time was very limited. As a result, I considered myself no different from my middle class Caucasian friends, though I knew I was of Japanese heritage.

It was not until I was an undergraduate on Long Island that I began to realize that my racial and ethnic identity was the grounds upon which others defined me. I was asked out by Asian foreign students, who thought I had an affinity for their culture, and by fraternity brothers who thought I was cute or exotic. I dated a few "real" Japanese men (from Japan), but found that I had little in common with them except race. I really had no opportunity to associate with *sansei* men, so marrying into my race or ethnic group was not of particular importance to me.

After marrying and moving to Colorado in 1970, I began teaching elementary school. I recall having a Japanese American teacher's aide who helped me design a unit on the Japanese culture for my first graders. It was an attempt to reconstruct my Japanese American roots. Throughout my professional career as an educator I had always been recruited to participate on multicultural education and ethnic studies program development. It wasn't until I taught at the university level that I realized the impact of affirmative action and the meaning of "token minority." My experiences in higher education created the catalyst for pursuing this research on Japanese American women. I have shared this portrait of my life and perceived ethnicity because it reflects in some manner what many of the Midwestern *sansei* women have also experienced.

The Japanese American women's perspectives

The sociopolitical contexts and life experiences of the *nisei* in my study differ greatly from those of the *sansei* and *yonsei*. With internment as part of their past histories, the *nisei* faced the overt racism of the 1940s and 1950s. They had been reared in a traditional Japanese home environment yet found it necessary to assimilate into mainstream society in order to survive. They kept a low profile and quietly reared the next generation. The *sansei* and *yonsei* in my study were acculturated into the middle class American society of the 1960s and 1970s, as beneficiaries of their parents' struggle to "make it". The world views of each generation of these women reflect these divergent contexts.

But all three generations, albeit to differing degrees, face the stigma of two stereotypical myths: the Model Minority and the Exotic Asian Woman. Japanese women, the cultured beauty of the orient, were stereotyped as graceful and delicate. Feminist Mitsuye Yamada points out that even if Japanese American women rejected the stereotype of subservience and submissiveness by which they were being defined, they still faced a lack of power. Reflecting on the dilemma of stereotypes, Yamada writes: "...the seemingly apolitical middle class woman and the apolitical Asian woman constituted a double invisibility."[11]

Her words are particularly relevant to professional *nisei* and *sansei* women who not only find glass ceilings in the workplace, but often have trouble getting on the first rung of the professional or corporate ladder. The *sansei* and *yonsei* women in my pilot study had experienced this double invisibility in their occupations as computer programmers, psychiatrists and teachers.

The model minority stereotype of high achievement and upward mobility proposes to define Japanese American women, but the real lives of the women in my study uncover some contradictions to this myth. For various reasons, the *nisei* women had mixed support for their education from their immigrant parents. In one case, the parents were unable to monitor their child's school work because they were too busy working in the fields and couldn't read or write English. The parents of another *nisei* informant wouldn't allow their daughter to attend college, even with a scholarship, because they believed she should learn cooking and sewing instead.

Of the *sansei* in my study, parental support for education was high in all cases. The *nisei* women were not all able to attend college, therefore higher education became an expectation for their *sansei* children. Mei Nakano points out that *nisei* women went to work for the purpose of earning their children's tuition. The monitoring of education was reported by all three groups as being "low key," with expectations of high effort and without tangible rewards. There was, though, variation in academic success among the women in my study.[12]

This study also uncovered the women's beliefs about the meaning of family. There is a difference between the traditional Japanese family, with its stem-family kinship network and the Japanese American family with its conjugal-family kinship network. Sylvia Yanagisako describes the stem-family system as one in which inheritance and responsibility are passed down in a linear fashion to the eldest son. First born sons are obligated by birth order to care for their parents. *Nisei* families in my study reflected the traditional family structure although most of the women resisted its continuation. They would endorse the conjugal network for the *sansei*, even suggesting that they wished to remain independent of their children in their later years.

In conjugal systems, the siblings share equal rights and responsibilities. Yanagisako's research reveals that the kinship patterns of Japanese Americans became women-centered. The *nisei* women transformed Japanese norms and symbols, giving them meanings that were relevant to an American life-style. The closeness and enduring cooperation between *nisei* sisters became attributed to "Japanese heritage" even though traditionally Japanese women joined the kinship network of their spouses.[13]

Multiple "voices" of Japanese American women

Literature by Japanese American women will become a data source and catalyst for communication in my future research. For example, as I read Akemi Kikumura's account of her *issei* mother in *Through Harsh Winters: The Life of a Japanese Immigrant Woman*, I think about my grandmothers' lives. What life experiences were never shared and will remain unwritten history? I am struck by the author's disclosure that her mother would not tell her story to anyone but a relative because of *haji* (meaning shame). "It's a shame to tell other people your problems," she explained. Mei Nakano writes about the brave women who gave testimony in 1980 at the Commission on Wartime Relocation and Internment of Civilians (CWRIC) hearings. The process was not a catharsis for them, instead it rekindled bitter memories.[14]

Jeanne Wakatsuki Houston's *Beyond Manzanar: Views of Asian-American Womanhood* provides some insight on ethnic identity formation. Her words describing her *issei* mother are poignant: "Thus, the chores and duties which she inherited as Japanese wife and mother were not her identity as such... She never confused her tasks with who she was. This concept of the inner self ...allowed her to form her own image, distinct from the one in the exterior world."[15] In my mind are images of my mother and grandmothers in camp, also in Manzanar. They are finding psychological spaces where little privacy exists. They have developed a strength that we *sansei* and *yonsei* cannot even imagine. Their voices will echo as passionately and eloquently as the printed words in Houston's book.

One of my favorite parts of Monica Sone's *Nisei Daughter* illustrates the confusion between cultural norms. In the chapter, "Henry's Wedding and a Most Curious Tea Party," the *nisei* plan an American-style wedding reception for Henry and his bride but fail to recognize that their *issei* guests were more used to Japanese tea parties. When the guests would not help themselves to the refreshments, saying instead, "*Dozo*, please don't trouble yourself over me," the young *nisei* found themselves confronted with a large culture gap. Even after the *nisei* demonstrated the American style of conduct for a buffet, their *issei* guests still remained seated. Finally, their *issei* mother suggested that the guests, nearly a hundred of them, should be served. The *issei* perception of formality was met with *nisei* informality.[16]

One of my study informants called it *enryo*, meaning you think of others before yourself, not obliging others. Her example was when someone offered to take her home, she would reply, "Oh, no, that's too much bother …I don't want to be an imposition to anybody." Even though she may have wanted or needed a ride she would politely refuse. This Japanese trait of *enryo* was evident in the literature and also reflected by my pilot study informants. Two voices echo the same cultural concepts.[17]

The findings of my pilot study indicate that while acculturation has changed the life-styles of each generation, the women have developed differing perceptions of ethnic identity. Commitment to the family and education appears to be strong across all three groups but the interpretation of family responsibility and educational achievement differs from generation to generation.

I end with one of my favorite poems written by Mitsuye Yamada. In *Mirror Mirror* she responds to her son's queries about his identity.

> *People keep asking where I come from*
> *says my son.*
> *Trouble is*
> > *I'm American on the inside*
> > *and oriental on the outside*
> > *No Doug*
> > *Turn that outside in*
> > *THIS is what American looks like"*[18]

This was first published in 1976. Today, in 1994, the message seems as cogent as it was 18 years ago. What shall the *sansei* tell the next generation, the *yonsei*, about their heritage? Will the biracial *yonsei* become "all blended in" and devoid of ethnicity or enriched by the diversity of their multiple roots? In years to come, I will be seeking them out, listening to their voices too.

Notes

1. Darrel Montero, *Japanese Americans: Changing Patterns of Ethnic Affiliation Over Three Generations* (Boulder, Co.: Westview Press, 1980); Harry H. L. Kitano and Roger Daniels, *Asian Americans: Emerging Minorities* (Englewood

Cliffs: Prentice Hall, 1988): 73.

2. **Amae** refers to the interdependency a Japanese mother and her child referred to by Japanese psychologist Takeo Doi in 1956. Doi's 1974 article defines amae as "to depend upon and presume upon another's benevolence." In 1986 Amy Iwasaki Mass described *amae* as "indulgent love." See Takeo Doi, "Amae: A Key Concept for Understanding Japanese Personality Structure," in *Japanese Culture and Behavior: Selected Readings*, eds. T.S. Lebra and W.P. Lebra (Honolulu: The University Press of Hawaii, 1975), 145-154.

3. **Gambare** has been translated in a variety of ways: most commonly as perseverance, as endurance (Befu, 1986) and as putting forth effort. John Singleton describes *gambare* as a verb form meaning "to persist, hang on or do one's best." See John Singleton, "The Spirit of Gambaru" in *Transcending Stereotypes: Discovering Japanese Culture and Education*, eds. Barbara Finkelstein, Anne Imamura and Joseph Tobin (Yarmouth, ME: Intercultural Press Inc., 1991), 119-125.

4. Harry H.L. Kitano, "Differential Childrearing Attitudes Between First and Second Generation Japanese in the United States," *Journal of Social Psychology* 53 (1961): 13-19.

5. Merry White, *The Japanese Educational Challenge: A Commitment to Children* (New York: Collier Macmillan Publishers, 1987); Harold Stevenson, "Learning from Asian schools," *Scientific American*, (December 1992):70-76; Susan Holloway, "Concepts of Ability and Effort in Japan and the United States," *Review of Educational Research* 58 (1988): 327-345.

6. Stanley Sue and S. Okazaki, "Asian-American Educational Achievements: A Phenomenon In Search Of An Explanation." *American Psychologist* 45 (1990): 913-920; Bob H. Suzuki, "Education and Socialization of Asian Americans: A Revisionist Analysis of the 'Model Minority' Thesis." *Amerasia Journal* 4 (1977): 23-52; Darrel Montero, *Japanese Americans: Changing Patterns of Ethnic Affiliation Over Three Generations* (Boulder, Co.: Westview Press, 1980).

7. George De Vos and Lola Romanucci-Ross. *Ethnic Identity: Cultural Continuities and Change* (Palo Alto: Mayfield Publishing Co., 1975): 17; Sylvia Yanagisako, *Transforming the Past: Tradition and Kinship Among Japanese Americans* (Stanford: Stanford University Press, 1985), 173; Maria Root, "Loyalty, Rootedness and Belonging: The Quest for Defining Asian American Identity," in *Asian Americans: Collages of Identities*, ed. L.C. Lee (Ithaca, N.Y.: Cornell University Asian American Studies Program, 1992): 183.

8. Marie Udansky, "For Interracial Kids, Growth Spurt." *USA Today*, 11 December 11, 1992. p. 7A Census: The Changing USA.

9. Louise Derman-Sparks, *Anti-bias Curriculum: Tools for Empowering Young Children*, (Washington DC: National Association for the Education of Young Children, 1989).

10. **Bon Odori** refers to a traditional Japanese celebration honoring the dead.

11. K. Osajima, "Asian Americans as the Model Minority: An Analysis of the Popular Press Image in the 1960s and 1980s," in *Reflections on Shattered Windows: Promises and Prospects for Asian American Studies*, ed. G.Y. Okihiro et. al. (Pullman, Wa.: Washington State University Press, 1987); Bob H. Suzaki,

"Asian Americans as the 'Model Minority' Outdoing Whites? or Media Hype?" *Change* (November/December 1989):13-19; Dennis Ogawa, *From Japs to Japanese: The Evolution of Japanese-American Stereotypes (*Berkeley: McCutchan, 1971); Mitsuye M. Yamada, "Invisibility is an Unnatural Disaster: Reflections of an Asian American Woman," in *This Bridge Called My Back: Writings by Radical Women of Color*, ed. Cherrie Moraga and Gloria Anzaldua (New York: Kitchen Table Press, 1983): 37.

12. Mei Nakano, *Japanese American Women: Three Generations 1890-1990*. (Berkeley: Mina Press Publishing & National Japanese American Historical Society, 1990).

13. Sylvia Yanagisako, *Transforming the Past: Tradition and Kinship Among Japanese Americans* (Stanford: Stanford University Press, 1985).

14. Akemi Kikumura, *Through Harsh Winters: The Life of a Japanese Immigrant Woman*. (Novato, Ca: Chandler & Sharp Publishers, Inc. 1981): 140; Mei Nakano, *Japanese American Women: Three Generations 1890-1990*. (Berkeley: Mina Press Publishing & National Japanese American Historical Society. 1990).

15. Jeanne Wakatsuki Houston, *Beyond Manzanar: Views of Asian-American Womanhood (*Capra Press. 1985): 9.

16. Monica Sone, *Nisei Daughter*. (Seattle: University of Washington Press. 1979).

17. The Japanese term **enryo** was defined by Harry Kitano in 1976 as "modesty in the presence of one's superior" but has changed meaning for Japanese Americans. First and second generation Japanese Americans used this behavior when responding to confusion, embarrassment or anxiety when dealing with persons outside of their ethnic community. See Harry H.L. Kitano, *Japanese Americans: The Evolution of a Subculture* (Englewood Cliffs: Prentice-Hall, 1976).

18. Mitsuye M. Yamada, *Camp Notes and Other Poems* (Berkeley: Shameless Hussy Press, 1986 3rd edition): 62.

5

Chinese American Servicemen in World War II

Yufeng Wang

World War II was a landmark in the history of Chinese Americans. It evoked, for the first time, widespread patriotic feelings among Chinese Americans and gave a new beginning to this long discriminated ethnic group in the United States.[1] Nowhere was the new Chinese American role better illustrated than in the military services, where over 12,000 served in the Army, and a smaller number served in the Navy and Air Force.[2] The Chinese American patriotic war effort represented one of the highest percentages of all ethnic groups in the United States.[3] Despite the increasing scholarly attention to Chinese American studies, the experience of Chinese American men and women in World War II has not been sufficiently addressed.

This article is a case study of Chinese American servicemen in World War II. It is based primarily on personal interviews with five World War II veterans: Lieutenant Colonel Chew K. Wong, Lieutenant Hong Lee, Sergeant David Hoy, Petty Officer Stanley Lim, and Mr. William Wong who served in the American Air Force and Navy in China and the Pacific during the war. It discusses their motivation in joining the war effort, their contribution to the American victory, the impact of the war on their lives and mentality, and how their patriotic war activities earned them greater social and legal acceptance in America.

Before the United States entered World War II, Chinese communities in America worked hard to mobilize support for China's resistance against Japanese aggression. They contributed millions of dollars and sent their sons into the battle in China.[4] The Japanese attack on Pearl Harbor increased patriotism among Chinese Americans. Community leaders urge young Chinese to enlist in the armed forces. New York Chinatown celebrated when the first draft numbers included Chinese Americans.[5] Chinese men and women were active in the battle fields and on the home front.[6] Over 20 percent of Chinese adult males in America enlisted in the military services.[7] It was common for several numbers in the family to join the service at the same time. For example, Rose Ong, a seamstress in San Francisco, sent her six sons to the armed forces.[8] While Lieutenant Hong Lee was stationed in China, his brother Sergeant Howard Lee was battling against the Nazis in Europe in General George Patton's army.

Lieutenant Colonel Chew K. Wong was one of the Flying Tigers in Major General Claire Lee Chennault's American Volunteer Group (AVG). He served in China from 1933 to 1945, and was promoted from first lieutenant major to lieutenant colonel. Wong was born, raised, and educated in the United States. After finishing high school, he went to the Aeronautical School in Oakland, California, where he learned flying and technical skills.[9] When he realized that China needed pilots, he went to Guangdong to serve in General Chen Jitang's airplane squadron as second lieutenant.[10] He later joined the AVG and became one of the Flying Tigers. Calling himself "one of the Chennault boys,"[11] Wong was very proud of his service in China and, particularly, his association with General Chennault.

As a staff officer directing ground operations, Wong was decorated the Legion of Merit for outstanding service. The Citation from the Army Air Force reads:

> First Lieutenant Chew K. Wong …is awarded the Legion of Merit for exceptional meritorious conduct in the performance of outstanding service as officer in charge of aircraft salvage and rescue work in East China during the period 13 April 1943 to 14 October 1944… Wong organized and personally supervised a number of aircraft salvage and rescue units composed of Chinese civilian mechanics and specialists in the reclamation and repair of more than 250 United States aircraft in East China. Except for Lieutenant Wong's excellent leadership, technical skill, courage in the face of danger, and intimate knowledge of East China, these aircraft would not otherwise have been returned to combat….[12]

During World War II, Chinese American servicemen fought in both Asia and Europe. They were, however, mostly active in China. Hong Lee was an American citizen by birth. In 1943, upon finishing high school, he volunteered to join the military service and became the only Chinese aviator in his outfit, the 11th combat cargo, and later in the 513th troop carrier and 332nd troop carrier units, in the 10th Air Force. Lee's duty in the war was to fly troops and supplies from inland China to the frontlines. His intimate knowledge and excellence in flying skills saved lives and won him respect among his comrades. After the war he was assigned to General George Marshall's Mission to China fl... ...nalist and Communist officials for political negotiations. He ... ...United States in 1946 after the Marshall Mission.

The 14th Air Service Group, cons... technical servicemen, was an energet... India Theater (CBI). This service g... General Chennault and Joseph S... United States Forces in CBI. Ser... served in this group. Hoy was United States as a "paper sor... New York before joining the New York Chinatown encou... a "forced volunteer." He... training and stationed in... in the message centers ... the American commar... charge of machine hc...

William Wong... receiving a high s... yard for two year... a supplyman in...

Stanley L... ...le United States... ...vas drafted by the Navy... ...ser-vicemen, he later became ... ...ment on USS *Ancon*. Stationed both in ... rom ...942 to 1945, he fought with USS *Ancon* from ... Normandy, to Okinawa. He was in the battle of Okinawa ... Japanese flew their remaining *kamikaze* planes at the American shi... crificing 35,000 of them and taking 50,000 American and British casualties on land and sea.[15]

Despite their actions, many Chinese American servicemen encountered racism during the war. In many cases their courage and determination prevailed. William Der Bong, an ex-serviceman in the Navy told his story:

> I was told [by a navy doctor] that "no Chinaman will ever fly in my outfit." ...He said, "I want you to know that I would do anything I can to fail you in your physical.' I looked at him and said, "If you do, it would be the most dishonest thing that an officer in this United States Navy could ever do to another member of the United Stated Navy.[16]

Hong Lee told of his confrontation with racial prejudice during cadet training:

> I was called to dress in a class A uniform to appear before the board that included five members. My instructor had decided to put me out.... Usually nobody would speak up and then he was out. I decided not to say I was out and instead to take him apart. I said that he was taking me out not because my true academic standard, maybe because I was not the student that he liked, which meant I was the only Chinese... I asked "how many students that you have in Air Force here graduated three and half years in high school and got into this corps up until now? I did that all in hard working!" After questions, they decided to let me stay. A couple of weeks later, the Chairman who had passed me said "I read your reports for the last two weeks.... You did so good, how come your own instructor gave you a bad grade on this?" What the instructor flunked me on was landfall, a way of navigating.... But on that particular item I hit 100 percent.[17]

Chinese American servicemen in CBI were usually bound by a double allegiance to defend China and fulfill their patriotic duty to the United States. Lieutenant Colonel Wong reveals his emotion and pride in being Chinese American:

> I went to China voluntarily. I was concerned about the Chinese people.... Once you are Chinese, you are Chinese forever.... I was very proud wearing the uniform of the United States armed forces, the best in the whole wide world!... The Chinese government honored us as Chinese and the American government honored us as American citizens. I was very proud. I could walk like a Chinese and act like an American.[18]

Hong Lee joined the military without hesitation. He recalled his decision almost fifty years later with a strong sense of pride and responsibility: serving the country "was everybody's patriotic duty at that time."[19] In China when he saw the war refugees begging for food and money he thought of his own mother in Guangdong with whom he had lost contact because of the war. "When I was flying over the rice patterns, my heart just pumped. You know, that's where you had come from."[20]

Chinese Americans' wartime activities and their patriotism left a mark on the Chinese American communities and earned them respect and greater acceptance. The 26 June 1933 issue of *Mariner*, a shipyard publication, carried the following comment: "We have learned that these Chinese Americans are among the finest workmen. They are skillful, reliable and inspired by a double allegiance."

The patriotic and hard-working Chinese in the armed forces and war industries were building up favorable opinion against legal discrimination to repeal the 1882 Exclusion Act. Chinese and their American friends worked hard to pressure the government to repeal the Chinese Exclusion Act. Among others, the Citizens Committee to Repeal the Chinese Exclusion Act, led by Richard Walsh, was most active.[21] It fought for months for the repeal.[22] It became obvious to the Roosevelt administration that the Exclusion Act served as a hindrance to cooperation between the United States and China during World War II, and as an excuse for Japanese propaganda to accusing the United States of being anti-Asian. In a message to the House of Representatives on 11 October 1943, President Roosevelt stated the need to abolish the Chinese Exclusion Act:

> I regard this legislation as important in the cause of winning the war and of establishing a secure peace... China is our ally.... China's resistance does not depend alone on guns and airplanes.... It is based as much in the spirit of her people and her faith in her allies... One step in the direction is to wipe from the statute books those anachronisms in our law which forbade the immigration of Chinese people into this country and which bar Chinese residents from American citizenship.... By repeal of the Chinese exclusion laws we can correct a historic mistake and silence the distorted Japanese propaganda.[23]

Ten days after President Roosevelt sent his message, the House passed the Magnuson Bill, and a month later the Senate gave its approval. On 17 December 1943, President Roosevelt signed it into law.

The legislation established an annual quota of 105 for Chinese to immigrate to the United States. Although legal discrimination continued, the law made about 40,000 foreign-born Chinese Americans eligible for U.S. citizenship. Following the repeal, the War Bride Act of 28 December 1945 made it possible for ex-servicemen to bring their wives and children to the United States as nonquota immigrants. To Chinese American servicemen, the Bride Act was not only a morale booster, it was a practical benefit. Many went back to China to marry or bring their wives and children to the United States; William Wong served in the American Legion as an officer to help Chinese American veterans bring their families to the States. The coming of "war wives" greatly changed gender balance and family structure in the Chinese American community. Women constituted 89 percent (8,947) of Chinese admitted to the United States between 1941-1950, while 11 percent (887) were males.[24] Hong Lee went back to China after the war and married a woman he had known before. Colonel Wong was married in 1935 while he served in the Chinese Air Force. After the war, his wife and children came back with him to the United States. Mr. Hoy's story was more complicated. He was married before he came to America as a "paper son." But on paper he was single. After the war he went back to China to "remarry" and brought his "separate wife" to the United States as a "war bride."[25]

The war and the repeal of the Chinese Exclusion Act indeed opened a new chapter in Sino-American relations and in the history of Chinese America. Looking back to the trying years of struggle, these ex-service men were very content. "I have no complaints now." Colonel Wong said, "I can live well. My sons and daughter were all well educated, and good citizens."[26] Wong was a professional soldier. To him the best way to serve his country was to join the service. His war experience and conviction influenced his relatives to a great degree. Two of his grandsons are now in the Army, and his grandnephews are in the U.S. Navy and Air Force.[27]

In sum, the war experience of Chinese American servicemen made a great contribution to the American war effort and the American society they lived in. The military service broadened their outlook and helped build their sense of confidence. These individuals had different backgrounds and served in different outfits, but they were driven by similar political and economic aspirations. They had mixed feelings as Chinese Americans who had been looked down upon in the United States but who highly valued American liberty. The dual heritage made them both very American and very Chinese. Their participation in the war contributed to the U.S. victory, helped change the attitude of the American society toward them, and improved their lives in the United States.

Notes

1. The Chinese in America experienced a 60-year legal exclusion from 1882 to 1943. Before the repeal of Chinese Exclusion Act of 1943, they were barred from naturalization and mostly restricted to Chinatown business. Diane Mei Lin Mark and Ginger Chih, *A Place Called Chinese America* ([n.p.]: The Organization of Chinese Americans, Inc., 1982 (revised).n.p., 1985) 91-93; Betty Lee Sung. *A Survey of Chinese American Manpower and Employment* (Washington, D.C.: U.S. Department of Labor, 1975): 25; Shihshan Henry Tsai, *The Chinese Experience in America* (Bloomington: Indiana University Press, 1986): 116.

2. It is estimated that 12,041 Chinese served in the U.S. Army and 214 of them became casualties. Shihshan Henry Tsai, *The Chinese Experience in America* (Bloomington: Indiana University Press, 1986) 194-95.

3. Jack Chen, *The Chinese of America* (San Francisco: Harper & Row, 1980): 203.

4. Mark and Chih, *A Place Called Chinese America*, 95; Tsai, *The Chinese Experience in America*, 113.

5. Ibid, 117; Rose Hum Lee, "Chinese in the United States Today: The War Has Changed Their Lives," *Survey Graphic* (October 1942): 444.

6. Judy Yung, *Chinese Women of America: A Pictorial History* (Seattle: Uni-

versity of Washington Press, 1986): 66.

7. Tsai, *The Chinese Experience in America*, 117.

8. Ibid., 71.

9. Chew K. Wong, interview by the author, tape recording, Pittsburgh, PA, 12 January 1993.

10. Commission from Chen Jitang, Commander in Chief of the First Army Corps, National Revolution Army. Chew K. Wong Collection, Pittsburgh.

11. "Pittsburgh 'Flying Tiger' Returns After Nine Years," *Pittsburgh Post-Gazette,* 7 October 1946.

12. Citation, USAF, Chew K. Wong Collection, Pittsburgh.

13. Hoy's real name was Yu Xianping. His father, who came to the United States in 1912 as a merchant, was not a naturalized citizen and was unable to bring his son to America. He spent $1,800 to buy a legal paper from a family friend, Lim Point, for his son. When Yu Xianping came to the United States his false name Lim Yi-Hoy was mistaken by the immigration officer as Hoy, Lim Yi. Thus Hoy became his last name. David Hoy, interview by the author, tape recording, Pittsburgh, PA, 21 December 1993.

14. William Wong, interview by the author, tape recording by telephone, Boston, MA, 9 January 1993.

15. Edwin O. Reischauer, *Japan: The Story of a Nation* (New York, 1990): 178.

16. Mark, *A Place Called Chinese America*, 96.

17. Ibid.

18. Chew K. Wong, interview by the author.

19. Hong Lee, interview by the author.

20. Ibid.

21. The Citizens Committee to Repeal Chinese Exclusion Act was founded in 1942 with over 180 non-Chinese members. Mark and Chih, *A Place Called Chinese America*, 98.

22. Franklin D. Roosevelt Library, Official File, Box 3, Hyde Park, New York.

23. *Congressional Record*, Vol. 89, 1943, 8199-8200.

24. Rose Hum Lee, *The Chinese in the United States of America* (Hong Kong: Hong Kong University Press, 1960): 22-24.

25. David Hoy, interview by the author.

26. Chew K. Wong, interview by the author.

27. Ibid.

Self-Identity

Self-identity is a concern that crosses all cultures of America's diverse society. Asian Americans' search for identity may be unique, however, when compared to their European counterparts. Initial generations of Asian immigrants frequently desired to disregard their cultural traditions, to become "Americanized" as quickly as possible. Just as frequently, however, later generations discovered personal loss of cultural identity as a result. That loss has led contemporary Asian Americans to seek a blending of the Asian and American heritages. The following papers represent some ways Asian Americans have dealt with their loss of cultural identity. Each seeks some way to find a new identity that allows them to embrace their heritages.

In Eric Chock's paper, "Diff'rent, yeah? Including Hawaii in Asian American Literature," his search for self-identity includes acknowledgment of the difference between Hawaiians and mainland Asian Americans. He also discusses the literary developments in Hawaii in the last twenty years, many of which have been directed towards bridging the gap between Hawaiian and mainland Asian Americans. The paper includes his own original poems written in Pidgin English and poems by Wing Tek Lum. He concludes with the suggestions that we need to continue to support Hawaiian ethnic literary networks within the context of multiculturalism in order to ensure the development of Hawaiian literature.

In continuing the search for self-identity, Marian Sciachitano and Rory Ong describe their personal experiences as bicultural and/or biracial members of their communities. In her paper, "Claiming a Politics of Biracial Asian American Difference," Sciachitano discusses her experiences as a biracial Asian American woman who has grown up without ties to a specific Asian American community. She expresses the necessity of a broader "non-essentialized" notion of differences which acknowledges the complexity of Asian American communities. Rory Ong's paper, "(Mis)Identifying Biracial and Bicultural Asian American Differences," discusses his relation to a Chinese American community as a biracial member while at the same time being mistaken as a member of other ethnic or racial groups by both white Americans and Asian Americans. He argues for further complicating the parameters of Asian American identity in order to critique a "white" ideology which continues to polarize Asian America and limit the possibilities of broadening the base of its communities.

In "Naming as Identity, Sui Sin Far," Annette White-Parks discusses the life and identity conflicts of Edith Eaton, aka Sui Sin Far, journalist and author who published the first essays and stories from an insider perspective of Chinese North Americans.

6

Claiming a Politics of Biracial Asian American Difference

Marian M. Sciachitano

In the powerful and moving 1988 documentary, *A Family Gathering*, film co-producer and narrator Lise Yasui claims not only her Japanese American family's history of struggle and resistance on the West coast during the early twenties and the internment years, but more importantly, she recovers and reconstructs the Yasui family's history for herself. She does this by weaving together images and narratives from old home movies, family photographs, letters, interviews, newspaper clippings, wartime newsreels, and F.B.I. documents. As *A Family Gathering* unfolds, moving images of Lise's childhood—swatches from her father's old home movies—quickly flash by on the screen. Lise begins narrating the film by remembering her father's stories while growing up "in Pennsylvania surrounded by her blue-eyed relatives on [her] mother's side."[1] While this narrative seems to get lost in the larger story of the Yasui family's internment experiences, and her grandfather Masuo's death, Lise Yasui's struggle to rethink and reconfigure the complexity of her identity as a biracial Asian American woman is an important subtext of this film.

Watching Lise Yasui's old home movies reminds me of a very similar family get together nearly a summer ago. I remember gathering in front of the entertainment center in my Uncle Joe's basement in Des Moines, Iowa—my hometown—to watch home movies of myself—movies I had never seen—of when I was just a toddler in Victorville, California, and then later as a four-year-old dancing with my dad at my Italo-American grandparent's golden wedding anniversary celebration. Like Lise, these images seemed so familiar to me because of the stories I had heard and the old black and white family portrait I'd seen commemorating that fiftieth anniversary. Looking at these film images, even though for the first time, only served to fine tune my memories of our family's past.

Having grown up as a biracial Asian American woman in the heart of the midwest, I have always been sensitive about my cultural and racial identity. In those days Asian Americans were a rarity in the city of Des Moines, in our northside neighborhood, and in the public school system. I usually found myself to be the only Asian American student in any of my classes. In fact, it wasn't until high school that I actually met another student who was biracial: Japanese and Anglo-Saxon. Although we were friends at school, it was difficult for me to accept him as a really close friend since he was one year my junior—needless to say at the time I couldn't handle the idea of hanging out with someone who was younger than me! But a more painful and perhaps ironic reason that kept us apart was that his mother and mine did not get along on religious lines. While his mom was a strict Buddhist, my mom had long ago accepted Catholicism—my father's religion—as her own.

What has been a continual and very familiar experience for me while growing up in the midwest, is having many curious Iowans come up to me on the street, on the bus, or at the mall and ask "What nationality I am" or "What country I am from." They are usually surprised to hear that I am "half" Italian. It is certainly not what they are expecting me to say. It is not what they hear when I pronounce my last name: Sciachitano. Even as a four-year-old little girl, I can distinctly remember strangers being considerably more curious about my "other half"—my Japanese half. I am now beginning to deepen my understanding and my critique of why it is that my Japanese half is so intriguing—so exotic to many European-Americans. Sometimes they want to know if I can speak Japanese or if I've ever lived in Japan, and when I tell them I don't speak Japanese or Italian—and I've never been to Japan, but I have lived briefly in Italy, they seem almost disappointed, even frustrated that "I don't know my own culture." The assumption being "my own culture" is only a Japanese culture and has nothing whatsoever to do with my having Italian roots or having lived in America all my life.

What is frustrating to me, however, is their general lack of recognition that I embody a biracial Asian American difference. Not only do I bring an awareness of my "Japanese side" via my *Shin issei* mother who hails from the northern island of Hokkaido—who worked as a nurse during the Second World War, as a dental hygienist for the U.S. Armed Forces during the Korean conflict, and later as a domestic once she arrived in the U.S. But I also bring an awareness of my second generation Italo-American father and his family and community. I actually knew and lived for a brief time with my first generation Italo-American grandparents Vito and Marian. I was even named after my grandmother. As a teenager, I grew up listening to my grampa's captivating stories of Sambuca, his coming to America *via* Louisiana, and a lifetime of back-breaking experiences working as a dock loader on the railroads. As a small child, I'll never forget his building me a rocking horse, chasing me around the "yellow bird house" in California as I playfully chanted "Catch me, Grampa, Catch me!" and later teaching me the proper way to transplant a tomato plant from a cold frame to the garden bed. I share these memories not just for "sharing's sake" or as some kind of simplistic and indulgent nostalgia for the past; on the contrary, these memories are important precisely because they have given me a complex bicultural and biracial identity. They are a part of my ongoing struggle to understand and critique how I am being positioned—by the gaze of strangers—by dominant cultural discourses, institutions, and their problematic categories. These memories also nourish my desire to not only find ways of negotiating my complex subjectivity and difference in a culture which still holds on to a notion of a unified, essential subject, but more significantly, to work towards what Cornel West has called "a new cultural politics of difference" where I can legitimately claim my complex standpoint—my positionality—as a biracial and bicultural Asian American woman.[2]

In an essay on "Cultural Identity and Diaspora," cultural critic Stuart Hall explains quite powerfully and eloquently that:

> Cultural identity …is a matter of 'becoming' as well as 'being.' It belongs to the future as much as to the past. It is not something which already exists, transcending place, time, history, and culture. Cultural identities come from somewhere, have histories. But, like everything which is historical, they undergo constant transformation. Far from being eternally fixed in some essentialized past, they are subject to the continuous 'play' [flux] of history, culture and power. Far from being grounded in a mere 'recovery' of the past, which is waiting to be found, and which, when found, will secure our sense of ourselves into eternity, identities are the names we give to the different ways we are positioned by, and position ourselves within, the narratives of the past.[3]

Lise Yasui's *A Family Gathering* was originally a film project that was going to document the internment of Japanese Americans—a simple project of historical "recovery"; however, as Lise herself became more involved in researching the film and the gradual uncovering of a long concealed and "missing" fabric of her family's internment history and their legacy of struggle and resistance, it became a much deeper and more serious project for her. Because these narratives of her family's past had yet to be spoken, Lise had to basically piece together and reconstruct a new sense of history from her standpoint as a biracial Asian American woman. Her film is in fact a powerful "practice of subjectivity" via a new cultural "politics of representation."[4] She is one of the many new cultural workers out there—a cultural producer whose film engages difference by problematizing the category of what it means to be an Asian American. Instead of allowing a dominant cultural discourse to position her as "outside" the history of Japanese Americans, Lise positions herself in history by critically engaging those past narratives and in effect reclaiming and revisioning the Yasui family's internment history from one of seeming tragedy and despair to one of ongoing resistance and hope "[which] challenges a politics of domination that would render us nameless and voiceless."[5] When Lise narrates *A Family Gathering*, she recalls that a favorite memory of hers is when her grandparents came to visit their family in Pennsylvania and she remembers staying up late into the night listening to her grandfather talk. Later in the film, however, she learns that her grandparents never made that trip and that she never met her grandfather or heard him talking into the night. And yet, what's so powerful about this documentary is that at the very end of the film Lise Yasui claims agency by choosing to keep that memory of her grandfather talking late into the night. This is a good example of what claiming a biracial, or even a multiracial politics of difference could be about.

In Michael Omi's "It Just Ain't The Sixties No More: The Contemporary Dilemmas of Asian American Studies," he observes that "the increasing diversity of the Asian American populations makes it difficult, if not impossible, to generalize about the state of Asian America. It, in fact, leads one to speculate as to whether such an entity exists."[6] Historically, Omi goes on to explain, the term "Asian American" emerged in the sixties as a "political label" that "was meant to convey similarities in the historical experiences of primarily Chinese, Japanese, and Philippinos [sic]."[7] However, given the arrival of new Asian immigrant groups in the U.S., Omi notes the limitations and difficulty of using the sixties definition of Asian American to continually "speak of a shared experience."[8] Furthermore, I would argue that the sixties definition, though political in its time, also never included the experiences of biracial, multiracial, gay, lesbian, or bisexual Asian Americans. Clearly the time for redefining what is meant by the term "Asian American" or "Asian Pacific American," in light of contemporary political and cultural realities, is long overdue. According to Stuart Hall, it is imperative to begin this conceptual process by naming ourselves and recognizing the "extraordinary diversity [and complexity] of subjective positions, social experiences, and cultural identities" that compose the category "Black," or in this case, "Asian."[9] Obviously, this process of naming and recognition extends to other ethnic and racial groups in the U.S. and most likely overlaps other borderlands. For example, Janice Gould, a mixed-blood American Indian, observes that there are an increasing number of mixed-blood writers, Leslie Marmon Silko, M. Scott Momaday, Louise Erdrich, Joy Harjo, and Paula Gunn Allen to name but a few, who are struggling to articulate the complexity of their experiences and identities.[10]

Within the diversity of Asian Americans who are also struggling for a new cultural politics of identity and difference, there are contemporary writers, poets, artists, and theorists such as, David Mura, recent author of *Turning Japanese: Memoirs of a Sansei* (1991), who discusses how "[he] grew up outside an Asian American community in the Jewish suburbs of Chicago."[11] The poet Ai, though Japanese, African-American, Choctaw, and Irish, identifies herself mostly with her Asian side.[12] Brenda Wong Aoki, a storyteller and performance artist, centers her work directly on the axes of her complex multiracial identity as a Chinese, Japanese, Australian, and Irish American woman. In a moving one-woman show, she mixes traditional stories such as *The Paper Crane* and stories of her Chinese-American grandfather through her knowledge and training in Japanese Noh theatre.[13] Brenda Wong Aoki also speaks about what it was like growing up on LA's West side by shifting easily from her familiar "valley girl" discourse to the everyday discourse of her Hawaiian-American high school boyfriend. Finally, bisexual feminist theorist Margaret Mihee Choe, a second-generation Korean American, articulates the complexity of her bisexual Asian American difference in a heterosexist culture which positions her not only in between the hegemonic racial categories of either black or white, but also in between binary sexual categories of either heterosexual or gay.[14] These are just a few of the Asian American men and women who are out there as "new cultural workers" struggling to creatively as well as critically interrogate their complex cultural identities and realities through personal essays, poetry, performance, and theory.

In my own struggles to begin seeing myself as a new cultural worker associated with a biracial politics of "Asian American" difference who is striving to define a broader "non-essentialized," more complex and diverse practice of that difference, I have recently found Gloria Anzaldúa's work on *mestiza consciousness*[15] to be extremely useful for re-thinking my own location—a biracial/bicultural politics of location. Anzaldúa, a Chicana dyke, calls for a new consciousness—a *mestiza consciousness* wherein the new mestiza copes by developing a tolerance for contradictions, a tolerance for ambiguity. She learns to be an Indian in Mexican culture, to be Mexican from an Anglo point of view. She learns to juggle cultures. She has a plural personality, she operates in a pluralistic mode—nothing is thrust out, the good, the bad and the ugly, nothing rejected, nothing abandoned. Not only does she sustain contradictions, she turns the ambivalence into something else.[16] In my daily life, I embrace and "juggle" my relations to Italo-American culture as well as Japanese American culture. Nothing rejected. Nothing abandoned. At the same time, I accept the contradictions, the uneasiness, and the ambiguity that often comes with taking up a bicultural and biracial politics of difference. While it may not seem obvious, it is very difficult and painful at times to call attention to or even name my difference. Everything in my cultural upbringing tells me "Not to tell"—to remain nameless and voiceless. Yet, I have gradually come to realize a politics of biracial or multiracial difference must be informed and spurred on by a new critical consciousness and a vision of the "not yet." Developing such a consciousness can in fact be "a source of intense pain" or invoke feelings of shame or guilt, but at the same time, Anzaldúa observes "its energy comes from a continual creative motion that keeps breaking down the unitary aspects of each new paradigm."[17]

Furthermore, what's particularly empowering about Anzaldúa's call for a new *mestiza consciousness* is that she recognizes that "the future will belong to the mestiza. Because the future depends on the straddling of two or more cultures. By creating a new mythos—that is, a change in the way we perceive reality. The way we see ourselves and the ways we behave.[18] As teachers or students, community workers or residents, mothers or fathers—we can "cultivate critical sensibilities and personal accountability."[19]

By legitimizing the complexity and heterogeneity of Asian America, we participate in creating a "new cultural mythos" and basis for political solidarity in the twenty-first century. As a biracial woman of color who teaches composition, I am very aware that there will eventually be students of color in my writing classes who may be attempting to negotiate and understand their biracial, multiracial, and perhaps even bisexual difference. If we are to move forward, what is needed is involved and complex. As Cornel West has rightly observed, "the new cultural politics of difference can thrive only if there are communities, groups, organizations, institutions, subcultures, and networks of people of color" who are deeply committed to this struggle and to forming alliances. This "will require all the imagination, intelligence, courage, sacrifice, care and laughter we can muster."[20]

Notes

1. Lise Yasui, co-producer and narrator. *A Family Gathering (*Independent film. PBS *American Experience*, 1988).

2. Cornel West, "The New Cultural Politics of Difference," in *Out There: Marginalization and Contemporary Cultures*, edited by Russell Ferguson, Martha Gever, Trinh T. Minh-Ha, and Cornel West (New York: MIT Press in association with The New Museum of Contemporary Art, 1990): 19.

3. Stuart Hall, "Cultural Identity and Diaspora," in *Black Looks: Race and Representation* (Boston: South End Press, 1992): 5; see *Identity, Community, Culture and Difference* edited by Jonathan Rutherford (London: Lawrence & Wishart, 1990).

4. Trinh T. Minh-Ha, "Outside In Inside Out," in *When the Moon Waxes Red: Representation, Gender and Cultural Politics (*New York: Routledge, 1991): 77; Stuart Hall, "New Ethnicities," in *Black Film/British Cinema*, edited by Kobena Mercer (London: ICA Documents Black Film, 1988): 27.

5. bell hooks, *Talking Back: Thinking Feminist Thinking Black* (Boston: South End Press, 1989): 8.

6. Michael Omi, "It Just Ain't the Sixties No More: The Contemporary Dilemma of AsianAmerican Studies." in *Reflection on Shattered Windows: Promises and Prospects for Asian American Studies*, edited by Gary Y. Okihiro, Shirley Hune, Arthur A. Hansen, and John M. Liu (Pullman, WA: Washington State University Press,1988): 32-33.

7. Ibid., 32-33

8. Ibid., 32-33

9. Hall, "New Ethnicities," 28.

10. Janice Gould. "The Problem of Being 'Indian,'" in *De/Colonizing the Subject: The Politics of Gender in Women's Autobiography*, edited by Sidonie Smith and Julia Watson (Minneapolis: University of Minnesota Press, 1992) 86-87.

11. David Mura, "Mirrors of the Self: Autobiography and the Japanese American Writer." In *Asian Americans: Comparative and Global Perspectives*, edited by Shirley Hune, Hyung-chan Kim, Stephen S. Fugita, and Amy Ling, (Pullman, WA: Washington State University Press, 1991) 251.

12. Ai. "On Being 1/2 Japanese, 1/8 Choctaw, 1/4 Black, and 1/16 Irish." *Ms* (May 1978): 58.

13. Brenda Wong Aoki, performance artist and storyteller. "Tales of the Pacific Rim." (Pullman, WA: Bryan Hall, February 1993).

14. Margaret Mihee Choe, "Our Selves, Growing Whole." *Closer to Home: Bisexuality & Feminism*, edited by Elizbeth Reba Weise (Seattle: The Seal Press, 1992) 20-23.

15. This expression belongs to Gloria Anzaldúa, "La Conciencia de la Mestiza: Towards a New Consciousness." in *Making Face, Making Soul/Haciendo Caras: Creative and Critical Perspectives by Women of Color*, edited by Gloria Anzaldúa (San Francisco: Aunt Lute Press, 1990): 379.

16. Ibid.

17. Ibid.

18. Ibid.

19. West, "New Cultural Politics of Difference," 34.

20. Ibid., 34, 36.

7

(Mis)Identifying Biracial and Bicultural Asian American Differences

Rory J. Ong

Where is my country?
Where does it lie?

Tucked between boundaries
striated between dark dance floors
and whispering lanterns
smoking of indistinguishablefeatures?

Salted in Mexico
where a policeman speaks to me in Spanish?
In the voice of a Chinese grocer
who asks if I am Filipino?

Channeled in the white businessman
who discovers that I do not sound Chinese?
Garbled in a white woman
who tells me I speak perfect English?
Webbed in another
who tells me I speak with an accent?

Where is my country?
Where does it lie?[1]

For me, "home" is Phoenix, Arizona the "Valley of the Sun," and it is where I spent most of my childhood, adolescence, and young adult years. The community I hail from, the one I most identify with whenever I return to Phoenix, is the Chinese American community that has been growing in the valley since the early 1900s. During the second World War, my father, a second generation Chinese American, was stationed in New York City where he met my mother, a second generation Italo-American. In the late 1940s they married, returned to Phoenix, and raised a family of four—all of whom are now married and most of whom have children of their own. Growing up as biracial, third generation members of this community made issues of identity all the more complicated for me and my siblings. On the one hand we only had to identify ourselves as Ongs, the children of our father John, or the nephews and nieces of my uncles or aunts, and the familial relations were understood by the community. It was a very comfortable place to be in, and growing up we felt very much a part of everything that went on in the community: cultural events, weddings, community dances, etc. On the other hand, our father did not require us to attend Chinese school like some of our peers. He wanted us to be 100 percent "American" so we never really learned our community's Cantonese dialect, nor were we taught any specific customs—although we did pick up a few just by being involved in the community. As we got older, however, particularly around the time we became interested in dating, community attitudes seemed to change. Suddenly we were not Chinese enough, in spite of the fact that we had always been embraced by the community and had come to think of ourselves as Chinese. Ironically, the community instilled in us (as it did in most of the young people) the idea that we should really only consider dating relationships, not to mention marital ones, with other Chinese Americans. Living in this contradictory space soon became a problem for us as we attempted, in a variety of ways, to negotiate the different directions in which we were being pulled.

Beyond that community, however, our identity was all the more complex. Because of the large groups of Chicanos, and American Indians in the Southwest, we were often identified with those communities. In fact, American Indian friends of mine would sometimes offer to take me on the Reservation because they thought "I could pass." When I changed high schools one year from a predominantly white working class school to one more racially diverse, those who befriended me were the Chicano and African American students in spite of my Asian background. I also remember many experiences when members of the Chicano community would approach me speaking Spanish, thinking that I was from that community. In fact, I remember a time when I filled out some affirmative action forms in high school and actually marked the "Hispanic" box because I was so commonly identified with that group. Contradictory though it may seem, I was often included in, and sometimes even identified myself with, these other racial and ethnic communities.

On the contrary, when members of the white community (my teachers, friends' parents, or employers) would inquire about my last name, the racial distinction for them became clear—I was Chinese. If perceptive enough, they would ask about my mother, and with eyebrows raised and heads nodding they would hum, "Hmmm... Italian!?" as if refiguring me in their mind's eye, attempting to distinguish the one from the other. As I have gotten older, and since "Otherness" has taken on such currency, the more common response has been "Gee, you don't look Chinese?" The query is actually quite problematic. Most often it is spoken with a presumption that I have lost all trace of my Asian background—racially as well as culturally. However, it actually reveals the dominant culture's overbearing concern with the presence of the Oriental as well as its unspoken desire for the centrality of the European—or, as Russell Ferguson calls it, "the phantom center"— "elusive," "absent," yet undeniably exerting its power.[2] In other words, I'm often thought of as not ethnic enough or not diverse enough to be considered for the emerging category of "multicultural" but also not white enough to be white. As a biracial and bicultural subject I'm not included in either category—that is, I do not embody the "presence of the 'Other'" nor do I possess the "absent power of the Center." I occupy an in between space—a contradiction—my biraciality having become another object for what Cornel West calls the "normative gaze"; that is, my "biracial" and "bicultural" identity is subordinate to the new western hierarchy of a plurality of "mono-racial" and "mono-cultural" peoples.[3] In these kinds of situations I, more often than not, become the responsible party, having mistaken myself for someone or something that I simply could not, or better yet should not be; my identity becomes misplaced, displaced, and erased in view of these "plural" cultural centers.

To identify myself as someone who is biracial and bicultural, means something much more complex and contradictory for me than the very narrow and limited parameters of identity delineated by the dominant U.S. culture. Not only does it mean that I identify with a very particular Chinese American community in Phoenix, but it means that I struggle for an identity, for a sense of agency and place, within that community as well. However, I think it is fair to say that in the midst of this struggle my biracial status also transgresses the boundaries of a particularly "Asian American" identity; it challenges the definition, and forces me to rethink and expand its perimeters. More importantly, my biraciality has enabled me to experience how an oppressive dominant ideology uses my contradiction to sharpen the lines of cultural and racial definition—lines that clearly mark the boundaries of the culturally and racially "pure," and blur, marginalize, and erase everything that falls outside those pristine boundaries.

In his critique of racial stereotypes in American popular culture, Michael Omi is quick to point out how dominant cultural notions of white superiority feed, generate, even construct the "traits, habits and predispositions of non-whites."[4] Despite the fact that their identities are often interchangeable in films, Omi observes that racial minorities often have unique qualities assigned to them—Latinos are angry, Blacks are physically strong, and Asians are sneaky, cunning, and evil. The differences which actually exist within communities of color are minimized, distorted, or obliterated altogether and thus the saying "All Asians look alike."[5] Omi's critique of this reduction is crucial, not so much because he identifies the stereotypes themselves, but because he acknowledges that the creation of stereotypes "underscores" and "highlights" the dominance and privilege of white culture.[6] This became clearer to me when I recently read Janice Gould's narrative "The Problem of Being Indian: One Mixed-Blood's Dilemma."[7] As a member of the Konkow tribe, she explains that her mixed background has often presented opportunities for members of the dominant culture to try and clue her in about her identity:

> I am sometimes perceived as Hispanic, sometimes as Asian. My first experience of racism as a child, in fact, had to do with a stupid misperception. A little girl called me a "dirty Jap" ... [and] thanks to that little girl, I understood that I was not seen as white by everyone.... Recently, something similar occurred to me. It lacked the viciousness of that little girl's hatred, but it smacked of similar ignorance. I was in an office in the English Department at my university, the University of New Mexico. The secretary, I could tell, was observing me. After a moment she asked, "Are you Asian?" "No," I answered, "I'm not." I hesitated, then decided to help the lady out. "I'm part Indian," I said. "Oh," she replied, "you are Asian. You people came over from China thousands of years ago!" Thus I was both corrected and informed about my origins. And maybe the lady felt better knowing she hadn't made a mistake. Somehow I became both more Indian and less Indian in this conversation. I was rendered invisible not only because of this woman's initial misperception of me... but also through the forced disappearance of my claim to Indianness...[8]

What I find interesting in this lengthy passage is that while Gould herself acknowledges that her mixed identity does not easily allow herself to be located in any particular ethnic category, this woman felt it her duty (re: it was her privilege) to explain to Gould the correct history of her Indian ancestry and culture. But as Gould rightly points out, her mixed identity is no more clear than it was when the conversation started. In fact, if anything, the complexity of Gould's identity has been further marginalized and silenced by this woman's self appointment as cultural authority. Stereotyping is much more problematic than mere media caricatures as Michael Omi has indeed suggested; the problem is one of dominant ideology in which relations of power and representation are formed to give some more than others the authority and privilege to create and define particular patterns of racial identity.

Gould's response to this cultural violation, her feeling more yet less Indian at the same time, is symptomatic of a dominant culture's oppressive discourse. Abdul JanMohamed and David Lloyd have argued that given the pervasiveness of this dominant discourse, it should come as no surprise that there has been an "historically sustained negation" of the voices of people of color.[9] They point out that the "inadequacy" or "underdevelopment" ascribed to the discourses of communities of color is due to the "limiting (and limited) ideological horizons of [a] dominant, ethnocentric perspective."[10] This is an important observation because, like Omi, both JanMohamed and Lloyd have managed to put their finger on the elusive, invisible center that wants to speak boldly for everyone, but only within the "absent" boundaries of its own paradigm. Therefore, when discussing the complex identities of biracial and bicultural Asian American subjects, and the struggles engendered by their multiple locations, it is important to understand how those struggles have been generated by the oppression of a dominant ideology which seeks to fix and bracket their identities to a wall of "white" supremacy. Stuart Hall articulates this best in his discussion of racism: "Racism, of course, operates by constructing impassable symbolic boundaries between racially constituted categories, and its typically binary system of representation constantly marks and attempts to fix and naturalize the difference between belongingness and otherness."[11]

If we are to alter this cycle of domination, we must question and challenge all attempts to suppress the kind of multiplicity and heterogeneity that biracial and bicultural subjects can bring into discussions about identity, representation, and power. We must resist oppression whether it be by those of the dominant culture, or those of communities of color. This resistance must include naming that which dominates, articulating it so that it becomes known. As Trinh Minh-ha puts it,

> In the current situation of over codification, of de-individualized individualism and of reductionist collectivism, naming critically is to dive headlong into the abyss of un-naming. The task of inquiring into all the divisions of a culture remains exacting, for the moments when things take on a proper name can only be positional, [and] hence transitional. The function of any ideology in power is to represent the world positively unified. To challenge the regimes of representation that govern a society is to conceive of how a politics can transform reality rather than merely ideologize it. As the struggle moves onward and assumes new, different forms, it is bound to recompose [both] subjectivity and praxis while displacing the way diverse cultural strategies relate to one another in the constitution of social and political life.[12]

By critically renaming and refiguring biracial and bicultural identities we unmask the discourse that subjugates, marginalizes, and silences these complex and contradictory histories. Renaming these subjects legitimates their place and stake in cultural production, social experience, and political life, and provides an alternate discursive space from which to speak—a critical location fashioned around a multi-faceted politics that recognizes the sometimes converging, sometimes conflicting, relations of power that are generated in the complex social, cultural, and political circumstances of daily life.

For example, I was reminded of my father during the recent celebration of St. Patrick's Day. My family was never really sure of his birthday except that it was thought to be sometime in March. Because of this, my father always liked to celebrate his birthday on the 17th, wanting to believe that it fell on that day. Active in many local organizations like the Optimists Club or the American Legion, my father met many people (non-Asians) who would ask about his name. "Ong? What kind of a name is Ong?" they would ask. "Don't you know?" he would stare back wide-eyed. "It's Irish!" Ironically, I was recently asked the same question. After succumbing to one of those lengthy telephone surveys, the interviewer wanted some basic information: name, address, telephone, and so on. When I told the interviewer my name, she asked, "Oh! What kind of a name is Ong?" "It's Chinese," I said. "No!" She responded in disbelief, as if I were joking. I went on to assure her that my name was indeed Chinese, but she still doubted. We went back and forth like this for a few moments, until she admitted that I didn't sound "Chinese."

My father was questioned about his identity because of his Asian features. I, however, was questioned because of the lack of them. In either case, as our respondents sought the specificity of particular racial signifiers, they were confused when we did not offer them. Mistaking our identities, in these instances, revealed not only the dominant culture's curiosity about difference, but its difficulty in acknowledging the diversity within difference. Misidentification is not simply a matter of confused people of color who, as biracial and/or bicultural subjects, misconstrue their identities or who simply "don't know their history or their culture." On the contrary, misidentification is a marker for the complexity of difference that multiple racial and cultural subjects bring to a polarized society—subjects whose complicated identities (their histories and experiences) disrupt and confound the dominant, mainstream discourse when their hybrid differences become articulated. The ways my father and I responded were examples of how this disruption functions in daily situations, and envisions the possibilities of a new kind of lived practice which problematizes the reductive discourse of the dominant culture. That is, a multiplicity and diversity of Asian American identities can engender what Lisa Lowe identifies as *heterotopic spaces* "from which new practices are generated at the intersections of unevenly produced categories of otherness, in the junctions, overlaps, and confluences of incommensurate apparatuses which are not primarily linguistic but practical and material."[13]

This practice, Cornel West tells us, cannot simply be a project that contests the mainstream in order to be included in it, nor can it simply be a "transgression" of the status quo for the sake of disruption alone.[14] Rather, it will be important to provide for a broader articulation of community, identity, and difference that will generate new cultural and political agents who will resist "mere opportunism, mindless eclecticism, ethnic chauvinism, and faceless universalism."[15] Once again, I think Trinh T. Minh-ha provides some very crucial insight into the difficult, yet necessary, implications of this new cultural practice. She points out that,

> The quest for the other in us can hardly be a simple return to the past or to the time honored values of our ancestors. Changes are inevitably implied in the process of restoring cultural lineage, which combines the lore of the past with the lore of the complex present in its histories of migrations. As soon as we learn to be "Asians in America"—that is to come to rest in a place supposedly always there, waiting to be discovered—we also recognize that we can't simply be Asians any longer... Listening to new sounds in the attempt to articulate a specific transcul-

tural between-world reality requires again that the steps backward be simultaneously a step forward.[16]

Embracing the "other in us," as Minh-ha puts it, is tantamount to embracing a revisioned identity that doesn't necessarily maintain traditional customs, remember the "correct" history of its origin, nor speak the traditional language. In fact, it is much more the case that these new subjects will be multivocal and multicultural, yet never forget their particular history as it pertains to them socially, culturally, and politically in the U.S. "Where is our country, and where does it lie?" I like how Nellie Wong has suggested, it is "[t]ucked between boundaries/ striated between dark dance floors/ and whispering lanterns/ smoking of indistinguishable features."[17]

Notes

1. Nellie Wong, "Where Is My Country" in *The Death of Longsteam Lady* (Los Angeles: West End Press, 1984): 32.

2. Russell Ferguson, "Introduction: Invisible Center." in *Out There: Marginalization and Contemporary Culture*, edited by Russell Ferguson, Martha Gever, Trinh T. Minh-ha and Cornel West (New York, Cambridge: The New Museum of Contemporary Art and MIT Press, 1990): 9-14.

3. Cornell West, "A Genealogy of Modern Racism," in *Prophesy Deliverance!: An Afro-American Revolutionary Christianity* (Philadelphia: The Westminster Press,1982): 53.

4. Michael Omi, "In Living Color: Race and American Culture." in *Cultural Politics in Contemporary Culture,* Ian Angus and Sut Jally, eds. (New York: Routledge,1989): 116.

5. Ibid.

6. Ibid.

7. Janice Gould, "The Problem of Being Indian: One Mixed-Blood's Dilemma," in *De/Colonizing the Subject: The Politics of Gender in Women's Autobiography*, Sidonie Smith and Julia Watson, eds. (Minneapolis: University of Minnesota Press, 1992).

8. Ibid., 84.

9. Abdul JanMohamed and David Lloyd, "Introduction: Toward a Theory of Minority Discourse: What Is To Be Done?" in *The Nature and Context of Minority Discourse* (New York: Oxford University Press, 1990): 4.

10. Ibid., 6.

11. Hall, Stuart. "New Ethnicities," in *Black Film/British Cinema*. Kobena Mercer, ed. (London: ICA Documents, 1988) 28.

12. Trinh T. Minh-ha, *When the Moon Waxes Red: Representation, Gender, and Cultural Politics* (New York: Routledge, 1991): 2.

13. Lisa Lowe, "Discourse and Heterogeneity: Situating Orientalism," *Critical Terrains: French and British Orientalisms* (Ithaca: Cornell University Press,

1991) 24.

14. Cornel West, "The New Cultural Politics of Difference." *Out There: Marginalization and Contemporary Cultures (*New York and Cambridge: The New Museum of Contemporary Art and MIT Press, 1990): 19-20.

15. Ibid., 26.

16. Trinh T. Minh-ha, "Bold Omissions and Minute Depictions" *Moving the Image: Independent Asian Pacific American Media Arts* (Los Angeles: UCLA Asian American Studies and Visual Communications, 1991): 87.

17. Wong, "Where Is My Country" 32.

8

"Diff'rent, Yeah?"

Including Hawaii in Asian American Literature

Eric Chock

A trip from Hawaii to the mainland is like a black hole around which time condenses. The days speed up as take off time approaches. Buying a thicker pair of shoes for the impossibly cold weather becomes incredibly difficult when Sears doesn't have your size of hiking boots, your brother-in-law's thermal underwear seems to tighten around your middle, and the TV continues to broadcast single digit temperatures one week before spring. Four time zones in one flight. Already, the body forgets how to sleep.

Therefore, it is not difficult to understand how our local Asian American literature can get lost in transition, even when we are bringing it ourselves. In fact, it can get so confusing that it will include poems like this one to my French Canadian wife, a resident of Hawaii for the last 15 years.

> ### Deux Langues
>
> *You say let's go "at my house"*
> *as your translation of "à la maison"*
> *You don't sweep*
> *you broom the room*
> *You want to buy a "nasal"*
> *for the garden house*
> *I try to correct your English*
> *but then you have "the taste for kissing"*
> *and who can resist that kind of twisting*
> *of our native tongues[1]*

So let me outline my talk. First, I would like to acknowledge the difference between Hawaii and mainland Asian Americans, and admit to our part in creating that gap. Secondly, I will briefly cover literary developments in Hawaii in the last twenty years or so, much of which has been directed towards bridging the gap between Hawaii and mainland Asian Americans. Third, I would like to suggest that we need to continue to support our ethnic literary networks within the context of the multiculturalism in order to ensure the development of our literature.

Let me start by admitting that we in Hawaii have been out of the mainstream of American culture for many years. We were raised on being another country, a territory, on our pidgin English, on eating poi, on a satellite delay for "Leave It To Beaver." It didn't matter to be a week or a month behind. Even though we have live satellite TV now and can see what clothes or music are in fashion, it still may take months before we get them for ourselves, if we decide to adopt them at all. After all, how many people are willing to wear all those oversized sweatshirts or sweaters in Hawaii just because they are seen everywhere on the mainland? Granted, I remember when I was young and did my best to put on whatever front I thought necessary to create the right image of myself.

Making Da Scene

In '66, our hair
was hitting da tops of our collars
and doing da surfa flip,
we neva tuck in da tails
of our button-down paisley shirts,
and you could still wear Beatle boots
and make da scene.
All summer we cruised Ala Moana,
Conrad and me, new wrap-around
sunglasses making everything green,
rolling along with da Stones and
getting no satisfaction
in his brother Earl's '63 Dodge Dart,
lifted, quad carburetor, could do 90
on da new H-1 Freeway, but
we neva even think we was mean.

Everytime around,
we just leaned down in his
blue vinyl seats, hoping
somebody would notice us
as we rumbled through da park,
those wrap-arounds like protection
and a tease
for those cute chicks
who was out there every day,
doing da same thing.[2]

So it was no surprise that we were different when we met dozens of Asian American writers from the mainland at the watershed 1978 Talk Story Writers' Conference in Honolulu. We in Hawaii were unfamiliar with the very term Asian American, preferring to be called "local." And I believe that, at least subconsciously, there was a kind of jousting between us to prove to the other that we each had our own kind of integrity. Perhaps this division dates back to World War II when the terms used by Japanese Americans were "buddhaheads" (Hawaii) and "kotonks" (mainland).

Initially, it was ironic that we saw in each other the weakness of being too assimilated, what we might call "haolefied." Locals noticed how mainland Asian Americans talked like haoles, so the reaction was: "Looks like a local but talks like a haole," which was a major component of being labeled a "banana," yellow on the outside but white on the inside. To avoid the label, it was a long-standing practice for locals to switch from pidgin to standard English only when appropriate; that is, only in the presence of haoles. So some of us felt that odd feeling that we were speaking to haoles in Asian bodies, which we got used to only if we went to college on the mainland, or to certain prep schools in Hawaii.

On the other hand, mainland Asian Americans said we were too apolitical, not aware of our own ethnic backgrounds, as far as they could tell from our writing. Not only were we unfamiliar with Asian American literature on the mainland, we were so "behind the mainland" again, that we were unfamiliar with our own local literary traditions. While they were celebrating their rediscoveries of camp journals or *nisei* novelists, University or Hawaii writing students were happy to be involved in a Joyce Symposium, or to become meditators and poets like Bly and Merwin. There was almost no mention of any non-white writers at the university. When I was a grad student in the 1970's and brought up the possibility of using pidgin as I had heard it in local comedy, I was steered away from that to my "real" audience, academic English. With attitudes like that, it was easy for mainlanders to say that we were passively assimilated into the white American mainstream culture, having no pride in our own, which of course was not true either. The kind of poem which would not have gone over well at the University of Hawaii would be the following.

Tutu On Da Curb

Tutu standing on da corna,
she look so nice!
Her hair all pin up in one bun,
one huge red hibiscus hanging out
over her right ear, her blue Hawaiian print muu muu
blowing in da wind
as one bus driver blows
one huge cloud of smoke
around her,
no wonder her hair so gray!
She squint and wiggle her nose
at da heat
and da thick stink fumes
da bus driver just futted all over here.
You can see her shrivel up
and shrink little bit more.
Bum bye, she going disappear
from da curb
foreva.[3]

But since 1978, things have changed. In Hawaii, we have established a literary network which functions to support a variety of new and established writers, and promotes the idea of local writers and local literature.

The prime example is the formation of Bamboo Ridge Press, a non-profit organization whose quarterly has provided a continuous showcase for local writers, who do have a harder time getting published on the mainland because of the distance and realities of literary politics. It has become a channel which allows for a multiplicity of voices to be heard, both in print and in live readings which occur with every issue. It has an ongoing track record of literary publication which is arguably better than any Asian American organization on the mainland. It has been at the core of a continuing workshop which has met monthly since 1980. Partly due to my position with the long-standing Poets in the Schools program which has been sending local poets into classes for twenty years, Bamboo Ridge has been instrumental in conducting a series of workshops for public and private school teachers on writing and local literature.

The Hawaii Literary Arts Council and the University of Hawaii have continued the series of visiting writers from overseas, but now there is at least one ethnic writer each year. This helps greatly in developing a sense of community between local and mainland ethnic writers. Although there is not yet an established program at any college which supports the development and research into ethnic literature, there have been a few classes specifically devoted to ethnic literature or Asian American literature, and several local writer/teachers use local books in their classes, often inviting the writers themselves to speak. However, we have yet to have an ethnic writer on the tenured faculty in the creative writing department at the University of Hawaii.

The University of Hawaii and a handful of smaller colleges have literary magazines, and there have been a few private publications as well. There are a few ongoing local readings series outside the University of Hawaii; local bookstores are beginning to pay more attention to local books, especially since the formation of the Hawaii Book Publishing Association, and local magazine and newspaper coverage of writers is more frequent than it used to be. *Honolulu Magazine* has established a fiction writing contest which is enormously popular.

We in Hawaii are learning to play the literary game. We have found a way to survive in a system that has not been quick to support us, forming our own literary institutions, networks, support systems, and making them work on our own while hoping someday to gain recognition from that larger system out there. We have sustained the struggle against an unsympathetic dominant culture, created ways to survive in spite of it, eventually producing material which does engender a response, secures a place for itself, and contributes to that other culture. We in Hawaii have had to fight to gain a kind of "multi-cultural" acceptance from mainland Asian Americans, as well as mainstream, white American society, and we have, to some extent, made it.

We are glad to be at dinner at someone's home and see among us recipients of a National Endowment for the Arts Fellowship, an American Book Award, a Pushcart Prize, or a nomination for the Pulitzer Prize. Although we do critique each other and make comments motivated out of envy as well as ideology, in the end, we basically are glad when one of us finds success. And we find ways to communicate our differences as well as our similarities, we find common ground on which to stand. We have the feeling that we are all moving forward. Isn't this what multiculturalism is about? As time goes by, we must find ways to get along without destroying the system which supports us, or life would be unbearable in our relatively small, geographically bound, multicultural community.

I like to refer to Wing Tek Lum's poem "Chinese Hot Pot" as a good working definition of multiculturalism. In the poem, he denies the melting pot image, and simply reworks it to provide more integrity to the various members who are not only partaking of the food, but are their own cooks, as well.

Chinese Hot Pot

My dream of America
is like da bin louh
with people of all persuasions and tastes
sitting down around a common pot
chopsticks and basket scoops here and there
some cooking squid and others beef
some tofu or watercress
all in one broth
like a stew that really isn't
as each one chooses what he wishes to eat
only that the pot and fire are shared
along with the good company
and the sweet soup
spooned out at the end of the meal.[4]

This may be contrasted with Wing Tek Lum's earlier poem, where the food metaphor is used to depict the divisions and hierarchies which are perceived in an unevolved America that has not yet had an open discussion of what it would mean to live in a multi-cultural society. In this poem, we are not even all seated at the same table, having been relegated to being the cooks, maids, or even the garbage from the food that is to be consumed.

Minority Poem

Why
we're just as American
as apple pie—
that is, if you count
the leftover peelings
lying on the kitchen counter
which the cook has forgotten about
or doesn't know
quite what to do with
except hope that the maid

when she cleans off the chopping block
will chuck them away
into a garbage can she'll take out
on leaving for the night.[5]

If we take these two poems to represent ethnic writers in America, we can see the progress to the point where we are sitting at the same table, even though we are cooking and eating our own different foods. In these terms, we have progressed from separate and lower, to separate but equal status, maintaining our own integrity even though we share the jointly created soup at the end.

While we were growing up in Hawaii, much changed on the mainland. While we were strengthening our literary network, mainland writers let theirs fade. Ethnic studies departments have proliferated, bringing in their wake an interest in Asian American literature, but mostly in a socio-political context. Their classes provide an audience, a market for ethnic writers, and the legitimization necessary for writers to continue with their craft. One would think that with the proliferation of ethnic studies departments, there would follow more literary journals and presses devoted to developing the field of ethnic literature. One would think that more criticism would emerge that would advance the literature.

But, the ethnic network for writers has not been strengthened. Although the Association for Asian American Studies continues its annual conferences—the last one in Hawaii—there is a predominance of history and sociology, as opposed to literature. Or Asian American literature seems most discussed in socio-political terms. Perhaps I'm being impatient, but there seems to be a lack of serious literary scholarship, except for a predominance of papers on Maxine Hong Kingston. So while we continue to talk about Asian American literature as if it were a legitimate field of study, in fact there are few concrete signs of it being treated as such.

In fact, it could be argued that there is a trend among mainland Asian American writers toward gaining acceptance as part of the mainstream, leaving ethnic publishing and criticism as a kind of backwater. Or there is a trend toward presenting to mainstream America an insider's look at a mysterious ethnic society, as opposed to telling a story which is based on the inherent humanity of the characters in and of themselves and in their own context, in their own eyes, not in the eyes of outsiders. Perhaps this presentation of duality to the majority is a necessity on the mainland. But this kind of writing does leave one open to criticism about using what is traditionally defined as exotic in Western eyes, whether or not the writing is good.

I'm not saying that it should be an either/or situation. I'm simply saying we should not abandon those networks which were instrumental in getting us as far as we've come. I believe that, 1) ethnic magazines and presses have been struggling and should be bolstered; and 2) literary criticism is lacking, except for a few usually historical or socio-political exceptions. Perhaps extended research in this area would eventually create its own arena, drawing attention to itself on its own merits and by its own standards, while nurturing the growth and refinement of our literature.

Are these weaknesses in publishing and literary criticism a sign that some of us are leaving behind the ethnic network that supports us, to progress out of the literary ghetto, as it were, leaving behind the ethnic presses and magazines? I would argue that the ethnic networks will continue to serve an important function for years to come; that it would be wise for us to build on them now; and that we should hold academic institutions accountable to their pursuit of scholarship and creativity. We must ensure that the system will be in place for generations of young writers. After all, this need is what gave rise to the establishment of ethnic studies departments or multicultural programs in the first place. If we want our writers to portray the many facets of our lives as ethnic Americans, we must continue to support our ethnic literary networks. The literature must be written, read, heard, critiqued, taught, and bought. Unless the goal is to blend invisibly into mainstream America, our separate subcommunities should maintain their own social, economic, and literary structures. It would be foolish to weaken the very network which has enabled many of us to enjoy what successes we have thus far achieved.

Notes

1. Eric Chock, *Last Day Here* (Honolulu: Bamboo Ridge Press, 1990).
2. Ibid.
3. Ibid.
4. Wing Tek Lum, *Expounding the Doubtful Points* (Honolulu: Bamboo Ridge Press, 1987).
5. Ibid.

9

Naming as Identity, Sui Sin Far

Annette White-Parks

The meeting and marriage between Sui Sin Far's (Edith Eaton's)[1] parents in Shanghai in 1863 reflects the tug between colonizer and colonized in the world of global politics where Sui Sin Far grew up. According to family legend, the mother, Lotus Blossom Trefusis (or Grace A. Eaton), was taken from China by missionaries as a young girl, educated in England, then returned to China, probably to convert her own people. The father, Edward Eaton, belonged to a silk merchant family of Macclesfield, England, whose ships were among the many plying Shanghai harbor in the decades following wars that the western nations provoked with China, resulting in treaties that opened China to increasing capitalistic commerce and Christian missionizing.

After the birth in China of a first son, Edward Jr., the parents returned to Macclesfield, where Lotus Blossom gave birth to a first daughter—Edith Maude or Sui Sin Far—in 1865. Birth records for a second daughter, Grace, from Jersey City, followed by records of more births in England, indicate that the Eaton family underwent one early, brief migration to North America, returned to England, then migrated a second time, stopping briefly in New York, then pushing on to Montréal, Quebec, where they would settle in 1873.

Here the birth of a new baby would take place almost every year, and nearly as frequently, the move to a new address. Family income plummeted, as Edward's occupation moved from "Clerk" to "Bookkeeper" to "Artist"—the work he had loved since a young man and that he stayed with from the 1880s till his death in 1915. All of the children were taken from school in their elementary years to, in Sui Sin Far's words, "help earn our living."

73

In an age of severe racialization[2] by Whites against Chinese in North America (The Exclusion Act in the U.S. and the Head Tax in Canada were both passed in the 1880s), with racist abuse heightened against children born of both races, there is every indication that the Eatons "passed" as an English Canadian family, with only neighbors, friends and other close associates being aware of the Chinese connection. All of the siblings, including Sui Sin Far, looked European and grew up with the border identity that society laid out for children who were both Chinese and White.[3] As an adult, Sui Sin Far, like most of her siblings, migrated to the United States where her family was unknown. Because her dual racial inheritance did not clearly show, she was faced with the excruciating choice, not only once but repeatedly, between hiding her Chinese ancestry and passing as English—with a continuing fear of exposure—or acknowledging her Chinese ancestry and facing discriminatory laws and social ostricization and violence. From a visible minority perspective, Sui Sin Far has been seen as fortunate, because she had the choice. The conflict involved, however, is one with which any homosexual American in the 1990s is clearly familiar: Will I be found out? Who can I tell?

Because Sui Sin Far (1865-1914) was, inasmuch as we know, the only one of her family to commit herself to the Chinese North American community and to actively seek her maternal inheritance both in her life and her writings, it is often supposed that this sister was frankly open about her "Chinese-ness"—in contrast to, say, Winifred, who is known for disguising it.

This is far from the truth.

The eldest sister's dream of dying at the stake to proclaim "how great and glorious and noble are the Chinese people," stood in continual conflict with her dream of "getting far away from where I was known, to where no mocking cries of 'Chinese!' 'Chinese!' could reach." It is on the tightrope between her deep pull toward her mother's people and the prejudicial demands of her father's that Sui Sin Far balanced all of her life. In this essay I will demonstrate how this sister's interplay between names illuminates her struggle to resolve her restless racial identity.

The name appearing on Sui Sin Far's birth certificate is "Edith Maude Eaton," the name appearing on her works as a mature writer is "Sui Sin Far," making it easy to assume that the former identified her role as a child with her family and the latter was taken as a pseudonym for her writing. Textual evidence, though, shows it wasn't that simple, rather that both names, or variations thereof, were part of the writer's identity from early childhood. In her autobiographical "Leaves from the Mental Portfolio of an Eurasian," she relates that a nurse said to her mother, "Little Miss Sui is a storyteller when she was age four. Meaning, in brief, "The Chinese Lily," Sui Sin Far was probably a pet name, given and used by her family. Other details point to the fact that during these first years in England, Sui Sin Far saw herself as an English child, not unlike other children around her, until "the day on which I first learned I was something different and apart from other children," a "difference" underlined with the words of a school chum: "I wouldn't speak to Sui if I were you. Her mamma is Chinese." The confusion about what "Chinese" meant to the questing child is capped in a scene after the Eatons arrive in New York and Sui Sin Far, with her older brother, sees two Chinese laborers, "drest in working blouses and pantaloons with queues hanging down their backs." "'Oh, Charlie... Are we like that?'" she cries, recoiling. "'Well, we're Chinese and they're Chinese, too, so we must be,'" her brother answers with seven-year-old logic.

When the Eaton family undertook their migrations to North America, it was most likely as British citizens, all covered with the "head of household" umbrella (Edward Eaton) under which immigration records were kept. In Canada, apart from close associates and neighbors who live "near us and [have] seen my mother"[4] everything indicates that the Eatons presented themselves and were seen by others as an "English Canadian" family. Public records—birth, baptismal, death—all are signed "Grace A. Eaton," the name the mother took with her marriage. It is a study in the way "invisible minorities" are formed, as, in the absence of foreknowledge, the researcher finds no clues that this family (Montréal residents during a time when it is said no Chinese were there) was either Chinese or had any Chinese relations.

In this context, the writer whom we in the 1990s know as "Sui Sin Far" grew in the 1890s into the public identity of "Miss Edith Eaton," the dutiful, hard-working eldest daughter of an English Canadian family who had to struggle not only with the prejudice leveled against her race and gender, but also with her own constantly flagging health and the burden of family poverty. When her father took her from school at age 11, to sell his paintings and the lace she crocheted herself, on Montréal streets, the older writer recalls that to survive she divided her mind into "two lives" or perspectives, creating a psychic division that underlies both her life and her writing: "I, now in my 11th year; entered into two lives, one devoted entirely to family concerns; the other, a withdrawn life of thought and musing..." To the latter, she describes "six keys," among them "the sense of being differentiated from the ordinary by the fact that I was an Eurasian" and "the impulse to create." [5]

It was the first, practical life, "devoted to family concerns," that would dominate as "Edith Eaton," then one by one her younger siblings, grew into their teens, and the second "withdrawn life of thought and musing" developed where "Sui Sin Far" would continue to flourish. Somehow, between earning a living and caring for 12 younger siblings, the young woman ferreted out cracks of time to launch a newspaper career and begin writing short fiction. Her first located pieces, a series of eight sketches printed in the *Canadian Dominion Illustrated* between 1888 and 1890, were on English and French Canadian subjects and, not surprisingly, were signed "Edith Eaton."[6]

The writer's identification with the Montréal Chinese community seems to have begun sometime in the early 1890s, when she accompanied her mother to "call upon a young Chinese woman who had recently arrived from China as the bride of one of the local merchants" (*Globe*) and recalls that: "From that time on I began to go among my mother's people, and it did me a world of good to discover how akin I was to them." A few years later (1894) when she opened "an office of my own" as a free-lance reporter, her stated purpose was "to fight the battles of the Chinese in the papers." Her evolution during this period into the role of "sympathetic outsider" is evident in that local papers gave her "most of their Chinese reporting" as she fought to champion Chinese Canadians against a growing onslaught of racist laws and practices. The fact that she used the name "Miss Edith Eaton" (listed under "M" in *Lovell's City Directory* 1894-97) indicates that she did not yet see herself as an insider. In an 1896 essay couched as a letter to the editor of the *Montréal Daily Star* (Sept. 21) captioned "A Plea for the Chinaman," she argued brilliantly against raising the Head Tax on Chinese Canadian immigrants from $100 to $500. Yet this letter was still signed as "E.E."

The eldest sister's struggle to negotiate identities through the decade of the 90s is clearly visible, as she is committed to the Chinese in her sympathies and her work, yet maintains her English father's name and public identity. This struggle was undoubtedly complicated by the friction any threat to their common mask would cause with her family. A reported conversation with "an acquaintance" who advises Sui Sin Far, "It isn't right" to walk "with a Chinaman," and her retort, "Not right to walk with one of my own mother's people? Oh, indeed!" is only one instance of how she reveals this conflict at the same time she uses anonymous characters to disguise it.[7] All of her sisters married White Canadian or American men, and her brothers (those who lived to adulthood) married White women. By blowing her camouflage (as an English woman, untainted), Sui Sin Far would blow theirs.

The writer's first "Chinese stories," five of them, appeared in 1896, the year before she left Montréal to undergo the migrations in and out of eastern Canada that would mark the rest of her life. All these stories were published in the United States, but signed from Montréal with a name that interestingly varies from the "Sui Sin Far" of her childhood: "Sui Seen Far."[8] Her effort to "come out," here and in 1890s stories to follow, betrays itself in scraps of thinly disguised autobiography: The "Eurasian" protagonist of the short story "Sweet Sin" reverses her author's case by having a Chinese father and a White mother, and cries out against the double-bind in which her author was similarly caught:

"But, Father, though I cannot marry a Chinaman, who would despise me for being an American, I will not marry an American, for the Americans have made me feel so [sic] I will save the children of the man I love from being called 'Chinese! Chinese!'"[9]

From the time Sui Sin Far leaves Montréal—first for Jamaica and then the United States West Coast, her Chinese identity begins to assert itself visibly and with a new confidence. By 1898—at age 33 and on the opposite side of the continent from her Montréal family—she appears to have been openly acknowledging her Chinese ancestry and—more far reaching—is ceasing to see Chinese North Americans as "other" in relation to Whites. In San Francisco, her observation that Chinatown residents see her as a pretender to their culture implies that she is publicly identifying herself as Chinese American: "Some little women discover that I have Chinese hair, color of eyes and complexion, also that I love rice and tea. This settles the matter for them and for their husbands also." She contrasts herself to "Chinese Eurasians" who masquerade as Mexicans or Japanese and live "in nervous dread of being discovered." In the following passage, she measures her own evolution: "My Chinese instincts develop. I am no longer the little girl who shrunk against my brother at the sight of the Chinaman," and expresses her growing personal identification with Chinese Americans, "Many and many a time when alone in a strange place has the appearance of even an humble laundryman given me a sense of protection and made me feel quite at home."

That by 1900, the writer saw both "Sui Sin Far" and "Edith Eaton" as integral to her personal identity is indicated in her response to a letter from a student at Dartmouth: "Of course I shall be glad to let you have my autograph… perhaps I should say *they* as I have both an English and a Chinese name." She closed with both signatures.[10] Though her business identity, signified by correspondence with editors, remained "Edith Eaton" (the practical side of her 11-year-old split), her byline in short stories and in a column for the *Los Angeles Express* becomes by 1904 "Sui

Sin Far."[11] In a series for *The Westerner* magazine (based in Earlington, Washington), entitled "The Chinese in America," the editor refers to his author as "Miss Edith Eaton," but describes her Chinese-English parentage in his introduction and uses the byline—*Sui Sin Far* (Edith Eaton).[12] It is notable that in this instance "Sui Sin Far" has been moved to the central, and "Edith Eaton" to the parenthetical position. The culmination of her writings in the book length collection *Mrs. Spring Fragrance* in 1912, and all future fiction, are similarly authored with both names, reflecting, I suggest, the mature writer's growing identity integration.

It does seem ironic, then, that at Sui Sin Far's death in 1914, the English mask she had fought to cast aside through her life again rose to meet her. Public notices and obituaries revert to "Miss Edith Eaton," and her name on Mont Royal cemetery records—in the English and Protestant section—is cited "Edith Maude Eaton." We can imagine this nomenclature was supplied by her family. The final word on their first daughter's identity was not theirs to supply, though, and had not yet been written. If we visit Sui Sin Far's grave in Mont Royal's "English section" today, we find English letters commemorating both names, "Edith Eaton, Sui Sin Far," in that order. Above the names, however, are engraved these words: "From Her Chinese Friends," and above the words, at the top of the monument, four Chinese characters roughly translate to: "It is right and good that we should remember China."

The place of naming in the publishing history of European women is well-documented; every student of women's literature knows the subversive nomenclature of George Sand and George Eliot; Acton, Currer, and Quentin Bell; and of Madame de Stael's Corinne, Ellen Moers' writes, she "has the problem professional women have always had with the social implications of a maiden or a married name; her own real name... simply will not do."[13]

The story of how much more complex this equation becomes for women writers whose names represent more than one race has yet to be closely examined and written. Sui Sin Far offers one example.

Notes

1. Although cited on her birth certificate as "Edith Maude Eaton," the name "Sui Sin Far" does not seem a pseudonym, but is rather a term of address her family identified her by from early childhood. In this text I purposefully use "Sui Sin Far," to underline the persona choice this writer made to distinguish herself from the English Canadian identity that most of her family maintained.

2. For more on theories of racialization, see Robert Miles, *Racism and Labour Migration* (London: Routledge & Kegan, 1982). As cited by Audrey

Kobayashi and Peter Jackson ("Japanese Canadians and the Racialization of Labour in the British Columbia Sawmill Industry, 1900-1930," paper presented at the Sixth BC Studies Conference, University of British Columbia, 2-3 November 1990), racialization follows the belief that "'race' is a social construction…," artificial, contrived and divisive.

3. Because the terms "white" and "of color" are literally inaccurate and reinforce a division that society constructs and enforces, when "white" is used, I choose to spell it in the upper case (White) or in quotes ("white") in the effort to make it equivalent with other racially descriptive words.

4. Sui Sin Far, "Leaves from the Mental Portfolio of an Eurasian," *The Independent* LXVI (January 21, 1909): 125-132. Quotes hereafter unless noted may be attributed to this source.

5. "Sui Sin Far: The Half Chinese Writer Tells of Her Career," *Boston Globe*, 5 May 1912, 6.

6. "A Trip in a Horse Car" (13 October 1888): 235; "Misunderstood: The Story of a Young Man" (17 November 1888): 314; "A Fatal Tug of War" (8 December 1888): 362-63; "The Origin of a Broken Nose" (11 May 1889): 302; "Robin" (22 June 1889): 394; "Albermarle's Secret" (19 October 1889): 254; "Spring Impressions: A Medley of Poetry and Prose" (7 June 1890): 358-59; "In Fairyland" (18 October 1890): 270.

7. L Charles Laferriére, a grand-nephew of Sui Sin Far's who lives in Montréal, says that all the characters in "Leaves" represent various members of the Eaton family.

8. Sui Seen Far, "The Story of Iso," *The Lotus* 2 (August 1896): 14-18; "A Love Story of the Orient," *The Lotus* 2 (October 1896): 203-206; "Ku Yum," *Land of Sunshine* 5 (June 1896): 29-31; "A Chinese Feud," *Land of Sunshine* 5 (November 1896): 236-37; "The Chinese Woman in America," *Land of Sunshine* 6 (January 1897): 60-65. Another name Sui Sin Far experimented with in the 1890s was *Sui Sin Fah*.

9. Sui Seen Far, "Sweet Sin," *Land of Sunshine* 8 (April 1898): 225-28.

10. Edith Eaton to Harold Rugg, 18 January 1900; courtesy of Barbara L. Krieger, Archives Assistant, Dartmouth College Library. Located by Xiao-Huang Yin, Arizona State University.

11. 2, 8, 14, 15, 22, 23 October and 3 November 1903.

12. May-August 1909.

13. Ellen Moers, *Literary Women* (New York: Doubleday, 1976): 184.

Insider/Outsider Perspectives

Asian Americans' experiences have long been excluded from the literary canon. And in this exclusion arises an implicit critique of the insider status: as dominating, hierarchical, judgmental. Thus, the aim of the outsider—the homeless exile in the margins of traditional literature—is *not* necessarily to find a home within the confines of the center (the central), but, to quote Qun Wang, to create a "dialectical relationship with traditional literature and balance out of the domination of tradition." In Wang's "In Search of Asian American Voices," this conversation among and between the insider and the outsider will bring about understanding and mutual acceptance, heretofore unheeded and unheard. As such, individual experiences and neglected human peculiarities, especially those which have been neglected by official history, will emerge, as is elucidated in Jun Xing's "Imagery, Counter-Memory, and the Re-visioning of Asian American History." History, decentralized (or de-officialized) within the counter-culture of memory, is attributed with more than one meaning, with numerous interpretations. The notion of the "other" recurs in Vidyut Aklujkar's "CheChi From Outer Space," in which the blatant play on "outer" emphasizes the insider/outsider (exile) status of an East Indian woman, returning from Canada, and regarded with skepticism by those in her own culture. She eventually becomes a sister (a "chechi") among the East Indian women who accept her differences by reworking their own visions of the other. To see and to be seen, with all their attendant implications, is central to Amy Ling's article, "Gender Issues in Early Chinese American Autobiography." Despite the double exclusion of being both Asian and woman, Ling argues that such early Chinese American women authors wrote in a style much richer and denser than their male counterparts, thereby reversing the established hierarchy. In this sense, these pioneering women created their own literature of exclusion. The creation of a specific literature, an outside voice, is integral to Darrell Lum's text, "Hawaii's Literary Traditions: Separating the Food From the Buta Kau Kau." In recognizing a native, Hawaiian pidgin literature, "Others will not define us," he writes, rather, "we must define ourselves." The notion of definition—of self and identity, within history and gender construction, and on the printed page—surfaces as the central issue in the following essays, which construct perspectives from the outside, simultaneously reconstructing the parameters of the insider(s).

10

In Search of Asian American Voices

Qun Wang

In Maxine Hong Kingston's *The Woman Warrior,* there is a description of an Asian American child's search for her voice. She felt that she had lost her voice when she had to speak English for the first time in kindergarten. Ever since:

> A dumbness—a shame—still cracks my voice in two, even when I want to say "hello" casually, or ask an easy question in front of the check-out counter, or ask directions of a bus driver. I stand frozen, or I hold up the line with the complete, grammatical sentence that comes squeaking out at impossible length. "What did you say?" says the cab driver, or "Speak up," so I have to perform again, only weaker the second time.[1]

The child's "silence" is apparently occasioned as much by her struggle with English as by her awareness of being different. In both cases, the traumatic feeling of alienation results from the child's having to deal with two cultural realities, that undermines the very sense of her true identity.

The prophetic power of Kingston's novels would be lost unless they are read as social allegories. Eighteen years after the first print of *The Woman Warrior,* mis(sing)-representation becomes a serious issue in the study of social and cultural diversity. The new cultural conservatives headed by William Bennett and Allan Bloom, preferring to preserve cultural and literary "tradition," would probably want to argue against the necessity of including the Asian American voice in revising the canon. But in doing so, they are also creating a social and cultural unreality which not only misrepresents the culturally diversified nature of American society but also, as is indicated by the struggle the child in Kingston's story had to go through, causes alienation and confusion in people's search for their true ethnic identity.

Michele Wallace, in her *Invisibility Blues: From Pop to Theory*, quotes Raymond Williams in arguing that the most accessible counter-hegemonic work has often been historical, but the rigorously selective process that defines "tradition" is always linked to "explicit contemporary pressures and limits." So while "history" may seem recoverable as "tradition," tradition's hegemonic impulse is always the most active: "a deliberate selective and connecting process which offers a historical and cultural ratification of a contemporary order."[2] Williams's deconstructionist approach to the study of the relationship between history and tradition in *Marxism and Literature* convincingly suggests that to dehegemonize tradition as an autocratic historical force is to recognize its arbitrariness and the possibility of change.

I understand that the use of the term "Asian American" is controversial. It loosely refers to people from more than 30 Asian countries and from close to a hundred ethnic groups. But the boundary of the Asian American community is not only geographically delineated by where these immigrants came from but also ontologically dictated by the communality in their struggle for social acceptance and for human dignity. After the U.S. Congress passed the Chinese Exclusion Act in 1882, for instance, the country turned to Japanese immigrants for a labor supply. But if history was read correctly, it would not be so difficult to predict the Asian Exclusion Act in 1924, which was mainly directed against the Japanese and Indian immigration. By the same token, Bret Harte's poem, "The Latest Chinese Outrage," makes no attempt at distinguishing people from different Asian countries, as the narrator laments:

> *Shall we stand here as idle, and let Asia pour*
> *Her barbaric hordes on this civilized shore?*[3]

The development of Asian American literature can be divided into two periods. The first period lasted for about a century. It started with the first print of Wong Sam's bilingual *An English-Chinese Phrase Book* in 1873 and culminated in Maxine Hong Kingston's publishing her two autobiographical novels, *The Woman Warrior* (1975) and *China Men* (1980). The period was marked as much by some Asian American writers' interest in using the autobiographical approach to define their experience and to identify their relationship with the mainstream American culture, as by a sharpened sensitivity built on the increased awareness of their own cultural heritage. Chinese American writer Pardee Lowe's *Father and Glorious Descendant* (1943), Jade Snow Wong's *The Fifth*

Chinese Daughter (1945), Japanese American writer Daniel Inouye's *Journey to Washington* (1967), Monica Sone's *Nisei Daughter* (1953); and Filipino American writer Carlos Bulosan's *America is in the Heart* (1943) use the genre of autobiography to describe the writers' struggle with not only inter- but also intra-cultural conflict. Chinese American writer Virginia Lee's *The House that Tai Ming Built* (1963), Chuang Hua's *Crossings*, Maxine Hong Kingston's *The Woman Warrior* and *China Men*, Shawn Wong's *Homebase* (1979), Japanese American writer Kazuo Miyamoto's *Hawaii: End of the Rainbow* (1964), and Filipino American writer Bienvenido Santos's "Scent of Apples," and Oscar Penaranda's "The Price" (1972) are fictionalized memoirs that can also be read as semi-autobiographies.

In the same period, there was also a group of writers who made efforts to portray the Asian American experience in more creative and artistic ways. Chinese American writer Louis Chu's *Eat a Bowl of Tea* (1961), for instance, presents a satirical but accurate depiction of the bachelor society in Chinatown. It is one of few works in Asian American literature that deals with the struggle of the lower middle class Asian Americans. Frank Chin's *The Year of the Dragon* and *The Chickencoop Chinaman* (1981) were pioneering works in dramatizing what Kai-yu Hsu calls "the Chinatown culture."[4] *The Year of the Dragon* was the first Asian American play on national television and *The Chickencoop Chinaman* was produced by the American Place Theater of New York in 1972. Chin's insistence on using the term "Chinaman" represents a tenacious effort on the writer's part to celebrate the Chinese cultural heritage. On August 2, 1970, Chin and Virginia Lee openly discussed the use of the term in an interview. Virginia Lee argued that she was "not so much concerned about being either Chinese or American or Chinese American or American Chinese" as she was "about being human." Chin responded by asking a rhetorical question: "Where's your identity, then?"[5] Twelve years ago, in the "Introduction" to *The Chickencoop Chinaman* and *The Year of the Dragon*, Dorothy Ritsuko McDonald observed that Chin's writing was "a feast of ideas, a sourcebook of themes and concerns" and she predicted that Chin's works "would... influence other Asian American writers."[6] Her prediction was right.

Toshio Mori's *Yokohama, California* (1949) is acclaimed by the Japanese American critic and writer Lawson Fusao Inada as "the first real Japanese-American book."[7] The fictional community of Yokohama, California, establishes a stage for the author to explore the richness of Japanese American culture from the thirties to the early forties. Mori's writing style is as colorful as his sense of humor is amusing. Like *Yoko-*

hama, California, John Okada's *No-No Boy* (1957) was also initially rejected by the Japanese American community under the control of the Japanese American Citizens League (JACL). "No-No boy" is a term used for Japanese Americans who signed "No" to questions 27 and 28 on the "loyalty" registration forms in the relocation camps during World War II. The novel takes a realistic look at the complicated feelings behind a Japanese American's decision to refuse to join the army during the war and at the lingering effect the relocation camps have had on the Japanese American community. Okada diverged from the use of the popular genre of autobiography in Asian American literature to create a believable character who struggles between his loyalty to his parents and to his country.

The second period of Asian American literature started in the mid-eighties. The Asian American Renaissance was heralded by anthologies such as Kai-yu Hsu's *Asian-American Authors* (1972), Frank Chin's *AII-IEEEEE! An Anthology of Asian-American Writers* (1974), Dexter Fisher's *The Third Woman: Minority Writers of the United States* (1980), and Joseph Bruchac's *Breaking Silence: An Anthology of Contemporary Asian American Poets* (1983). These anthologies provided a forum for some fledgling Asian American writers whose works were rejected by the mainstream culture because they were considered either inferior in quality or not exotic enough to appeal to the reading public. Kai-yu Hsu, for instance, included works produced by his students at the California State University, San Francisco, in *Asian-American Authors*. The anthology represents one of the initial efforts of Asian American writers to canonize their own voice.

The Asian American Renaissance gathered its momentum in the late eighties and early nineties. There are two noticeable changes in the development of Asian American literature in this period; both are related to diversity. First, autobiography has lost its reign as the predominant form of expression in Asian American literature. Asian American writers in this period are more interested in experimenting with various literary genres and styles in search of a medium that would reflect and depict their feelings accurately. This period has witnessed an increase in the publication of short stories and poems. Secondly, writers from ethnic groups other than Chinese, Japanese, or Filipino start to make waves. Their writings have contributed to democratizing the canonization of the Asian American voice. These writings also present a more colorful and more pluralistic interpretation of the Asian American experience.

Both Japanese American writer Jessica Saiki's *Once, A Lotus Garden* (1987) and Hisaye Yamamoto's *Seventeen Syllables* (1988) are collections of short stories. Their description of the Japanese American experience in Hawaii and the mainland is both exquisite and smooth. David Mura's *After We Lost Our Way* (1988) is a collection of poems. In the book, the voice of anger is intermingled with that of agony. The poems, nevertheless, possess a dignified tone in celebrating the human spirit. Mura also published *Turning Japanese* in 1991. The book fits into the genre of travel literature. It describes his trip to Japan and the development of his appreciation of the Japanese culture. Chinese American writer Frank Chin's collection of short stories, *The Chinaman Pacific & Frisco R. R. Co.* was published in 1988. Typical of Chin's writing style, the stories are as powerful and vitriolic as Chin's other works.

In 1988, *M. Butterfly* opened in Washington D.C., at the National Theater where *West Side Story* and *Amadeus* had premiered. The play won the Tony for best play, the Outer Critics Circle Award for best Broadway play, the John Gassner Award for best play, and the Drama Desk Award for best new play. *M. Butterfly* was not Chinese American playwright David Henry Hwang's first success in theater. His *FOB* (Fresh-Off-the-Boat) was presented at the New York Shakespeare Festival's Public Theater in 1980 and *Rich Relations* premiered at New York's Second Stage in 1986. The play, nevertheless, marks the playwright's, as well as the Asian American theater's, maturity. In *M. Butterfly*, Hwang dramatizes the pernicious effect of the illusory world built on stereotypes and false assumptions. The story of the play is based on French diplomat Bernard Bouriscot's involvement in espionage activities in China. It develops along the same line of the trickster tradition in African American folklore and literature.

During the same period, Asian American writers of Korean, South, and Southeast Asian descent become more productive and are ready to take on the challenge to diversify the approach and voice in the portrayal of the Asian American experience. Korean American writer Kim Ronyoung's *Clay Walls* (1986) experiments expressionistically with the narrative point-of-view. It describes a Korean couple's settlement in Los Angeles before World War II from three characters' perspectives. Mary Paik Lee's autobiographical depiction of her family's struggle in the *Quiet Odyssey: A Pioneer Korean Woman in America* (1990) is as moving as it is inspiring. The hardships the author went through as a child in both Korea and in the United States did not diminish her hope for a better future; nor did they shake her determination to fight for human dignity.

Nineteen eighty-nine saw the publication of Indian American writer Bharati Mukherjee's *Jasmine* and Vietnamese American writer Le Ly Hayslip's *When Heaven and Earth Changed Places*. *Jasmine* describes the metamorphosis of an Indian woman in America and how she helps change the ideological contours of the country. *When Heaven and Earth Changed Places* (1989) uses an autobiographical approach to examine the painful memory of the Vietnam war. Its description is sincere and convincing. Hayslip published another book, *A Child of War, A Woman of Peace*, in 1991. She is one of the first Asian American writers from Southeast Asia to break into the publication circle. *Hmong Tapestry: Voices from the Cloth* opened on March 7, 1991, at the 7th Place Theater in St. Paul, Minnesota. It is a play written and performed by first generation Hmong immigrants. While the artistic value of the play is debatable, it stands out as a commendable effort by the Hmong immigrants to explore the richness of their own heritage and to define their own identity.

In 1989, Amy Tan published *The Joy Luck Club*. The writer was not surprised by her success with the book, since she had been publishing short stories in some "prestigious" magazines in this country. But Tan probably was not able to foresee the impact the book would have on the development of Asian American literature in general and on that of Chinese American literature specifically. Besides rekindling hope in the heart of some struggling Asian American writers, Tan's success also opened the publishers' door a little bit wider for them. Nineteen ninety-one was a busy year for Chinese American writers. Amy Tan's *The Kitchen God's Wife* was another success. Gish Jen's *Typical American* received rave reviews from both *People* magazine and the *New York Times Book Review* magazine. David Wong Louie's *Pangs of Love* explores themes of universal significance, such as: intercultural and intergenerational conflict. The narrator's struggle with the clash of cultural values is further compounded by the communication problem with his parents. Frank Chin published his first long piece of work, *Donald Duk* and Gus Lee, a lawyer from California, wrote an autobiographical novel, *China Boy*.

Among the anthologies published in this period, two of them have pointed at a new direction in the development of Asian American literature. Both *Making Waves: An Anthology of Writings By and About Asian American Women* (1989) and Shirley Geok-Lin Lim's *The Forbidden Stitch: An Asian American Women's Anthology* (1989), as the titles indicate, take feminist approaches to the treatment of the Asian American experience. In the "Preface" to the anthology, the editors of *Making Waves* declare that the book includes "primarily unpublished works by and about Asian American women since the early 1970s."[8] The editor of *The Forbidden Stitch*, Shirley Geok-Lin Lim, also announces that the anthology "resulted from an open call for submissions."[9] It is quite obvious that editors of both anthologies intend to give voice to the female Asian American writers who have been struggling with obscurity and to those who haven't thought about using writing as a medium to fight both racism and sexism.

Nineteen ninety-one also saw the publication of *The Big AIIIEEEEE! An Anthology of Chinese and Japanese American Literature*, edited by Frank Chin, et al. The selections in the anthology are as controversial as Chin's article, "Come All Ye Asian American Writers of the Real and the Fake." King-Kok Cheung, in the "Preface" to the *Asian-American Literature: An Annotated Bibliography*, notes that the "Introduction" to *AII-IEEEEE! An Anthology of Asian-American Writers* (1974) "distinguish sharply between Americanized Chinese Authors and Chinese American authors." Cheung argues that: "the influence of overseas Asian—be they sojourners or immigrants with American-born offspring—cannot be ignored in a study of Asian American literary history."[10] In the article, "Come All Ye Asian American Writers of the Real and the Fake," Chin makes another judgment call: he names Pardee Lowe, Jade Snow Wong, Maxine Hong Kingston and Amy Tan the "Christian autobiographers"[11] (Chin's polemics with Kingston are legendary; in fact, Kingston's third novel, *Tripmaster Monkey: His Fake Book*, is a parody of Chin's ideology); and he posits that: "Kingston, (David Henry) Hwang, and Tan are the first writers of any race, and certainly the first writers of Asian ancestry, to so boldly fake the best-known works from the most universally known body of Asian literature and lore in history."[12]

Frank Chin's arduous effort to defend the purity of the Chinese culture in its reproductive form in Asian American literature is admirable. His attempt to problemize the configuration by redefining Asian American literature is also helpful to developing a healthy critical discourse. However, to reject autobiography as an inappropriate form in depicting the Asian American experience is arbitrary. The rejection is also tantamount to denying the achievement of Asian American literature in its early stage. Kai-yu Hsu, while being critical of the autobiographies that "confirm rather than modify a stereotyped image of the Chinese and their culture," admits that autobiography is "the path of development of many writers."[13] While the merits and weaknesses of the so-called "slave narrative" are open to discussion, nobody can deny the instrumentality of Frederick Douglass's three autobiographies, *Narrative of the Life of Frederick Douglass*, *An American Slave*, and *My Bondage and My Freedom*, to the development of African American literature and political movements.

Frank Chin's argument for maintaining the "real" Chinese culture in Asian American literature is also question-begging. For one advantage of being Asian American is that we are blessed with two cultures and can have the freedom and luxury to be selective. Or as Brave Orchid, the dynamic mother in *The Woman Warrior*, puts it: "When you come to America, it's a chance to forget some of the bad Chinese habits."[14] I believe that the change Maxine Hong Kingston, David Henry Hwang and Amy Tan have made in using the traditional Chinese culture, rather than being a result of "a faulty memory,"[15] epitomizes an attempt at accurately defining the Asian American experience and describing it accordingly. Besides, as mentioned in the beginning: to accept history as a changing process is to recognize tradition's hegemonic impulse. The use of traditional Asian culture should serve to broaden, rather than restrict, our understanding of the dialectical relationship between the Asian American experience and our cultural heritage.

The development of the Asian American Renaissance hasn't shown any sign of losing momentum. In 1988, King-Kok Cheung and Stan Yogi published *Asian-American Literature: An Annotated Bibliography*. The book would certainly be helpful to scholars who are interested in defining the Asian American voice and to those who want to see its representation in the canon. To canonize the Asian American voice by developing a critical discourse on Asian American literature and culture is to recognize the struggle behind the cracked voice of Maxine Hong Kingston's narrator in *The Woman Warrior*; to respond to the narrator's earnest call for understanding; and to avoid inflicting the same kind of pain the narrator suffers on people who are caught in what W. E. B. Du Bois calls the struggle of "double consciousness." It is not only necessary but also crucial to building a multicultural society.

Notes

1. Maxine Hong Kingston, *The Woman Warrior* (New York: Vintage, 1975): 165.

2. Michele Wallace, *Invisibility Blues: From Pop to Theory* (London and New York: Verso, 1990): 214.

3. Bret Harte, "The Latest Chinese Outrage," *Asian-American Authors*, Kai-yu Hsu and Helen Palubinskas, eds. (Boston: Houghton Mifflin, 1972): 7.

4. Hsu and Palubinskas, *Asian-American Authors*, 11.

5. Hsu and Palubinskas, *Asian-American Authors*, 1.

6. Dorothy Ritsuko McDonald, "Introduction," *The Chickencoop Chinaman* and *The Year of the Dragon*, Frank Chin (Seattle and London: University of Washington Press, 1981): xiv.

7. Lawson Fusao Inada, "Standing on Seventh Street," *Yokohama, California,* Toshio Mori (Seattle and London: University of Washington press, 1949): v.

8. *Making Waves: An Anthology of Writings By and About Asian American Women*, Asian Women United of California, ed. (Boston: Beacon Press, 1989): ix.

9. Shirley Geok-lin Lim, "Introductions," in *The Forbidden Stitch: An Asian-American Women's Anthology*, Shirley Geok-lin Lim, et al., eds. (Corvallis, OR: Calyx Books, 1989): 10.

10. King-Kok Cheung, "Preface," in *Asian American Literature: An Annotated Bibliography*, King-Kok Cheung and Stan Yogi, eds. (New York: The Modern Language Associating of America, 1988): v.

11. Frank Chin, "Come All Ye Asian American Writers of the Real and the Fake," *The Big AIIIEEEEE! An Anthology of Chinese American and Japanese American Literature*, Frank Chin, et al., eds. (New York: Meridian, 1991): 33.

12. Frank Chin, "Come All Ye," 3.

13. Hsu and Palubinskas, *Asian-American Authors*, 10.

14. Kingston, *The Woman Warrior*, p. 139.

15. Frank Chin, "Come All Ye," 3.

11

Imagery, Counter Memory, and the Re-visioning of Asian American History

Rea Tajiri's History and Memory for Akiko and Takashige

Jun Xing

> I remember having this feeling growing up that I was haunted by
> something... That I was living within a family full of ghosts... There
> was this place that they knew about I had never been there, yet I had a
> memory for it. There was a time of great sadness before I was born. We
> had been moved, uprooted. We had lived with a lot of pain. I had no idea
> where these memories came from... yet I knew the place.[1]

This is the voiceover for *History and Memory: For Akiko and Takashige*
(1991). Directed by Asian American video artist Rea Tajiri, it is a documentary on the Japanese American internment experience during World
War II. Like 110,000 other Japanese Americans, Tajiri's mother and father
were viewed as "sympathetic to the enemy" after Japan bombed Pearl
Harbor in 1941. Forced by the U.S. government to sell their property,
homes and businesses in 1942, her parents' families were forcibly relo-
cated to two different internment camps: her father's family was dislo-
cated to Santa Anita, California, in spite of the fact that her father was
serving in the U.S. army, and her mother's family was sent first to Salinas,
California, and later to Poston, Arizona, where they lived in barracks on
the Colorado River Indian Reservation. Guarded by armed soldiers, both
families were confined behind barbed wire until 1944. Some 40 years
later, haunted by a ghost-like memory and equipped with a camera and
tape recorder, Tajiri began to reconstruct her family's camp experience.

Despite this simple story line, *History and Memory* is a rich and complicated cultural text for both its artistry and historical consciousness. As
its title suggests, the video is a poetic blend of history, memory and visual

imagery. Interweaving multiple voices and texts, it raises significant questions concerning historical representation, collective memory and the role of an all-encompassing visual media in historical discourse.

History is usually thought of as something real and tangible, a collection of past events, dead people and fixed dates. However, history also represents a point of view, a selective process of inclusion and exclusion. "Who Chose[s] What Story to Tell," as a boldface line of text states at the beginning, very much decides the point of view represented by the historian. Tajiri twice told her viewers in the video: "I began searching for a history, my own history, because I had known all along that the stories I had heard were not true and parts had been left out."[2] As an illustration of her point, Tajiri metaphorically borrows the image of Spencer Tracy's search for Kimoko, a Japanese-American man murdered the day after Pearl Harbor, from the Hollywood movie *A Bad Day at Black Rock* (1954). "Spencer Tracy makes this search throughout the whole film," the voiceover explains, "to find a Japanese American man. He never appears, not even a picture or a photograph... Kimoko's disappearance from Black Rock was like our disappearance from history. His absence is his presence. Somehow, I could identify with this search. This search for an ever-absent image and the desire to create an image where there are so few."[3]

In Tajiri's attempt to recover her family history, she reveals gaps in both public and private discourse. If the public discourse, dominated by the mainstream vision of history, selects what to leave in and or to take out to influence public opinion, this struggle of remembering and forgetting at the individual level becomes a defensive mechanism of self preservation. As Zora Neale Hurston wrote in *Their Eyes Were Watching God*, "Now women forget all those things they don't want to remember and remember everything they don't want to forget."[4] This "refusal to remember" characterizes Tajiri's mother's psychological response to her traumatized experience in WW II. As a victim of incarceration in relocation camps, her intuitive response to her daughter's inquiry about the experience was painful self-denial. In a tape-recorded conversation between the two, the mother said,

> No, that's the truth I don't remember... When you hear people on television and everything how they felt and everything, I don't remember any of that stuff. All I remember is... when I saw this woman... This beautiful woman, young, you know, and uh, I thought to myself, why did this happen you know? You can go crazy, you can go out of your mind, so you just put these things out of your mind, you know.[5]

Her mother's loss of memory is a conscious action for self protection. As one scrolling text reads, "She tells the story of what she does not remember but remembers one thing: why she forgot to remember."[6]

The meaning of historical memory, individual and popular alike, has always been a publicly contested terrain that has often been corrupted by the mainstream, especially visual, media. As Janice Tanaka, a prominent Asian American video artist has noted,

> Memories are not always an understood compilation of linear ideas. They seem instead to be fragments of stored, synthesized, edited sensory stimuli; bits of personalized perceptions. Film and television oftentimes play a major role in the process of subliminal inculturation by creating a criteria for self-evaluation. Consequently, our self-image, our role models, what we know and expect of our society and the world, are greatly influenced by the media.[7]

History and Memory provocatively probes the impact of visual images on historical memory. In the beginning of the video, Tajiri recalled that her sister had a huge box filled with pictures of movie stars that she continually pored over. "The strange thing, of course, when I thought about it later," Tajiri reflected retrospectively, "was that the photos were of white people. I often wondered how the movies influenced our lives"[8] Accompanying her reflections were a series of shots taken from the Hollywood musical *Yankee Doodle Dandy* (1942), *From Here to Eternity* (1953), and from the documentary made by the Office of War Information, *Apartment (Relocation of Japanese Aliens)* (1942). Graphic images flip over the screen: Japan's sneak-attack on Pearl Harbor, leaving a trail of thick black smoke; the Japanese Americans' willing relocation to the camps; and a Roosevelt-like American soldier marching with a band, singing: "We're one for all and/ All for one/ Behind the man, behind the gun/ And now that we're in it/ We're going to win it..."[9]

If film and video can construct history, they can also deconstruct it, depending on the stance of the filmmaker. Even though the story is deeply personal, *History and Memory* becomes a subversive tool, challenging the dominant historical narrative and formulating a counter-cultural voice based on the memories of Japanese Americans. In recent years counter-memory, or collective memory, as some scholars call it, has become a powerful concept in cultural studies. French structuralist philosopher Michel Foucault, in his discussion of language and history, defines counter-memory as "the affirmation of particularities and trivialities that official history either neglects or glosses over in order to tell a grand story."[10] George Lipsitz, in *Time Passages*, offers a slightly different interpretation by emphasizing the oppositional nature of counter-memory. Counter-memory, Lipsitz asserts, "focuses on localized experiences with oppression, using them to reframe and refocus dominant narratives purporting to represent universal experience."[11] In studying the esthetics of Third Cinema, Teshome H. Gabriel demonstrates how popular memory negates an official history that "claims a 'centre' which continually marginalizes others." "For popular memory," Gabriel argues, "there are no longer any 'centres' or 'margins,' since the very designations imply that something has been conveniently left out."[12]

Despite the apparent differences of emphasis, the three scholars seem to agree that, as an alternative way of remembering and forgetting rooted in the personal, immediate and particular counter-memories create an autonomous cultural space for subjugated social groups which helps them reclaim their history. Rea Tajiri's documentary, in drawing upon the Japanese American community's counter-memory, exemplifies the potential of the fledging Asian American cinema in re-visioning their own American history.[13]

An alternate vision of Japanese American history

Michel Foucault, in proposing an alternative to the vision of traditional history, suggests using genealogy as "effective" history."[14] Traditional history, according to Foucault, produces continuities that "link events into a united, coherent story... Writing genealogy, on the other hand, involves the recognition of disparity, of the dispersion of origins, and links, of discontinuities and contradictions."[15] *History and Memory* is one of a growing number of Asian American films making up the genre of family histories or "family portraits," as Elizabeth Weis calls them, where the filmmakers' public and private lives intersect.[16] According to Weis, "there is a trend among independent filmmakers to make documentaries about their own families... The urge behind these films comes from the filmmakers' desire to understand themselves through their origins—genetic and ethnic."[17] Though in filming *History and Memory* Tajiri does not appear to convey a personal sense of urgency about her roots, she certainly shares this desire to find her own cultural identity through an exploration of her family's history. She poetically explains her feelings of uprootedness as *sansei* by saying, "I began searching because I felt lost, ungrounded, somewhat like a ghost that floats over terrain witnessing others living their lives and yet not having one of its own." What emerges from her search for roots is a sympathetic portrait of the lives of her extended family during the war years (the video recollects the images and voices of her grandparents, parents, sister, uncle, four aunts, niece and nephew). The significance of this personal and family story is in its immediacy and credibility. Until quite recently, Asian American history was essentially faceless, with the story usually told in terms of an anonymous "they." As a counterpoint, *History and Memory* fills the anonymous void with "authentic" images and voices from Tajiri's own relatives—the people she knows, cares for and respects—by giving them a forum to express their pride, happiness, hopes, discontent, frustration and longings for change. This emotional dimension has given Asian American history a human face which functions as an important corrective to the widely held stereotype of Asians and Asian Americans as stoic, emotionless people. The genre of family history becomes the vehicle for Asian American filmmakers to counter stereotypical Hollywood images. Loni Ding, a prominent Asian American filmmaker, for example, stated about her strategies as a filmmaker: "My preferred approach is to displace stereotypes by creating vital images of Asian Americans as real human beings, with individual faces, voices, and personal histories that we come to know and care about." [18]

The significance of this family genre, or genealogic narrative in Foucaultian terms, also lies in its collective subject. As Third Cinema critic Gabriel puts it,

> Here I do not mean autobiography in its usual Western sense of a narrative by and about a single subject. Rather, I am speaking of a multigenerational and trans-individual autobiography, i.e., a symbolic autobiography where the collective subject is the focus. A critical scrutiny of this extended sense of autobiography (perhaps hetero-biography) is more than an expression of shared experience, it is a mark of solidarity with people's lives and struggles. [19]

Indeed, this "multi-generational and trans-individual autobiography" is characterized by a plurality of voices. Like the new social historians, Rea Tajiri has drawn upon oral traditions and reclaimed information from her own family and the Japanese American community that is rarely available in any written form. In recreating her family's camp experience, for example, Tajiri uses a myriad of both unconventional and conventional sources—personal diaries, private letters, family albums, artifactual evidence, and amateur video footage from the National Archives. But her most important sources of historical information come from oral histories. Utilizing direct interviewing techniques, Tajiri sought to excavate collective memory as a set of events stored, preserved, and shared in the minds of three generations of her family members. These personal memories are often scattered, sometimes nightmarish and even contradictory. As the text in the prologue reads, "The spirit of my grandfather witnesses my father and mother as they have an argument about the nightmares their daughter has been having on the twentieth anniversary."[20]

To recover these scattered human memories and knit them into a coherent story, Tajiri literally collected every family resource available. She brought in the images of her father's army picture, her grandfather's alien I.D. card and a carved wooden bird her grandmother made in a camp class in 1942. She arranged a series of screen images from *Topaz 1942-45*, a film David Tatsunos shot with a contraband 8mm movie camera: a bowing man, a work crew digging a ditch, a woman with a frying pan, people making *mochi* and a woman skating alone; she interweaves several excerpts of the letter from her uncle Shinkichi in Holland; and most importantly, she recorded oral histories from her Aunts Betsy, Yoshiko, Helen, and Mineko. To reclaim her mother's "lost" memory, in 1988 and 1989 Tajiri made two separate pilgrimages to Salinas Rodeo Grounds camp and the camp in Poston, Arizona, where her mother stayed. She compares her own mission in Poston for the recovery of human memory to that of Spencer Tracy in Black Rock. In the process, *History and Memory* became a repertoire of collective memory. As Tajiri states in the conclusion, "I could forgive my mother her loss of memory and could make this picture for her."[21]

The importance of the video certainly transcends its familial value. What is most significant is the fact that the filmmaker has articulated a new historical consciousness—that how individuals and groups remember their histories, often in bits and snatches, is equally as important as what "actually" happened. The richness and complexity of Asian American history could only be grasped by this inclusive approach through the means of collective memory. A few years ago Russel Leong, editor of *Amerasia* journal, called for Asian American scholars "to open [them]selves to alternative forms of history." Using metaphor, he asked that a ballad be composed, sung and contributed by many different voices. *History and Memory* contributes to this ballad by becoming the guardian of collective memory.

Collective memory may not carry effective countercultural values for marginalized groups until it is related to the present situation. Put differently, collective memories are only meaningful insofar as they "teach us" about our current actions. In recreating her family history, Tajiri not only tries to rescue human memories, but also, and more significantly, to establish links between reminiscences about the past and the present struggle. This existential theme is conveyed by the way she juxtaposes past and present images and texts, both visual and literary. For example, when she revisits the scene of Poston barracks, she contrasts the camp as it is today with government photos showing it under construction in 1942. She creates a montage of images from the Japanese relocation, where we see men, women and children disembarking from a bus, barrack shots taken in 1988, and scenes from *Come See the Paradise* and *Alien Roundup*, from the National Archives. The most eloquent example might be this scene: while showing the clips from *A Bad Day at Black Rock*, the text from the *New York Times* of August 28, 1990 rolls into the frame, "Assemblyman Gil Ferguson, Republican Orange County, California, seeks to have children taught that Japanese Americans were not interned in 'concentration camps' but rather were held in 'relocation centers' justified by military necessity."[22] To heighten the contemporary meaning for the audience, she reads from Uncle Shinkichi's letter,

> You asked what I thought I gained or lost from the evacuation. Gained? Very little except a unique situation that a very tiny percentage of the American public had ever explained. What I lost was my faith in the American Constitution and it is for that reason that I left the U.S. 43 years ago, a year after I returned from the war.[23]

In short, Tajiri formulates a historical narrative which not only attempts to reshape our memory of the past, but also can inform the present political dialogue. In a sense, this struggle of memory against forgetting as represented by the video could become a source of community empowerment.

Having said all the above, *History and Memory* is, after all, a work of art and not historical scholarship restrained by verifiable evidence. However, as a powerful medium which is able to evoke emotions, shape ideas and communicate a message, *History and Memory* has performed an important function in re-visioning Japanese American history.

Notes

1. *History and Memory* script, version 8/12/91, p. 15, available from Video Data Bank, The School of the Art Institute of Chicago, Chicago, Illinois.

2. Ibid., 9.

3. Ibid., 18.

4. Zora Neale Hurston, *Their Eyes Were Watching God* (Champaign, Illinois: University of Illinois, 1979): 1.

5. *History and Memory* script, 10.

6. Ibid., 11.

7. Janice Tanaka, "Electrons & Reflective Shadows," *Moving the Image*, Russell Leong, ed. (Seattle: University of Washington Press, 1991): 206.

8. *History and Memory* script, 3.

9. Ibid., 6.

10. See Michel Foucault, *Language, Counter-memory, Practice: Selected Essays and Interviews by Michel Foucault*, Donald F. Bouchard, ed. (Ithaca, New York: Cornell University Press, 1977).

11. George Lipsitz, *Time Passages* (Minneapolis: University of Minnesota Press, 1990), 213.

12. Teshome H. Gabriel, "Third Cinema as Guardian of Popular Memory: Towards a Third Aesthetics," *Questions of Third Cinema*, Jim Pines and Paul Willemen, eds. (London: The British Film Institute, 1989), 53-54.

13. By definition, Asian American films in this essay means "films by, for and about Asian Americans."

14. Foucault, "Nietzsche, Genealogy, History," in *Language, Counter-memory, Practice*, 139-164.

15. Ibid.

16 For a definition of a family portrait, see Elizabeth Weis, "Family Portraits," *American Film*, 1: 2 (Nov. 1975), 54-59.

17. Ibid., 54.

18. Loni Ding, "Strategies of Asian American Filmmaker," *Moving the Image*, 47.

19. Gabriel, "Third Cinema as Guardian of Popular Memory," 58.

20. *History and Memory*, 1.

21. Ibid., 21.

22. Ibid., 19.

23. Ibid., 20.

12

Gender Issues in Early Chinese American Autobiography

Amy Ling

"Male-female conversation is cross-cultural communication,"[1] says linguist Deborah Tannen. This statement may explain the decades-long controversy in Asian American literature which has split the community primarily along gender lines into what has unfortunately become, to simplify issues greatly, the Maxine Hong Kingston and the Frank Chin camps. Since Elaine Kim and King-Kok Cheung have ably and thoroughly analyzed the phenomenon and the issues, I shall not enter the fray here.[2] Instead, my contribution to the discussion of gender issues comes from a close analysis of the four earliest autobiographical texts of Chinese American literature: *When I Was a Boy in China* by Lee Yan Phou;[3] "Leaves From the Mental Portfolio of an Eurasian" by Sui Sin Far;[4] *My Life in China and America* by Yung Wing[5] and *Me, A Book of Remembrance* by Winnifred Eaton[6] but published anonymously. Having discussed the female authors' writing in *Between Worlds*,[7] I will focus primarily on the texts of the male authors.

Though four texts is undoubtedly a small sample, and though large generalizations are always slippery and especially explosive in the area of gender studies, they are also of great interest. I noted immediately certain salient points which, when I read more deeply into feminist studies of autobiography, fit patterns noted by other scholars, particularly Estelle Jelinek:[8] the male writers seem more concerned with expressing what they have done, while the female writers are more concerned with expressing who they are. The men explain how they have acted upon the world; the women how they have been acted upon. The men assume what seems to them an appropriate public posture, for they are clearly addressing the world; the women, on the other hand, unafraid of the personal and

101

the intimate, seem to be speaking either to themselves or to a close friend and allowing us as readers to look over their shoulders.

A closer examination of the four texts will make my points clearer. But first, we need to establish briefly the historical contexts and the identities of these four writers.

As far as we know, the first Asian American text published in English by an Asian living in the United States is Lee Yan Phou's 1887 *When I Was a Boy in China*. Lee's mentor, Yung Wing (1828-1912) was the first Asian to immigrate to the U.S. and to graduate from a major American university—Yale class of 1854. However, Yung Wing's autobiography did not appear until 1909, when he was 81, while Lee Yan Phou published his autobiography at age 26. The first Asian American fiction writers were two Chinese Eurasian sisters—Edith Maud Eaton (1865-1914), or Sui Sin Far, and her younger sister Winnifred Eaton (1875-1954), who employed the pseudonym Onoto Watanna. Sui Sin Far's "A Chinese Feud" (*Land of Sunshine*, 1896) is, as far as is presently known, the first Asian American short story, while Onoto Watanna's 1899 *Miss Numè of Japan* is the first Asian American novel.

In the latter part of the nineteenth century, when sinophobia was rampant in the Western portion of the United States and Chinese were so rare in the Eastern portion that they were displayed in Barnum's Chinese Museum,[9] Yung Wing, by his own account, received a cordial reception in New England in 1846 (at age 18) upon his arrival in the train of the missionary, Reverend Samuel Robins Brown (Yale class of 1832). Yung Wing's autobiography tells us that his ship's passage had been a gift of the ship owners, the Olyphant Brothers of New York. His expenses for two years as well as provision for his aging parents on Pedro Island, where he was born, near Macao, were provided by several generous patrons. Though Yung Wing was too polite to question the motives of his benefactors, attributing their generosity only to their goodness, we may speculate that the philanthropists and missionaries may have been interested in answering the question: Can a Chinese, a heathen, if taken young enough, be transformed into an American, a Christian? The answer was yes.

Having attended Miss Gutzlaff's boarding school in Macao from age seven onward, Yung Wing had received early preparation. His command of the English language enabled him to attend Monson Academy in Monson, Massachusetts, where he did college preparatory work, and then Yale, where he nearly flunked in mathematics but won prizes in English composition.

From other sources we learn that between 1847 and 1854, Yung Wing converted to Christianity, attending the Congregationalist church, and became a naturalized American citizen before the passage of the law excluding Asians from citizenship. Before the miscegenation laws prohibiting marriages between "Mongolians" and whites, he married an Euro-American woman and reared two sons in Hartford, Connecticut. But these facts about his religion and marriage may not be found in his autobiography.

Instead, the emphasis is on his patriotism. Well aware of the privilege conferred on him, for as "the first Chinaman who had even been known to go through a first-class American college, I naturally attracted considerable attention...,"[10] nonetheless, Yung Wing did not forget his origins. He shuttled back and forth between his countries, trying to be of service to both. While still an undergraduate at Yale, he noted that, "the lamentable condition of China was before my mind constantly and weighed on my spirits."[11] Acknowledging the technological superiority of the west, he sought to assist his native land by importing American technology into China and exporting Chinese youths to the United States for a western education. As he put it:

> Before the close of my last year in college I had already sketched out what I should do. I was determined that the rising generation of China should enjoy the same educational advantages that I had enjoyed; that through western education China might be regenerated, become enlightened and powerful. To accomplish that object became the guiding star of my ambition.[12]

Back in China after graduation, he pursued a variety of occupations. Finally, in 1863, he won the confidence of Tsang Kwoh Fan, the Viceroy of China and the general who had quelled the Taiping Rebellion, who was "literally and practically the supreme power of China at the time."[13] Tsang commissioned Yung Wing to buy arms-making machinery from the West. After visiting factories in France and England, Yung Wing purchased the machinery from a manufacturer in Fitchburg, Massachusetts, and shipped it to China where it later became, an impressive "establishment that cover[ed] several acres of ground and embrace[ed] under its roof all the leading branches of mechanical work."[14]

In 1871, with the support of Tsang Kwoh Fan, Yung Wing's dream of extending to other boys the educational advantages he had enjoyed became a reality. The Manchu government established the Chinese Educational Mission, which was to sponsor 120 Chinese boys between the ages of 12 and 15 for 15 years of study in the U.S. They were to be sent in four yearly installments of 30, accompanied by a teacher of Chinese to ensure the boys' facility in their native tongue. The Mission flourished for ten years until conservative elements in China and sinophobia in the U.S. brought it to an end. The students were recalled to China before any group had been able to complete the program. Lee Yan Phou was one of the students recalled, but he later returned to the States and graduated from Yale University in the class of 1887.

Of his meetings with important officials of China and religious ministers and benefactors in the United States, Yung Wing is expansive and detailed in his autobiography, providing many names and dates. But of the details of his personal life, apart from his voyages between his two nations, he reveals little. Such information emerges only obliquely. For example, on February 24, 1875, Yung Wing married Mary Louise Kellogg, but this fact cannot be found in his 246-page autobiography. His marriage is alluded to only in a nonrestrictive clause, referring to his wife only by association when recounting his trip to Peru to investigate the living conditions of the Chinese coolies. He writes, "My friend, the Rev. J. H. Twichell, and Dr. E. W. Kellogg, who afterwards became my brother-in-law, accompanied me on my trip." His brother-in-law's name deserves mention, and later even his mother-in-law's, when she assists him with their two sons after his wife's untimely death, but his wife's own name never appears in Yung Wing's text. Furthermore, that miscegenation was illegal in approximately one half of the United States and that Chinese were being driven out of the Western states are topics on which he is completely silent. However, he devoted an entire chapter to his investigation of the inhumane treatment of the coolies in Peru and to his role in stopping the coolie traffic there. Undoubtedly, it was far safer to write of racist exploitation in a far-off land, than to treat such matters close to home.

Clearly, Yung Wing's intended audience is a white readership. His tone is polite and restrained. As a Yale graduate and a Confucian gentleman, he bears the weighty responsibility of service to two countries and two traditions. Like an earlier American autobiographer, Ben Franklin, Yung Wing recognizes that he has played a singular and significant role in history, and while he believes he should assume the cloak of modesty, at the same time he is revealing with obvious pride all his civic accomplishments.

Both Yung Wing's *My Life in China and America* and Sui Sin Far's "Leaves from the Mental Portfolio of an Eurasian" were published in 1909; both texts appeared close to the end of their authors' lives, though Sui Sin Far, dying at age 49, lived only slightly more than half of Yung Wing's 84 years. Her ten-page autobiographical essay is but a fraction of his book, but both are works of summing up, of looking backward over a lifetime of accomplishment, and both are written from a perspective between worlds. Sui Sin Far's between-world perspective is apparent in the essay's focus on her Eurasian identity, while Yung Wing's position must be interpolated from his numerous oceanic crossings and a single explicit disclosure of his difficulty with the Chinese language upon his first return to China.

Though Sui Sin Far is reluctant to reveal specific dates and names of persons and places, the very focus of her essay—what it was to be an Eurasian in the English-speaking world (Macclesfield, England; Hudson City, New York; Montreal, Quebec and Kingston, Jamaica)—requires personal disclosure. Contrary to Jelinek's conclusion, that painful and intimate memories are not usually divulged in autobiographies,"[15] "Leaves" centers on the uncomfortable subject of racism, specifically sinophobia and its ramifications. Though she never names the disease, Sui Sin Far provides a catalogue of symptoms. The poignant anecdotes which structure her entire essay all emphasize the alienation and awareness of difference imposed on her from age four through 40.

Since "Leaves" has been discussed in *Between Worlds*, and is now readily available in a number of texts, I will not take up space providing specific examples. Suffice it to say that Sui Sin Far's reaction to sinophobia was directly confrontational. Proud of her Chinese heritage, she was entirely self-taught:

> Whenever I have the opportunity I steal away to the library and read every book I can find on China and the Chinese. I learn that China is the oldest civilized nation on the face of the earth and a few other things. At eighteen years of age what troubles me is not that I am what I am, but that others are ignorant of my superiority. I am small, but my feelings are big—and great is my vanity.[16]

Her racial pride led her to choose a Chinese pseudonym, and her courage made her a word warrior in the battle for just treatment of the Chinese:

> I meet many Chinese persons, and when they get into trouble am often called upon to fight their battles in the papers. This I enjoy. My heart leaps for joy when I read one day an article signed by a New York Chinese in which he declares "The Chinese in America owe an everlasting debt of gratitude to Sui Sin Far for the bold stand she has taken in their defense."[17]

This is the only passage in "Leaves" that may be construed as focused on Sui Sin Far's work as a means of making a mark on the world, but the thrust of the episode is not so much to boast about public recognition as to show what she has done with the heightened consciousness of her chosen ethnicity.

Sui Sin Far's sense of purpose and her desire to serve her mother's people was no less strong than Yung Wing's, yet her autobiographical essay is not filled with her accomplishments, nor the names of the famous people she met.[18] She does not tell the reader about the national magazines in which her stories were published nor the positive reviews she received from such influential publications as the *New York Times* and the *Independent*. Instead, she focuses on the development of her own identity and pride, forged in the furnaces of pain and humiliation.

Of the experience of being Chinese in a white society, Yung Wing writes not a word. Nor, as we have noted, do courtship and marriage enter his text. Sui Sin Far, on the other hand, devotes a disproportionately large space to a marriage that didn't take place in the story of "one Chinese Eurasian," very likely her own story. Despite the fact that unmarried women were regarded with opprobrium, Sui Sin Far called herself "a very serious and sober-minded spinster indeed."[19]

Though their texts reveal a shared love for China as well as a strong independence of spirit, the tone and content of both writings clearly differ. Yung Wing's autobiography is a public document, written with an eye to posterity. He reveals his attempts to bring China out of her feudal somnolence into a technologically advanced modernity. Sui Sin Far's essay, by contrast, is an intimate piece, more a personal musing directed to herself than a public statement. Aware of an audience, of course, she is not forthcoming with names and dates, but she courageously probes the troubling intimate questions which plagued her as a child:

> Why are we what we are? I and my brothers and sisters? Why did God make us to be hooted and stared at? Papa is English, mamma is Chinese. Why couldn't we have been either one thing or the other? Why is my mother's race despised? I look into the faces of my father and mother. Is she not every bit as dear and good as he? Why? Why?[20]

Engaged in introspection, she explores her own complex identity as an Eurasian, the subject of some of her best stories in her collection *Mrs. Spring Fragrance.*[21]

In contrast to the texts by Yung Wing and Sui Sin Far, Lee Yan Phou's *When I Was A Boy In China* and Onoto Watanna's *Me: A Book of Remembrance* are both rather strange texts. Though both claim to be autobiographies, the former seems the brainchild of a publisher[22] with an eye to the travel-book market, and the latter reads like a novel. To write what purports to be an autobiography but to publish it anonymously and to give oneself a fictional name throughout is to produce a text that is a violation of the genre itself.

Lee's book is very consciously addressed to an audience that knows little or nothing about Chinese culture and customs, and the author takes up the role of tourist guide, or as Elaine Kim puts it of another Asian American author, "transmitter of Chinese 'culture' to non-Chinese" and "ambassador of good will."[23] Lee's text clearly has an anthropological and didactic thrust, as evidenced in the chapter titles: "The House and the Household," "Chinese Cookery," "Games and Pastimes," "Girls of My Acquaintance," "Schools and School Life," "Religions," "Chinese Holidays." Lee is most conscientious; for example, he devotes an entire paragraph to his birthdate because this simple fact entails a lengthy explanation of the Chinese calendar. Here is how his book begins:

> On a certain day in the year 1861, I was born. I cannot give you the exact date, because the Chinese year is different from the English year, and our months being lunar, that is, reckoned by the revolution of the moon around the earth, are consequently shorter than yours. We reckon time from the accessions of Emperors, and also by cycles of sixty years each. The year of my birth, 1861, was the first year of the Emperor Tung-che. We have twelve months ordinarily; and we say, instead of "January, February," etc., "Regular Moon, Second Moon, Third Moon," etc. Each third year is a leap year, and has an extra month so as to make each of the lunar years equal to a solar year. Accordingly, taking the English calendar as a standard, our New Year's Day varies. Therefore, although I am sure that I was born on the twenty-first day of the Second Moon, in Chinese, I don't know my exact birthday in English; and consequently, living in America as I have for many years, I have been cheated of my birthday celebration.[24]

Lee's explanation of the Chinese calendrical system, in its minute specificity and complexity, verges on the ludicrous, but it is offset by the direct address to his non-Chinese audience, his awareness of their lack of information, and, at the very end, this passage is redeemed from the level of a cumbersome encyclopedia article by a humorous touch. The book follows the same pattern. To counteract the deadening effect of a compendium of facts, Lee seeks to make the experience immediate. After telling us that the household servants are going to market, he writes, "Let us follow them," and proceeds to describe in visual and auditory detail the sights along the way, in the fashion of a *National Geographic* film: "Here are incense-shops, butcher-shops and grocery-stores, fish-stalls and vegetable-stands. The stone pavement is slippery with mud. The din is deafening."[25]

Lee Yan Phou presents himself as a reasonable, urbane, well-read, Christian Chinese gentleman guide, equally comfortable alluding to the witches in MacBeth and also asserting that few books in English are the equal of the Chinese classic, "the unfailing delight of all classes; ... the *History [Romance] of the Three Kingdoms*."[26]

The illustrations in the book, however, appear to be inserted in total disregard of the text. For example, while Lee is describing the floor-plan of his grandfather's fifteen-room mansion and its furnishings, we are given the irrelevant photograph of a barefoot "Chinese beggar boy." The discrepancy is startling and inexplicable. Another jarring juxtaposition is the book's cover and the author's photograph. The cover drawing shows a highly-exoticized slant-eyed boy flying a bat-shaped kite; his queue flies tail-like in the wind while the kite string trails tail-like at his back. By contrast, the author's photograph, opposite the title page, reveals a wide-eyed young man with short cropped hair and a mustache in a double-breasted western jacket, looking bright and intense. The two images clash in their intent: the cover exoticizing and estranging, the author's photograph familiarizing and engaging. It is very unlikely that Lee Yan Phou, who later married an American woman and became a journalist in the United States, would have selected these particular images and this cover to represent himself. In fact, the topics of the chapters themselves may not have been the ones he, given his choice, would have written.

The text gains in interest in the last three chapters, which finally become a personal narrative and describe Lee's preparations and earliest experiences in the United States. The book's most amusing sentence occurs in the last chapter, in which Lee describes his railroad journey cross-country:

> Nothing occurred on our Eastward journey to mar the enjoyment of our first ride on the steam cars—excepting a train robbery, a consequent smash-up of the engine, and the murder of the engineer.[27]

The understatement of the bland assertion "nothing occurred" is counteracted by the series of catastrophic events: "train robbery," "smash-up," "murder," indicating that the author is in jest. This introduction is followed by a brief description of the mishaps in which the author's sense of adventure is readily apparent. But since Lee, at this point, has begun to deal with life in the United States, he is falling outside the stated scope of the book—his boyhood in China—and the narrative is abruptly cut short. Though I have focused on these few humorous and personable passages, they are the exception in a text given to rather dry explications of culture and customs.

Me, on the other hand, is an entirely personal book—so revealing that the author published it anonymously for fear of dispelling the persona she had created for herself as a best-selling Japanese author. In *Me*, Winnifred Eaton clearly states that she was born in Montreal, the eighth in a family of 16 children. She reveals the poverty of her childhood home, where her father set up his easel in the kitchen because that was the only warm room in the house and where the noise and confusion of so many siblings became her image of hell. Of her mother's ethnicity, she writes only vaguely, "She was a native of a far-distant land, and I do not think she ever got over the feeling of being a stranger in Canada."

Winnifred mentions others' curiosity about her ethnicity, noting that they looked at her, "as if I interested them or they were puzzled to know my nationality. I would have given anything to look less foreign. My darkness marked and crushed me, I who loved blondness like the sun."[28] Nothing in either Yung Wing's book or Lee Yan Phou's gives the slightest indication of their awareness of or concern about how others perceived them, despite the sinophobia of the period and the fact that a Chinese man in the Eastern United States in the late nineteenth century was undoubtedly a rarity and must have provoked numerous and varied responses. For the men, this facet of life in the United States seemed to be beneath notice. Yung was concerned with relating how he had made his mark on the world; Lee with explaining the world from which he had come. Winnifred Eaton also explained her early world in order to show how far she had had to come to write her first book. Though she gives her protagonist a fictional name, Nora Ascough, her narrative is filled with personal revelations, with the inferiority complex of a dark-haired girl in a blond-loving society, with the emotions of unrequited first love, with the hopes and fears of a beginning writer, with the sexual harassment a young woman encounters when making her way in the world without the insulation and support of a wealthy family.

In conclusion, I realize that the smallness of my sample limits the validity of my generalizations. Other factors also need to be taken into account, such as the age of the authors when they arrived in America; Sui Sin Far was six and Onoto Watanna was born in Montreal. The men immigrated in their late or mid teens, with their sense of identity already formed in China. For the women, growing up as a racial minority was an experience that deeply marked their sense of self and thus colored their life stories. However, the four texts themselves clearly substantiate certain gender differences noted by scholars of women's autobiographies. Men are more concerned with conveying information, with solving problems, with themselves as actors upon the world. Women are more concerned with weaving relationships and interacting with others and with their own subjectivity, their inner, emotional, and psychological lives.

Yung Wing's autobiography is totally focused on his struggle to modernize China through the importation of Western technology and through Western education. Lee Yan Phou's purpose was to make more familiar what he knew his readers found alien about Chinese people and culture. He served as a bridge between nations. Sui Sin Far also felt herself a bridge between races; her life experiences spoke against the constraints and artificiality of racial, sexual and cultural hierarchies, whose boundaries she wished to break. These three, in their efforts to create social change, may be seen to be sharing more with each other than with Winnifred Eaton, whose autobiography was focused on her individual and personal experience in relation to her professional growth. However, though Sui Sin Far may have shared a goal with the men, she shared a method with her sister. For both women, the larger picture is to be inferred from the specific details, the intimate personal disclosures. For the men, the larger picture is the primary point, the personal disclosures are extraneous.

Our ways are different, but gender roles are by definition learned ways.

Despite the Chinese ethnicity of these four turn-of-the-century writers, an ethnicity that would put them at a disadvantage in the dominant American society, the males nonetheless clearly wrote from a position of strength and confidence, while the women wrote with an awareness of weakness stemming both from their ethnicity and their sex. This would seem to corroborate Bell and Yalom's assertion that "males [are] almost universally in a position of dominance." However, in the genre of autobiography, greater awareness of the interior self and greater revelation of this interiority result undoubtedly in more interesting and engaging autobiographies. Thus, the hierarchy is inverted.

Notes

1. Deborah Tannen, *That's Not What I Meant!* (New York: Ballantine, 1987): 125.

2. See Elaine Kim, "'Such Opposite Creatures': Men and Women in Asian American Literature," *Michigan Quarterly Review* 29:1 (1990): 68-93 and King-Kok Cheung, "The Woman Warrior versus The Chinaman Pacific: Must a Chinese American Critic Choose between Feminism and Heroism?" in *Conflicts in Feminism*, Marianne Hirsch and Evelyn Fox Keller, eds.(New York: Routledge, 1990).

3. Yan Phou Lee, *When I Was a Boy in China* (Boston: Lothrop, Lee & Shepard, 1887).

4. Sui Sin Far, "Leaves from the Mental Portfolio of an Eurasian," was originally published in *The Independent* (21 January, 1909): 125-132. It may now be found in Vol. 2 of the *Heath Anthology of American Literature*, p. 885-895 and in *Visions of America*, edited by Wesley Brown and Amy Ling (New York: Persea Books, 1992): 22-33.

5. Yung Wing, *My Life in China and America* (New York: Henry Holt, 1909).

6. [Winnifred Eaton], *Me: A Book of Remembrance* (New York: Century, 1915).

7. Amy Ling, *Between Worlds: Women Writers of Chinese Ancestry* (New York: Pergamon, 1990).

8. In the past ten or twelve years, research in women's autobiography has mushroomed. Note the books assembled and edited or written by Estelle Jelinek, Sidonie Smith, Shari Benstock, Celeste Schenck and Bella Broadzki, Valerie Sanders and Carolyn Heilbrun, Susan Bell and Marilyn Yalom. Estelle C. Jelinek's "Introduction: Women's Autobiography and the Male Tradition" in *Women's Autobiography* (Bloomington: Indiana University Press, 1980): 7-8 accords well with my comparisons.

9. See Judy Yung, *Chinese Women in America* (Seattle: University of Washington Press, 1986).

10. Yung Wing, *My Life in China and America*, 39.

11. Ibid., 40.

12. Ibid., 40-41.

13. Ibid., 142.

14. Ibid., 153.

15. Jelinek, *Women's Autobiography*, 10.

16. Far, "Leaves," 128.

17. Ibid.

18. One newspaper clipping in the LaFerriere family archives reports that Sui Sin Far met with Dr. Sun Yet Sen, the first president of the Republic of China during his visit to Montreal.

19. Far, "Leaves," 130.

20. Ibid., 127-8.

21. Sui Sin Far, *Mrs. Spring Fragrance* (Chicago: A.C. McClurg, 1912).

22. Indeed, I note after writing this sentence that Elaine Kim has stated that the publisher initiated this series: "At the turn of the century, a series of books by young men from various lands was solicited by the D. Lothrop Publishing Company. Lee Yan Phou's *When I Was a Boy in China* (1887) was one of the first of these, and New Il-Han's *When I Was a Boy in Korea* (1928) was one of the last." See *Asian American Literature: An Introduction to the Writings and Their Social Context*, (Philadelphia: Temple University Press, 1982): 25.

23. Kim, "Such Opposite Creatures," 72. 24.

24. Lee, *When I Was a Boy in China*, 7-8.

25. Ibid., 27.

26. Ibid., 82.

27. Ibid. 107.

28. [Winnifred Eaton], *Me*, 3, 166.

13

Hawaii's Literary Traditions
Separating Food from the Buta Kaukau [1]

Darrell H.Y. Lum

I believe that writing and literature validates our lives. That is, until we appear as the major characters in novels, plays, stories, poems, movies and television programs about the islands, we can never really see ourselves as heroic in our own communities. Until our lives are validated in literature, we do not truly exist. Until this happens, we are left with someone outside of ourselves to tell us about ourselves; just as James Michener did with the novel, *Hawaii*.[2] Now there's nothing wrong with Michener writing about Hawaii except when we begin to believe in his fiction more than we do the truth of our own lives;[3] when we ignore the fact that at around the same time as *Hawaii* there were countless other examples of poetry, fiction, plays and novels written by local writers. The novel *Hawaii* was predated by Shelly Ota's *Upon Their Shoulders*,[4] a saga of immigration describing the struggles of Taro Sumida and his family and community. Shortly thereafter, books by Margaret Harada *The Sun Shines on the Immigrant*,[5] Kazuo Miyamoto, *Hawaii End of the Rainbow*,[6] and Milton Murayama, *All I Asking for Is My Body*,[7] told stories far different from Michener's dream of a homogenized Golden Man. The stories told by Ota, Harada, Miyamoto and Murayama never spoke of the melting pot. Instead they spoke of individual struggles, of ethnic and class solidarity, of pride in one's culture, and told tales full of the conflicts within a family and within an ethnic group that were far more real to me than Michener's *Hawaii* ever was.

Island literature, or as it has been termed, local literature, has been systematically and deliberately suppressed for at least 150 years, since the start of the public educational system in the Kingdom of Hawaii. Literary voices have been ignored and we have been duped into believing that we have no literature, that we have no literary history, that we have no literary traditions.

How many times have we heard:

"Local literature is just Hawaiian legends or stories from the old country, from Japan and China."

"Nobody except locals can understand it."

"Our parents and grandparents were too busy making a living, working on the plantation to think about writing." or

"Native Hawaiians only had an oral tradition, not a written one.

And the suppression has come from ourselves as well as from the outside as we repeat these fallacies: *We have no literature, we have no literary history, we have no literary tradition.*

There should be little wonder then that students in Hawaii often think that writers are dead and that writing is about people and places and things that are far away, geographically as well as emotionally. It's a hard lesson for writers to learn: that they must write from their own experience. Yet the dishonesty depicted by the Hawaii Visitors Bureau and popular media continues to define us. How many times have we watched "Hawaii 5-0" or "Magnum P.I." or "Jake and the Fatman" and discovered stereotypic depictions of Asians and Pacific Islanders (usually a thug or a flunkey) speaking bad pidgin or simply heading off in the wrong direction as they go to the airport? How many books, movies, or TV programs will it take before we throw up our hands and say, "Get it right!" Why haven't these writers bothered to get it right? Have colonial attitudes, paternalism and language oppression been around for so long that we simply have come to accept it? Or worse, fail to recognize it?

These inaccuracies cannot be easily dismissed by saying that the existing literature is inaccessible or that there is a conspiracy of publishing houses and university professors who are deliberately ignoring these works. Rather, I believe that there is a conspiracy of attitude and spirit that has kept our voices, if not silent, certainly suppressed and has convinced us that we have no literature and what there is, is not good enough. And we've repeated this enough times, perhaps unconsciously to our students and to our children, that it has become self-fulfilling: *We have literature, no literary history, no literary tradition.*

My discovery of the existence of a Hawaii literature came at the first Talk Story Writers Conference held in Honolulu in 1978. Until that time, I felt that I had been working in a vacuum; that I was the first to use pidgin in short stories and it was very, very lonely. Imagine my surprise when I met Milton Murayama whose pidgin novel *All I Asking for is My Body* helped me realize that I wasn't a pioneer after all. I learned that creative writing dating back to the 1920s has always been available in readily accessible collections, but had been largely ignored by readers, teachers, scholars and other writers.[8] Instead of being a pioneer, I was, in fact, part of a long history of pidgin literature.

At the conference, Maxine Kingston pointed out that the pidgin-speaking grandmother in my play[9] sounded just like her grandmother in Stockton; that I had written about a kind of universal grandmother. The Talk Story Conference was important because for the first time, I met other local writers and felt a part of a community of writers who chose to write about the islands and its people as we know them. We realized that we did not carry the burden of telling the whole story by ourselves; that there were other people with similar backgrounds and concerns: "How do you use pidgin or Japanese or Chinese words without a glossary? "Who is your audience?" "Will mainland people understand this?" Will local people think we're 'talking stink,' airing dirty laundry?"

We looked for models among the other writers at the conference. The visiting Asian American writers seemed to have a history. Perhaps we were like them. They had a tradition that drew on the black and the sixties hippie experience. Maybe we were like them. But then they accused us of being politically naive. "Where are the politics in your writing," they demanded. We couldn't answer. We knew we were not like them. They had a different history and tradition. Was our writing apolitical? What was our tradition? Did we have one at all? Were they right? What were our politics?

As with all other things, we had begun to believe that we were simply a few years behind the mainland. We felt we were in the literary backwaters of America. "Give us time," we told ourselves, "we'll catch up." After all, K-Mart arrived in Hawaii only last November. "Mainland prices have come to Hawaii," the ads boasted. Eventually we do get all the fast food franchises, a few years after they open on the mainland. But even McDonalds made concessions to island tastes and started serving fruit punch and *saimin*. Perhaps like other aspects of local life, our writing was similar in some ways but different in other ways from those mainland writers. Ours was a little more subtle, more indirect and non-confrontational; more concerned with the intricacies of interpersonal and family relationships. Ours was the politics of living on an island; the fragile balance of being interconnected by family, by school, by job, by neighborhood; ours was about the necessity of reciprocity and the reality of "no talk stink, you might be related." Our literature was characterized by a sense of place, by a "talk story" narrative style and a history inextricably linked to a paternalistic plantation system and a colonized people. Is it possible that we had an identity of our own?

A. Grove Day's bibliography of books about Hawaii published in 1977, *Books about Hawaii, Fifty Basic Authors*,[10] lists only one Hawaii-born fiction writer, Ozzie Bushnell, in the top 50. It does list other creative writers like Michener, Robert Louis Stevenson, Jack London, Earl Biggers (who gave us *House Without a Key*, the first Charlie Chan novel) and a single poet, Genevieve Taggard. What kind of Hawaii do we get in this, Day's "must read" list of books about Hawaii? It is largely the same list of authors who appeared 20 years earlier in a book Day and Carl Stroven edited called *A Hawaiian Reader*[11] published in 1959. The book features 37 selections ranging from the Kumulipo (a native Hawaiian creation chant), to Rev. Abraham Akaka's Statehood Service at Kawaiahao Church but contains no creative work from a Hawaii-born writer. It does include other works such as a racist short story called "Chun Ah Chun" by Jack London[12] wartime accounts ("Bombs Fall on Hawaii: Dec. 7, 1941") and "Sukiyaki on the Kona Coast" a story in which the narrator, a dinner guest at a local household, is horrified by the sight of geckos on the wall. Was there so little literature that the editors had to stoop to racist stories, war accounts or anecdotes about insects?

In fact, in the 30 years since *A Hawaiian Reader,* it appears that Professor Day has not discovered any new writers of note. In 1988, when asked why he had not mentioned the contributions of Chinese and Japanese Americans and other writers born in the islands in *Mad About Islands: Novelists of a Vanished Pacific,*[13] Day replied:

> I have always been aware that there are excellent but untranslated writings about the Pacific Islands in a dozen languages. As a teacher at Manoa of several thousand students, I have strongly repeated the advice that they should write about their own experiences, to exploit the unique treasures of a Pacific heritage to be found in their own backyards... the native people of Oceania have had their own fictions that differ markedly from the mode of writers in English... [14]

According to Day then, it's too bad more literature by writers born in the islands isn't in translation, that our writing differs from other writers of English, that he has always encouraged his students to write from their own experience, and that we local-born are not even Americans but Oceanians.

Contrast this with our own efforts to find selections by Chinese Americans to include in *Pake: Writings by Chinese in Hawaii,*[15] an anthology published in commemoration of the 200th anniversary of Chinese immigration to Hawaii. We tracked down a playwright whose work, written as a university student in the early fifties, we wanted to use. We found him living in Connecticut and asked him about professors or writers who might have influenced him. He recalled a Professor Day who told him, in no uncertain terms, that if he ever wanted his writing to amount to anything, he should have only *haole* (Caucasian) characters and set his stories on the mainland. Who are we to believe?

It is unfortunate that the distinguished professor who taught the Hawaii and Pacific literature course at the university failed to find any literature worthy of note over these 30 years. It is truly unfortunate that he fails to recognize that English is our native language.

Thus not only did Day overlook a century or so of local literature, he has in part, perpetuated the notion that we have no literature. He has denied what our literature is and who we are as a people by his choices and omissions. And what is worse, we let him.

Can this be true? In 1977 Stephen Sumida and Arnold Hiura compiled a bibliography, *Asian American Literature of Hawaii,* and found over 700 entries written by Asian Americans in the University of Hawaii, Hawaii Pacific Collection, the Hawaii State Library and in other public collections—the same places that Day's and Michener's researchers must have looked. Is this poor research, or poor scholarship or the deliberate oversight of important work, in English, literally sitting on the shelves right next to the entries in Day's anthologies.[16] Was he too, blinded by the belief that we have no literature?

And what of native Hawaiian literature? In Kiki Mookini's study of Hawaiian language newspapers from the 1830s to the 1940s, there were 14 different Hawaiian language newspapers being published.[17] The Hawaiians had rapidly become a literate society, and the Mookini study discovered that Letters to the Editors page had become a public forum as well as a kind of inter-island mail system to communicate with friends and relatives. In the letters she found a wonderful sense of playfulness of language, riddles, puns, and gossip. In every issue there was a funeral hymn, elegy or dirge; travelogues and poetic descriptions of geographic locations, wordplays and clever poetry with multiple meanings, songs, detailed genealogies and serialized stories. What she discovered could well be called an emerging literary tradition of native Hawaiians.[18]

How often have we have come to believe that the native Hawaiian tradition was solely an oral one. Yet here was evidence of a written tradition. Who are we to believe? *We have no literature, no literary history, no literary tradition.*

Similarly, immigrant groups brought their own literary traditions which were transformed by the Hawaii experience. The myth that immigrants did not write is still more garbage, *buta kaukau.* At the Talk Story Conference on the Big Island in 1979, those in attendance met members of the Hilo Shou Kai (the Literary Society), a haiku club founded in 1903

and the oldest continuously active haiku club in *the world*. The club is even older than clubs in Japan and continues to meet, write and publish books of Hawaii haiku that have their own unique characteristics to fulfill the formal season word requirements: the mention of certain fruits, flowers or crops or the sight of snow on Mauna Kea. Here clearly was a traditional literary form that had been transformed into a Hawaii literature.[19]
We have no literature, no literary history, no literary tradition.

How is it that we have come to believe in these myths, this *buta kaukau*? Where have we acquired the notion that somehow we are incapable of creative expression, inferior in our ability to use language, that our language isn't even a language? Our literary traditions were nearly erased by the movement to ban foreign language schools,[20] the "Speak American" anti-pidgin movement,[21] and the system of education elitism in the English Standard schools[22] under the guise Americanization. This too is a part of our history: The deliberate effort to eliminate whole languages and cultures in favor of standard English.

In a curious way, the attempts to ban pidgin actually ensured its perpetuation. Since the standard English speakers were concentrated in the English Standard schools, the regular schools lacked a mix of standard English and pidgin speaking students and despite teachers' efforts to discourage it, pidgin flourished. At the same time, progressive educators ran the regular schools and turned to an activity-centered curriculum, one that allowed more free expression and the integration of school, community and vocational interests. The net effect was an educational system that was segregated by race and economic class and the vivid depiction of the inherent contradictions between American democratic values and a plantation system that was characterized by paternalism, contract labor, ethnic segregation of living quarters, pay differences based on ethnicity, and labor treated as a commodity.

Talk like one haole... every parent's wish

"Speak good English," my father used to say to me. He'd be sure to point out to me whenever he met a local kid who spoke standard English, "Too good, eh? Dat kid, he talk like one *haole*!"

The desire of parents for their children to "talk like one haole" is a commonly held assimilationist attitude that not only devalues pidgin but sees it as something to "overcome, like a bad habit."[23] This dread "pidgin peril" has been the bane of the educational system since the 1880s when it was called "hideous mongrel jargon," "a barbarous perversion of English," and a "bastardized language."[24] It has continually been the scapegoat for the poor language skills of some of Hawaii's children,[25] despite evidence as early as 1934 that established pidgin as a creole and suggested that it was not necessary to eliminate pidgin in order to teach standard English.[26]

As recently as 1987, the Hawaii Board of Education attempted to ban pidgin on and off campus because pidgin speakers were "severely limited" and would be unable to "move up the ladder of success."[27] The board chose to ignore nearly 60 years of evidence that established pidgin as a language and linked it to identity and local culture.[28] After much debate, the measure was passed in a watered down form after a surprising amount of testimony defended pidgin as a cultural symbol.[29]

Still, the attitudes which devalue pidgin are with us and are likely to remain with us. This too, is part of our history. And unless we watch for books, movies, histories and our own writing that perpetuate these attitudes we will truly be doomed to believe: **We have no literature, no literary history, no literary tradition.** We must question our assumptions about who we are and continue to define ourselves, write about ourselves, the way we know we are. We must refuse to merely accept how others have defined us as the only truth. We must acknowledge and celebrate our long literary history.

I'd like to end by reading a short story which I think acknowledges some of these traditions: traditions of the islands, traditions of a language and traditions of being American.

Giving Tanks

The brown and orange crayons always run out at Tanksgiving time. You gotta use um for color da turkeys and da Indian feathers la dat. Yellow run out fast, too. My teacher, Mrs. Perry, used to tell us dat we suppose to use dose colors cause ass da autumn colors. Supposed to be when all the leaves on da trees turn color, like da orange and brown crayons or do funny kine brown one in da big crayons box, burnt something. I couldn't see how if da leaves turn color, was pretty. For us, dat jes means dat da tree going die, or maybe stay dead awready. Or maybe like our lychee tree in da backyard, when da leaves turn color, they fall off and Daddy tell me I gotta go rake before I can go play.

Tanksgiving was when you gotta learn about da Pilgrims and all dat. Ass when da Indians and da Pilgrims went get together, eat turkey or something. Kinda hard to believe though, yeah. Me, I like da Indians mo bettah den da Pilgrims. Da Indians had da kine leather pants wit da fringes and da small kine beads and dey fight wit bow and arrow la dat. Da Pilgrims had to wear da black suits, even da small kids, and da funny kine hat. Dey even had funny kine gun dat was fat at da end. My brother told me dat was one blundahbuss, dat da olden days guys wanted da bullets to spread all over so da gun was funny kine. He said da gun couldn't shoot straight, though. Ass why da Indians mo bettah. I betchu arrows could shoot moo straight den dat.

Da teacha told me to do one report on da Pilgrims and draw one cornucopia. I nevah know what dat was. Even aftah I saw da picture, I still couldn't figure out what dat was.

"Ass one horn of plenty," Louise went tell me. She smart, so she oughta know. "Stay like one basket fo put fruits inside, fo show you rich, dat you get food."

"Well, how come always stay falling down and all da fruits spilling out?" I went ask her. "Funny kine basket, eh?" I not so dumb. So when I went home, I went try draw one horn of plenty but I couldn't figure out what was fo. Look more like my brother's trombone den one basket. And you no can play music wit one horn of plenty. Ho, sometimes da teacher make us do crazy stuffs.

In school we always had to do the same old ting. You know, make one turkey out of one paper plate: da plate is the body and you paste on the head and tail and the legs. Sometimes we make one napkin holder turkey: you staple half a paper plate to your turkey so get one place fo put da napkins. Den you paste da neck and da head and da feet and you gotta color dat too...brown and orange and yellow. Den you fold up da paper napkins and put um inside da plate and if you use color-koa napkins, look like da turkey tail. Mama really went like that one. She went hang um up on da wall and fill um up with napkins and put away da regular napkin holder until came all had-it and da head went fall off.

Everybody like go to Auntie Jennie's and Uncle Jim's house fo Tanksgiving dinner cause Mama said Auntie's turkey always come out moist. Me, I only like eat skin and gravy. Auntie Jennie make good gravy and I like the cranberry sauce da best. I no like da stuffing cause I tink they hide all da ugly stuff from inside da turkey in dere.

Auntie Jennie's house was nice. Her kitchen table had real cloth kine tablecloth not da plastic kine on top and she no put sheets on top her couch and had anykine knitted stuff, like those hat things that cover the extra toilet paper on top the toilet tank. And get anykine neat stuff all around her house... anykine souvenirs from all over da world, da places they went go visit. J'like everyplace they went, she went but one salt and pepper shaker. Fo collect. Some look like animals and look like one house or one car or one famous building. Some you couldn't even figure out where da salt or pepper come out!

Uncle Jim has this teeny tiny collection of knives dat was da best. Wasn't real, was imitation; each one was about one inch long or maybe two inches long. Was anykine knives, like bolo knife and swords from all over the world and put on one piece of wood, j'like one shield. Maybe he went collect knives from everyplace he went.

Uncle Jim was da fire chief so always had firemen at his house. And he park his car right in front his house, one big red station wagon. Da license plate says, "HFD 1," Honolulu Fire Department One. Dat means he da chief. Uncle Jim was tall and skinny and bolohead. Errybody call him "chief" and I know he da *fire* chief but he remind me of one Indian chief, tall and old and plenny wrinkles on his face. I betchu he get one Indian knife someplace, wit one leather holder, too.

My grandma, Ah Po Lee, was always dere too, sitting down on the couch in her plain stay-at-home clothes talking Chinese to my Auntie. I think she get nice clothes, one time I seen one silk cheong sam hanging up on her door with the plastic from the dry clean man but I nevah seen her wear um. And she wear one wide cloth headband dat make her look like one old Indian lady: all small and bent ovah, plain blue khaki jacket and black Chinese pants and fancy cloth slippahs wit small beads making one dragon and anykine wrinkles and spots on her face. Look j'like warpaint.

So ass what we did Tanksgiving time. Go Auntie Jennie's house and eat turkey and make paper plate turkeys and try fo figgah out what one cornucopia was. And in school, I kept tinking, when we going learn about one Indian holiday? Would be neat if we could, yeah? We could dance around...whoa, whoa, whoa, whoa! Anyways, all dat was jes one fairy tale. Like wrestling at da Civic Auditorium, fake. Same like da uddah tings in da books and da National School Broadcast, all fairy tales. Ah Po told me one time, dat real Tanksgiving stay everyday. Ass why every day she pray fo my grandfahdah. No miss. She burn incense and pour tea and whiskey fo him outside on da porch where get da bowl wit sand fo stick da red candles and da skinny kine incense. Sometimes I watch da ashes curl up, hanging on, hanging on. Da ting can go long time before it fall off.

I no can remembah my Ah Goong, my granfahdah, except fo da big picture on da wall in da living room. But even ny bruddah Russo said dat he nevah look like dat. He said he look mo old. Da picture stay one young guy. I guess ass one fairy tale, too. Ah Goong was old, Russo said. Tall and skinny and old. So Ah Po burn candles and incense and pour whiskey and tea fo dis tall, skinny, old guy and I watch da ashes curling and da smoke go up like smoke signals. Once, I went ask Ah Po how come she pray so much and she tell me she pray dat Ah Goong stay okay, she pray dat us guys, Russo and me, be good boys, she pray "tank you" she get rice to eat. She tell me she get lots to pray about.

Everytime get sale, she go buy one bag rice. Could tell she felt rich when she had one bag rice extra in the closet. And toilet paper. Lots of toilet paper. And Spam and vienna sausages and Campbell's soup and can corned beef. Nevah mind she kept fixing and fixing her stay-home dress ovah and ovah, cause was stay-home anyways. Nevah mind dat she had one old washing machine you had to crank da clothes through da roller stuffs. Nevah mind sometimes she went eat *hahm gnee*, salt fish, and rice fo dinner for three days when me and Russo went sleep her house and we wanted to eat plain meat and not all mixed up wit vegetables kine.

And I seen her finish eating da little bit meat off da bone from my piece of meat and how hardly had any slop for da slop man and how she went look in her button bottle for two quarters fo wrap up in red paper fo give us *lee-see* fo buy ice cream from da ice cream man. Ass how I knew dat my cornucopia wasn't one basket wit fruit and vegetables spilling out. Wasn't Indians and Pilgrims sitting down fo eat turkey. Was Russo and me sitting down at da table while Ah Po put her oily black frying pan on da stove and turned da fire up high until da oil smoke and she put noodles and carrots and a little bit oyster sauce and three, maybe four, pieces of green onion cut big, so that we could see um and pick um out of our plates. She nevah used to have one big fat turkey fo Tanksgiving.

"Lucky," she used to say anyways. "Lucky da ice cream man come," even though he always pass by about 3:30 every Thursday. "Lucky you get *lee-see* to spend. Lucky. Lucky you come visit Ah Po," she would say. And we would tink about what if we nevah come and miss out on noodles and quarters and ice cream.

I guess we was lucky, yeah?[30]

Parts of this address were previously presented to the Ka Hui Helu Helu Reading Association conference, December 1, 1990. I would like to acknowledge the assistance, support and scholarship of Ralph Stueber and Stephen Sumida which provided the foundation for these remarks. Stephen H. Sumida, And the View from the Shore: Literary Traditions of Hawaii (Seattle: University of Washington Press, 1991).

Notes

1. *Buta kaukau*, pig food or slop, is an example of a truly pidgin term. *Buta* is the Japanese word for pig and *kaukau* is Hawaiian for food (actually the Hawaiian pronunciation of the Chinese pidgin word for food, *chow-chow*, according to E.B. Carr in *Da Kine Talk* (Honolulu: University Press of Hawaii, 1972): 135. In this chapter, the term pidgin is used in reference to Hawaii Creole English (HCE) rather than to the pidgin of the early immigrants.

2. James A. Michener, *Hawaii* (New York: Random House, 1959).

3. The Hawaii Mission Children's Society in 1967 issued a pamphlet protesting the depiction of the missionaries in the novel. The outcry was apparently great enough for Michener's biographer, A. Grove Day to defend the depiction of the missionaries and others as remarks "from a few racial bigots." A. Grove Day, *James A. Michener* (New York: Twayne Publishers, Inc., 1964): 112. He goes on to state that, "Those who had lived in Hawaii for years and had read its history were probably least qualified to judge this book objectively" (Day, *James A. Michener*, 113). Despite being a novel, Michener himself calls the work "true to the spirit and history of Hawaii" (Michener, *Hawaii*, iii).

4. Shelley Ayame Nishimure Ota, *Upon Their Shoulders* (New York: Exposition Press, 1951).

5. Margaret N. Harada, *The Sun Shines on the Immigrant* (New York: Vantage Press, 1960).

6. Kazua Miyamoto, *Hawaii: End of the Rainbow* (Tokyo: Charles E. Tuttle, 1964).

7. Sections of Milton Murayama's, *All I Asking For Is My Body* (San Francisco: Supa Press, 1975, reprinted Honolulu: University of Hawaii Press, 1988) were published as early as 1959.

8. Arnold T. Hiura and Stephen H. Sumida, *Asian American Literature of Hawaii, An Annotated Bibliography* (Honolulu: Hawaii Ethnic Resources Center: Talk Story, 1979).

9. Darrell H.Y. Lum, "Oranges Are Lucky," in *Sun, Short Stories and Drama* (Honolulu: Bamboo Ridge Press, 1980): 44-61.

10. A. Grove Day, *Books About Hawaii: Fifty Basic Authors* (Honolulu: University Press of Hawaii, 1977).

11. A. Grove Day and Carl Stroven, eds. *A Hawaiian Reader* (Appleton-Century-Crofts, 1959, reprinted Honolulu: Mutual Publishing Co., 1984).

12. Michener, referring to Jack London, said, "he actually denigrated an entire body of people, largely on racist grounds. The story… was founded upon events occurring within a real Chinese family, but is, I fear, a pathetic misreading of both the Chinese and of the spirit that activates Hawaii. I have never understood how he [Jack London] could be one man in California, and such a different man in Hawaii. I still cannot understand how he could be practicing socialist on the one hand and a race supremacist on the other." (Day & Stroven, *A Hawaiian Reader*, xv).

13. A. Grove Day, *Mad About Islands: Novelists of a Vanished Pacific* (Honolulu: Mutual Publishing, 1987).

14. Gay Sibley, "Conversations with a Nesomaniac, an interview with A. Grove Day," *Literary Arts Hawaii*, No. 88&89 (Spring & Summer 1988).

15. Eric Chock and Darrell Lum, eds., *Pake: Writings by Chinese in Hawaii* (Honolulu: Bamboo ridge Press, 1989).

16. Stephen H. Sumida, "Waiting for the Big Fish: Recent Research in the Asian American Literature of Hawaii," in *The Best of Bamboo Ridge* (Honolulu: Bamboo Ridge Press, 1986): 305, 317.

17. Esther K. Mookini, *The Hawaiian Newspapers* (Honolulu: Topgallant Publishers, 1974).

18. Esther K. Mookini, interview Honolulu, November 1990.

19. Sumida, "Waiting for the Big Fish: Recent Research in the Asian Amer-

ican Literature of Hawaii," 306-307.

20. In 1922 the Territorial Legislature tried to require teacher certification as well as control over the curriculum of all language schools. The Japanese language schools protested and the law was challenged and struck down by the U.S. Supreme Court in 1927. The issue arose again in 1943 when the legislature mandated that language school instruction be limited to children above the age of nine. The law was opposed by the language schools and was declared unconstitutional in 1947 and later upheld by the U.S. Supreme Court. Ralph Stueber, "Hawaii: A Case Study in Development Education, 1778-1960" (Dissertation, University of Wisconsin, 1964) 363.

21. The "Speak American" (i.e., speak standard English) movement associated speaking standard English with patriotism and was supported by many *nisei* (second generation) Japanese Americans as a reaction to anti-Japanese sentiment. C. Sato, "Linguistic Inequality in Hawaii: The Post-Creole Dilemma," (Unpublished paper, UCLA, 1981. University of Hawaii, Hawaii Pacific Collection): 17; reprinted in N. Wolfson and J. Manes, eds. *Language of Inequality* (Berlin: Mouton, 1985).

22. The English Standard school system established a dual public school system that was segregated ostensibly by English ability but effectively created an ethnically segregated system, one for *haole* (Caucasian) children and one for native Hawaiian and immigrant children. Those who could pass a spoken English test were allowed to go to an English Standard school (which appeared to have better trained and more "college prep" teachers) while the others (generally pidgin speakers) attended a regular school. The system remained in place from the 1920s until 1960 when the last English Standard class graduated from Roosevelt High School.

23. C. Sato, "Linguistic Inequality in Hawaii:: The Post-Creole Dilemma," (Unpublished paper, UCLA, 1981. University of Hawaii, Hawaii Pacific Collection), 18; reprinted in N. Wolfson and J. Manes, eds. *Language of Inequality* (Berlin: Mouton, 1985).

24. Ralph Stueber, "Hawaii: A Case Study in Development Education, 1778-1960" (Dissertation, University of Wisconsin, 1964): 148.

25. John Reinecke, *Language and Dialect in Hawaii* (Honolulu: University Press of Hawaii, 1969).

26. Bernhard Hormann, "Speech, Prejudice and the School in Hawaii," in *Community Forces in Hawaii: Readings from Social Process in Hawaii*, Sociology Club Publication (Honolulu: University of Hawaii, 1968) 232.

27. State of Hawaii Board of Education minutes of September 17, 1987 meeting and appendices.

28. Richard R. Day, "Pidgin English: Hawaii's Unique Resource," plenary address, 16th Annual TESOL Convention, Honolulu, 1982, p. 17.

29. C. Sato, "Linguistic attitudes and sociolinguistic variation in Hawaii." *University of Hawaii Working Papers in ESL*, Vol. 8, No. 1, May 1989, 191-216, reprinted in J. Cheshire, ed. *English Around the World: Sociolinguistic Perspectives* (Cambridge: Cambridge University Press, 1991).

30. Darrell H.Y. Lum, "Giving Tanks," in *Infant Tongues: The Voice of the Child in Literature*, Elizabeth Goodenough, Mark Heberle and Naomi Sokoloff, eds. (Detroit: Wayne State University Press, 1994).

14

Chechi from Outer Space

Vidyut Aklujkar

Hotel Purna, Trivandrum

June 8, 1989

My first day in this city. Having spent a week in Madras, I arrived here at noon today. On the very last day in Madras, I was successful in obtaining a copy of the Sanskrit manuscript for which I came there. Now we shall see what happens here.

Ever since I started from Poona on the conquest of the South, I am being made aware of my femininity in more ways than one. Take the bus ride, for example. In Madras, I stayed in the Dasa Prakash hotel and I used to take a bus to go to the university which is located at Marina Beach. It was wonderful to go to the beach day in and day out and sit watching the dance of the waves. The first day I was there, I climbed on the bus and as the conductor pointed to the back seat, I sat on it quickly. When I looked ahead, the whole bus looked divided like Ardhanari-nate-sha, the androgenous form of God. That is to say, that all *sarees*, half-*sarees* and flowers in hair were sitting on the left side seats and all the *lungis*, *mundus* and trousers and shirts and ties were sitting on the right hand side. This division was not only evident among the seated passengers, even the standees were segregated likewise. In that over-crowded bus, the men were standing on the right hand side, almost glued to the men on the seats, while all the women were standing leaning onto the left hand side where the women were seated. Like Moses, the bus conductor was deftly passing through the opening in the middle of this sea of humanity. Since that day, I took upon myself to be a leftist as soon as I climbed aboard. The locals observed this segregation policy with such a zeal, that even if there were free seats on the women's side, hardly a man

125

would step forward to occupy one, so there was no question of the women doing likewise by crossing the boundary.

By the time I got used to this segregation of left and right in Madras, I arrived in Trivandrum. A new province, a new policy. The other day, I came out of the Sanskrit Department conversing with a couple of professors, and came down to the bus stop where we stood together talking. Soon Dr. Vijayan said to me, "Madam, your queue is separate." I did not follow the reason and asked why. He said, "Ladies queue is separate from the gents, ma'am." I looked in surprise. And truly, the spectacle that I now noticed was thus: the bus stop was an open shed. Right at the centre of this stop two separate lines had started but the line of the women had turned itself on the left hand side of the shed and stretched out in the sun while the men's line had turned to the right hand side of the shed. Literally two separate gender lines emerged sharing only the origin, as in the womb, and stretched in opposite directions. They were not even parallel. There must be a philosophical moral in this, but the bus stop with two lines on left and right reminded me of a picture of Chingi or a Pippi Longstocking with two braids around her face flying in opposite directions. I was the only non-conformist there so I bowed to their division of the sexes and stood on the left hand side. I did notice a couple of Keralite girls hiding their laughter at my being so devoid of decorum in the first place.

The empty bus arrived. It had only one door right in the middle of its long side where its navel would be, and it opened as the bus came to a stop at the middle of the shed. At that the two men standing near me climbed up. I was after them, or so I thought and I climbed up too. While I grabbed a window seat I heard the same girls giggle again. And then it dawned on me fully. The etiquette here was that when the bus door opens, the first line to get in is that of the men. The entire line of men gets in from the middle of the bus, they head straight to the back end of the bus and start grabbing all the backside seats, left and right or stand there. When all the men are in, only *then* does the women's line start to board the bus, and they in their turn, get seated or stand up only in the front half of the entire bus. The bus conductor alone stands at the middle door of the bus and lets passengers in or out from the door. He looked quite like the sandlewood dot that they apply to the middle of the forehead otherwise smeared with long lines of ashes. So the bus that was sporting a left-right gender split in Tamilnadu was now divided back to front in Kerala. I was obviously pardoned my recalcitrant behavior out of courtesy today, but I must remember to observe this new split from now on while in this province.

There are visible advantages of this separation. All the women in the front half of the bus seem to be friends with each other. The seated ones hold the sacks and lunch-boxes of the standees so that they stand with ease, leaning on to the seats and chatting with friends. The men in the back of the bus seem to enjoy the ride too, chatting and joking and arguing with gusto. But I was amused to see even Radha and Potti do the same. They are husband and wife and work in the same department here but they too observe this segregation on the bus stop and on the bus, and do not talk to each other until they alight the bus. Perhaps that is what keeps their marriage fresh. Ashok, my husband, has a theory that half the divorces in North America happen because the married couple stays together too much. He thinks that if the American married women start to imitate us Indians and go to the father's house every now and then leaving their husbands behind, their marriages will last longer. Perhaps he is right. And to test his theory, I have now come to India all by myself, to conduct my research while he in Canada will be looking after our kids and the house. Of course, many friends both here and there are surprised with my decision, but I am very happy to find uninterrupted time to follow my work after a long hiatus. Of course, it is true, that in all our married years Ashok has never once cooked a meal, but I think he will find ways of feeding the kids and himself. Didn't I learn to cook when I had to? So will he. But I must write my grammarian husband about the gender differences in the grammar of the bus.

University Women's Hostel

Kariavattom Campus,

Trivandrum

June 20, 1989

My last day here today. Time seemed to fly for the past ten or twelve days while I was engaged in my work. I was busy copying the old Sanskrit manuscripts in my own handwriting for almost twelve to sixteen hours per day. I was also making others work just as much. Thanks to Dr. Unni, I was staying with Lalita in her room in the Ladies Hostel on this campus. Lalita is a doctoral candidate in Sanskrit and she assisted me to read the old Sanskrit manuscripts written in the old Malayalam script and preserved in the Oriental Library here. The palm leaf manuscripts are at least four hundred years old, and so brittle, that if handled carelessly, they crumple like cookies. So of course, Xeroxing is out of the question. And even if it were possible, I cannot read the old Malayalam script so the Xerox copy would not be of much use anyway. So while here, I must make the most of my time. Lalita reads one manuscript letter by letter with me and I write down everything in Devanagari, and then I go to the library where the librarian Mr. Shaji reads the other manuscript with me and I jot down the variant readings on the copy that I have with me. The third manuscript is so decrepit, that I must give up on that at least for the time being. Lalita and I sit in her room in the residence from seven to ten in the morning, then from eleven to three in the afternoon I work with Shaji in the library, and then again from four p.m. till twelve at night with Lalita in her room.

The only time we take a break in this writing marathon is due to the 'load shedding' in Trivandrum. They cut off electricity at least three times daily for one to two hours at a time. It is not so bad during daytime, since the only inconvenience is that the fan doesn't work, and the room becomes hot and humid. But when the power fails around dusk and the monsoon clouds have already made everything dark, we have to work in candle light, and at night it is much worse, since even in candlelight, we cannot read very well the letters on the palm leaves. The tired eyes feel the strain. Then we are forced to take a break, and we go down to the mess to finish our meals. Sometimes when the power fails at ten p. m., all the girls gather in Lalita's room and we sing songs, or play at capping Sanskrit verses.

These hostel residents who were rather awed by my presence earlier, and kept their distance from me are now quite close to me. They are candidates for their Masters, and Doctorates, but they are quite innocent and straightforward compared to such students in Maharashtra. Even the residence seems to be arrested in the middle ages. The girls have to return to their nests every evening by six thirty p. m.! The campus is far away from the town and with these regulations it is very inconvenient for me to stay here and get any work done in town. It takes a whole hour to go to town by bus.

In 1966-67, I was the superintendent at the Ladies Hostel of Fergusson College in Poona. After so many years, here I am in this hostel, living by myself. But I must say, I find that the Marathi girls living in the hostel even in the sixties were a lot more inquisitive and assertive than these Keralite girls. These girls seem to be more traditional. Many of them get up early in the morning, bathe, catch a six o'clock bus from campus to go to the town, so as to be at the temple to worship, circumambulate and come back to get their breakfast by eight o'clock in the residence, and then go to attend lectures in their classes. Poor Lalita has to miss this morning routine due to my work with her, but she is particular not to miss her evening prayer, and chanting in the room. She has got several pictures and idols of the Gods in her room, and she says a long prayer to them in Sanskrit every night. She is not alone in this. Almost all the girls in the residence are like her. The Christian girls sing songs to Christ in their rooms, and a Hindu girl called Gita, who worships Christ since "He cured her of an illness," has got on her door a sign which proclaims, "Jesus Saves." This sign reminds me of the graffiti I once noticed on the walls of a New York subway station, where underneath the claim, "Jesus, Saves" was an addition, saying "Moses invests."

The other day, at four p.m., I saw Lalita waiting patiently outside the door of her professor's office to get his signature on her application for a fellowship grant. I knew that she and I had come at ten in the morning here and she had already submitted the application to the professor then. So I asked her why she didn't get him to sign in the morning when she had submitted the application. Her answer was that the time then was *Rahu kala*, which was inauspicious according to the stars, so she had to wait until three for the professor to actually sign. This answer stumped me.

On the other hand, the girls here think I am queer. They do not understand how I could have spent almost a fortnight in Trivandrum and not once have visited the temple of the Great Padmanabh swami. Lalita is quite surprised by my behavior. I told her that I did go all the way to the temple once. However, since I was dressed in Salwar Kameez then, I had to turn back without seeing the image of the God, because the regulations do not permit a married woman to enter the temple unless she is wearing a *saree*. But Lalita did not understand why I did not go again to visit the temple and pay respects to the God, since I did have a couple of sarees with me anyway. I did not try to explain to her that to me getting my work done was worship enough. Lalita has decided to take it upon herself to escort me personally to all the eminent temples in the vicinity. And I submit to her wishes, since she has been so helpful.

For quite a few days now, Lalita and her friends have watched my non-conformist ways, and they must think of me as coming from outer space rather than from Poona or from Canada. What a queer woman, they must think. She says she is a researcher of Sanskrit, but she has no interest in observing religious rituals, does not say a prayer, does not visit temples, does not observe any fasts. She says she lives in Canada, but she has not cut her hair, does not wear any makeup, nor have any western clothes. She says she is a Brahmin, then how does she sit at the same table with the untouchables and Christians to eat her lunch? She wears *sarees* like us, and does wear a few pieces of jewelry, but shows no interest whatever in finding out whether our jewelry is real gold or not. The funny woman cannot tell whether her bracelets are true gold or not, but she asks us every single name of the birds she sees and every single tree she passes. She talks to the cats in the mess in her own funny tongue, but has no pictures of her own children with her. She works all day long and never even remembers her children. What kind of mother is she? Oh, the girls had seen spinsters who were academic women all their unmarried lives, but they had not seen a married woman like me who had young children like mine leave them ten thousand miles away with their father, and come all the way to work on her own project. I was queer on all counts. When Lalita had asked me to show her the picture of my family, I had no picture with me to show her, neither of my husband nor of my children, which they thought was strange, to say the least.

In short, I was quite a basket case, for most of them. Nevertheless the girls were sweet by nature, and so they treated me with generous hospitality. Since my arrival here, I had showered them with so many questions, that by now they were getting used to at least being asked "why?" every now and then. To quote one instance, the Department of Sanskrit and the Oriental Institute Library were situated on one hill, and the residence buildings were on the other hill opposite the first one. Between the two hills was a lush expanse of green lawn going up and down. But instead of crossing that distance from one hill to another in a straight line, Lalita would always make me walk for forty minutes on a long winding roundabout road on that campus. One day I asked her, why not go from here to there climbing up and down the hills? She said that the warden had instructed the girls not to use the hilly road, since it was secluded. I said, that I could see the cowherds in the valley and to me that was a sign of humanity enough to go across the hills in a straight line. They were ready to follow me if I ventured. I did and they did. Since then, we used the straight line to cross the distance every time and saved at least thirty minutes per trip.

Yesterday all the girls wanted me to go for a walk with them, on the hill nearby, and since I had finished the work at hand, I did go with them. The hill had lots of medicinal herbs and bushes. The girls were all chatter. They wanted to ask me so many questions about myself, about Poona, my birth place, and about Canada, my work place. I thought, just when I am about to fly off again these sparrows have started to chirp.

By now, Lalita no longer takes me to be a creature from outer space. Instead, she calls me Chechi. Chechi means sister in her language. One day she said to me, You are just as old as my chechi. Of course her chechi is a mother of four girls, and is constantly worried about the marriages of those daughters. Lalita must have compared my queerness with the traditionality of her own Chechi, but the dear girl had decided that I was all right after all.

After we came back from the walk, Lalita's friends invited me to visit their rooms. After dinner the power had failed again, so taking a candle in hand, I visited each friend's room in that residence. Lalita and a couple of friends accompanied me from room to room. Every girl was pressing me to sit down on the single chair in each room while they would all huddle on the bed or stand by beside me. I did not always respond to the pressure, and often I would only stand. Finally they all looked at each other, giggled, and said to me, "Madam, you must sit down in each girl's room, because we have a superstition in our hostel." I asked them what it was, and got lots of shy glances, and giggles in answer. Finally Muthu-Lakshmi overcame her shyness and said, "Madam, we believe that if our guest does not sit down in our room and accept our hospitality, then we may not get the husband that we want." On hearing this, I had to sit down in each one of their rooms, of course, and I had to bless each one of them that they find the groom of their dreams. This went on into the wee hours of the morning, all of them singing with me in Malayalam, Marathi, Sanskrit. Today, while returning, I have with me not only the Sanskrit manuscripts that I came for, but the Indian coins Lalita gave for my children, the Kathakali mask that Muthu-Lakshmi gave for my son, and other such gifts of love. All the girls have made me promise that I would send them the pictures of my family on my return to Canada, and also that I will write to each one of them. Thus having a glimpse of their budding lives, I am on my way back, a thousand times more enriched than I was before I came here.

Writing in Anguish
Vidyut Aklujkar

"Why don't you write in English?" you ask,
"Why, after half your life in Canada, do you still write in Marathi?
Isn't it like always making a long distance call?"
"Oh, yes, it's more than that." I say,
"It is more like herding the sheep while sitting on a camel."
You nod in disbelief, and prod further,
"But why not write in English? After all,
you speak, teach, argue in it!"
Now it's my turn to nod.
"Well, not just yet. You see, writing poems in English
will be like trying to wear your shoe.
It may be a size larger and come off my foot
just when I enter the race;
or it may be a little too tight
and pinch me out of step.
Oh, I'm not worried of falling down and scraping my knees.
No, no... I am afraid that
if I wear the shoe that's not mine,
then even if I go places, win a race, or climb a peak,
the traces I will leave
will not be mine.
But, just you wait,
gimme some time to learn
to use the skin of your tongue.
In time I shall wear that shoe
so much that my heels will peep out of the soles
and then,
only then I shall write in Anguish."

Savitri Mane
Vidyut Aklujkar

As soon as I turned fifteen,
my people wrapped me in a saree,
and strangers licked and licked
and licked me with hungry glances from all around
I shut my mind like a wet umbrella while climbing a bus,
but droplets of insult went on trickling here and there
Every wedding season prospective grooms
turned me around, tested and tried me and discarded me
like a stale bunch of vegetables back in its basket.
So I grabbed a scholarship that easily came my way and
landed in America as one lands in heaven on a single thread of Karma
grabbing that thread I kept climbing
up and up and above the rest.
I reached the top and felt lonely for a sec
but just for a sec.
Those fastidious groom-gods of yore
are long through the race,
now they are busy in the routine arithmetic
of balancing the budget.
The only thing they have to vie with my fat salary check
is the spread of their fat married middles.
No, I didn't meet any soul-mate here
but I'm so used to my lone pillow, that I ask,
why invite a cloud in a clear sky?
On Vata-paurnimá?
Oh, I rinse my mouth on that day with wine,
put the red dot of ketchup on the face of my dinnerplate,
and ask for the blessing:
"May I get the same boon,
the same groom, life after life:
Wisdom."

Educational Challenges

There is perhaps no other setting in the United States today that contains deeper contradictions for Asian Americans as academia. Because of the traditionally high premium that Asian Americans place on education, they view academia as the gateway to success and acceptance to American society. However, because of the lack of opportunity or outright discrimination, education is not always a sure or secure avenue for the Asian American. Because of the stereotype of Asian Americans as the "model minority," academia has high expectations of them. This stereotype sometimes becomes an excuse to ignore the special needs of this minority. In addition, it can create undue pressure to those who do not live up to the stereotype. Finally, because academia is traditionally viewed as a haven of civility and progressive thinking in social relations, Asian Americans can find in this the opportunity to thrive. Yet, academia does not always live up to the image of a tolerant and nurturing environment.

The next set of papers point out some examples of how academia and the educational process generate contradictions for Asian Americans.

In instances where academia opts to recognize the multicultural campus, there are unintended effects on some ethnic groups. Monica Chiu's introspective look at multiculturalism in "Asian Americans in the Multicultural Composition Classroom" provides a revealing analysis of the relationship between and among minority groups on campus. She raises the possibility that the literary focus on the struggles of African Americans and Hispanics obscures the struggles that all people of color, including Asian Americans, must endure. As a result, Chiu concludes, even in writing and literature the Asian American voice seems to be lost in the struggle of all ethnic groups. She warns that multiculturalism needs to focus on all the voices of people of color because "to privilege one is to silence the other."

Aside from the dilemmas that Asian American students must face, those who come from mixed racial backgrounds face unique problems stemming from their less well-defined ethnic identity and the challenges of straddling two cultures. The multicultural Gardiner family takes a look at this issue in "Support Groups in Higher Education: The Asian American Experience." They place special emphasis on gathering information about the types and availability of Asian American support groups all over the country and the recent development of a model support group.

The contradictions Asian Americans face in academia are not limited to students but apply to faculty as well as shown by Gabriel and Cecilia Manrique in their new study of immigrant faculty. In "Asian American Faculty in U.S. Colleges and Universities: American Higher Education and the New Wave of Immigration," they examine the discrimination and prejudice endured by Asian American faculty on their campuses—the very progressive places that we expect to be ahead of the rest of society. But even if Asian American faculty understand that campuses are not race neutral, they expressed ambivalence towards the hiring of more racially diverse faculty.

Education will remain an important gateway for Asian Americans on their way to achieving the American dream. However, the voices from academia that are heard in this set of papers suggest that education is not a paved highway to success but a winding road that requires careful steering.

15

It's an Asian Thing. You Must Try to Understand

Asian Americans in the Multicultural Classroom

Monica Chiu

...[Johnnetta Cole] hates the sweatshirts at Spelman and around the country [which state]: "It's a black thing. You wouldn't understand." [She prefers:] "It's a black thing. You must try to understand."
—Susan Chira, *The New York Times*[1]

Addressing race relations in the multicultural classroom presents a unique challenge in both approaching the subject with sensitivity as well as in engaging students in constructive discussions about themselves and others. Unfortunately, many of us believe that speaking about race is easier when the class is predominantly White. Is it easier because we can then formulate stereotypes about the non-inclusive "other" with impunity, perhaps with less discomfort? Comfort was not a priority in my composition classroom last year when I decided that the diverse students would become the course backbone, supplying most of the questions and many of the answers. As the semester progressed, the students became more and more excited about addressing race relations, finally engaging in loud debates and heated discussions stemming from multicultural readings and personal experience. My students were coming to voice.

Recently, within the academy, formerly silent and silenced ethnic voices now speak out in anthologized essays, stories and poems. I am an enthusiastic advocate of multicultural literacy, especially since the majority of African American students in my course celebrated the inclusion of authors such as Alice Walker, Malcolm X, and bell hooks, to name a few; those with Hispanic backgrounds enjoyed essays by Gloria Anzaldúa and

Eduardo Galeano. Unfortunately, those texts addressing Native American, feminist and Asian American issues elicited little interest and almost no discussion. Even the Asian and Asian American students in the classroom remained relatively silent when we attempted to discuss work by Japanese and Chinese American authors.[2] In many cases, the conversation gradually returned to issues of slavery and Black-White racial relations.

The introduction and promotion of African American studies within colleges and universities over the past 15 years has sparked a plethora of interesting dialogues about theoretical approaches to African American literature, and other multicultural texts, as well as discussions about race relations on and off the campus. In addition, college catalogues now boast courses in Chicano/a and Latino/a literature as well as gay and lesbian studies.[3] The widespread visibility of these voices throughout the years has encouraged both instructors and students to demand a change from the hegemonic classroom material of the past. However, Asian American studies lacks this foundation; the term "Asian Studies" usually refers to Asian languages, Asian history or Asian philosophy. Rarely, until very recently, have I seen course listings for Asian American literature.

In addition, compared to many of my African American students for whom the text remained secondary to first-hand experiences with racism, Asian American students offered few arguments against the stereotypical image of the Asian or insights into their own encounters with racism, if such encounters existed. Here, I do not want to commit an act of stereotyping by assuming that all minorities will necessarily experience racism. Rather, I would like to discern the reason behind the relative silence of Asian Americans concerning issues specific to them. Part of the problem lies within the paucity of almost all students' basic knowledge of Asian American history, whether Chinese, Japanese, Korean, Filipino or others. If the histories of Japanese internment camps, or those of Chinese railroad workers and sugar cane laborers, have been left unattended, how can uninformed students condemn an uninvestigated Asian racism?

In so far as multiculturalism is a unification of people, I do not propose that universities and colleges meticulously equalize and compartmentalize the scope and extent of individual minority struggles. Rather, the most efficacious solution entails linking them. Abdul JanMohamed and David Lloyd, editors of *The Nature and Context of Minority Discourse*, explain the task of such a critical discourse as a method "to describe and define the common denominators that link various minority cultures. Cultures designated as minorities have certain shared experiences ... and should be able collectively to examine the nature and content of their common marginalization and to develop strategies for their reempowerment."[4] In examining the unification of their similar struggles, students will be encouraged to talk about their experiences in a larger context.

Bell hooks, in her *Z Magazine* column "Sisters of the Yam," recently endorsed the importance of linking Black and Jewish marginalization in an article titled "Keeping a Legacy of Shared Struggles." She recognizes the lack of "a complex language to talk about white Jewish identity in the United States and its relationship to blackness and black identity."[5] Similarly, Johnnetta B. Cole, president of Spelman College in Atlanta, emphatically stresses the need for mutual understanding through her disgust with sweatshirts at Spelman and on hundreds of other college campuses nationwide which read: "It's a black thing. You wouldn't understand." In this January *New York Times* article, Cole's alternative slogan says: "It's a black thing. You must try to understand."[6] Human empathy, not antagonism, is the goal toward which students and instructors must work when asking the question Cole poses, "How do we get under each others' skins?"[7]

Empowering students in the multicultural classroom to speak, to think critically and eventually to write revolves around an education in which diversity is regarded as a strength to be encouraged, not a weakness to be exploited. However, in her article "Defining Asian American Realities Through Literature," Elaine H. Kim states, "clumsy racial fantasies about Asians continue to flourish in the West, and these extend to Asian Americans as well."[8] These so-called "fantasies" project undesirable images of difference which work to negatively define Asians. In the introduction to her text *Asian American Literature: An Introduction to the Writings and Their Social Context*, Kim speculates that Americans are more familiar with Asian film characters—such as the 1950s effeminate Fu Manchu and those Hollywood Asians advocated through Rambo films rather than actual Asians and Asian Americans.[9] In a sense, then, the limited view one can construct from Hollywood's unsubstantiated representations of Asians merely reveals ignorance, fear and perplexity about another race. The perpetuation of these stereotypes serve as "the roots of racism," says Amy Ling in her text *Between Worlds: Women Writers of Chinese Ancestry*, for the negative image created of the "other" continuously posits them in a place of inferiority.[10]

Equally pernicious stereotypes define, and therefore confine, other minority groups. Bell hooks, in her article "Reflections On Race and Sex," discusses the manufacture of a pernicious myth: that is, the Black rapist and his desire for the unattainable, White woman.[11] Similarly, in her autobiographical novel *Lakota Woman*, Mary Crow Dog elucidates how the so-called benevolent Christian nuns and priests believed that dirty, lazy Native Americans could learn only through severe beatings.[12] While these stereotypes have slowly eroded, partly through greater interest in and awareness of such cultures as advocated by multiculturalism, the destruction of false Asian American representations—those "clumsy fantasies"—lags far behind.

This gap allows non-Asian students to condemn racial stereotyping directed toward them while simultaneously condoning such activity involving Asian Americans. One such incident is exemplary: I was invited to a basic composition course, engaged in a multicultural unit, to speak about my two-and-a-half year experience living and working in Japan. One particular student asked whether the Japanese still chopped each others' heads off with swords, either as criminal acts or as a form of capital punishment. I responded in the negative quite politely, and a bit incredulously, explaining that the days of feudal Japan were long over. However, the student remained dissatisfied with this image of Japan, one unreflective of Hollywood's rendition continuously recreated for him on the large screen. Consequently, he insisted on posing the question as if I, and not he, were somehow misinformed. Only when I reminded him of stereotypical and blatantly incorrect representations of African Americans—those which he vehemently contested—did he understand how his vision and version of the Japanese were grossly distorted. Here, the recognition that Japanese and subsequently Japanese Americans, like other minority groups, are culturally constricted in many ways, indicates a step toward linking minority struggles.

I suspect that such scenes occur frequently and, therefore, are hardly surprising. However, when professors and instructors react as this young man did, I am truly shocked. Recently, in an interview for a graduate fellowship, a professor asked how I felt about my low GRE math score, especially since this is one of those perceived Asian success areas. Later, when I inquired about the environment for Asians within the campus and city, the same professor mentioned several markets where I could find "my Asian spices." I was visibly taken aback at both these comments. Ironically, I was interviewing for a minority fellowship, one whose aim included populating the campus with students of color in order to gain a certain intellectual richness and diversity from them (this notion itself contains the possibility of presenting the minority as different, unusual and perhaps exotic). Evidently, the task of destroying minority myths begins with students as well as instructors.

Taking these incidents as cues, in a subsequent composition course I selected a few essays from the reader *Making Waves: An Anthology of*

Writings By and About Asian American Women, which aims at destabilizing the myth of the Asian as the model minority. In the essay "The Gap Between Striving and Achieving: The Case of Asian American Women,"[13] Deborah Woo explains that the notion of the successful Asian American—both economically and socially—was invented from outside the Asian community itself. In other words, the Western world around Asians conceived an Asian American idea and ideal contributing to their so-called success. Consequently, because Asian Americans were seen to "save more, study more, work more, and so achieve more,"[14] the government eventually revoked its funding from certain Asian programs.[15]

This misconception works against other minority groups as well. In upholding Asians as an exemplary model for all struggling minorities, the supposedly unsuccessful groups are perceived as lazy or inept. Johnnetta Cole speaks to this pernicious myth of the model minority when it allows whites to "throw Korean successes in Blacks' faces."[16] This, according to Cole, allows Blacks to think, "Their kids [Korean children] are smart, their families stick together, save and get ahead. We've already had built into our heads a kind of—'Why should I like these people? They are getting ahead and I'm not.'"[17] In addition, when minorities fight among and between each other, rather than against a larger society perpetuating destructive falsehoods, the situation is perceived as a minority problem.[18] Once established as such, those considered outside the situation—whether non-Blacks or non-Koreans—decline intervention.

Once again, while Asian and Asian American students in the classroom offered little or no comment supporting or destroying these misconceptions, other students reified the image of the hardworking, self-supportive Asian based on their own image making. Despite articles denouncing an inherent Asian intelligence, and instead stressing an Asian commitment to education and unrelenting work as a means to their social and political achievements, students insisted that Asian Americans succeeded in the U.S. because they were so smart.[19] I pointed out that this statement, therefore, could suggest that other minority groups were naturally inferior in intelligence. I expressed how this ran counter to earlier discussions in the semester, those in which African American and Latino/a students alike resented an educational "tracking" system, especially prevalent within New York's inner city schools. These programs looked at students' skins and not their intelligence, therefore placing a significantly unequal proportion of minorities in lower level reading and mathematics groups. These actions reveal how minorities, here African Americans, come to view themselves as less capable than other students. Or, as one student put it quite succinctly, "I always supposed I was stupid." However, instead of steering the class back to the model minority issue, as I hoped this comment would, the class remained silent. Finally, a Jamaican American student dismissed the entire subject by suggesting that because she was Black, she could not speak for another minority group; the discussion folded.

It is difficult *not* to anticipate that Asians or Asian Americans will speak out about issues concerning them. However, this expectation can become increasingly frustrating when they do remain relatively quiet and seemingly uninvolved in discussions. Instead of pitting one minority group against another, as perhaps my earlier attempts to remedy the discussion did, I would suggest finding readings among and between authors whose main ideas intersect. These reading selections should exemplify how work by diverse authors can provide material from which students can draw connections and unify struggles, thereby engaging all students to talk about people from cultures other than their own.

In subsequent discussions and papers, students are encouraged to address not only Asian and Asian American issues, but to look at their own representation, self-representation, ethnic identity and its roots. I may ask the students to write about how they identify themselves as well as how they would like to be identified: as Asian American? American Asian? American? Korean? Or, if the student is African American, would s/he like to be called Black? African American? Jamaican? West Indian? Does the state of being White in a world concentrating more and more on ethnicity and multiculturalism become problematic? What does it mean to problematize race? What is it like to live on a border, straddling two cultures?[20]

In future courses, I will spend classroom time generating an abundance of stereotypes surrounding many ethnic groups and discussing their origins, their purpose and their perceived benefits to others. Students' personal experiences and firsthand knowledge of how these stereotypes work to keep minorities "in their place" will hopefully uproot their intent. What kinds of biases do Asians have against other minority groups? How can these be destroyed? We often speak of the rift between Black women and Black men in the struggle between racism and sexism; do similar struggles exist among Asians and Asian Americans? These questions may constitute the beginnings of several other successful discussions in which the struggles of one group open a segue into the struggles of another.

In the end, we read to avoid the kind of myopic vision inherent in a recent *New York Times* letter to the editor. Here, a young man of Australian descent chastises what he considers to be a group of whining Korean Americans complaining of a racist United States. His basic tenet: if my ancestors had to adjust and adapt to the American community, so must those of Korean descent. Unfortunately, he overlooks the obvious differences between the Western looking Australian who already speaks English, and the Asian looking Korean who may not. In other words, the disgruntled writer conveniently forgets that the dominant Western culture more easily accepts the more familiar over those of other colors, tongues, religions and thought.

If we can think beyond the limitations of the skin, then perhaps, according to Ling, ancestors of those who labored on the transcontinental railway will not be asked if s/he is from a foreign country. And perhaps the Asian American professor in an English department will not be asked why s/he has no accent.[21] As Kim mentions, being White is not a precondition for being American.[22] As students acquire more knowledge not only about Asians and Asian Americans, but about all cultures within the U.S., this shared information will redefine minority discourse as "a legacy of shared struggle."

Notes

1. Susan Chira, "A Scholar's Convictions Keep Her Pushing the Power of Words," *The New York Times* (January 10, 1993): Eastern ed., sec. 4, p. 7.

2. While the terms "Asian" and "Asian American" include people with diverse backgrounds—from Thailand, Korea, Laos, Vietnam, to name a few— most of the students I have taught include those of Chinese, Japanese and Korean descent. I recognize, however, that the imposed term "Asian" is an all-inclusive one which, unfortunately, tends toward blurring the distinctions among people from all Asian countries. As is the aim of my course, therefore, I work toward allowing each student to identify and name him/herself.

3. Abdul R. JanMohamed and David Lloyd, "Introduction: Toward a Theory of Minority Discourse: What Is to Be Done?" in *The Nature and Context of Minority Discourse*, JanMohamed and Lloyd, eds. (New York: Oxford University Press, 1990): 1-2. Originally published as "Introduction: Minority Discourse—What Is to Be Done?" JanMohamed and Lloyd, in *Cultural Critique* 7 (Fall 1987): 5-17. All further references will be to the former citation.

4. Ibid., 1-2.

5. bell hooks, "Keeping a Legacy of Shared Struggle," *Z Magazine* (September 1992): 23.

6. Chira, 7.

7. Ibid.

8. See JanMohamed and Lloyd, 148. Kim, in *Asian American Literature: An Introduction to the Writings and Their Social Context* (Philadelphia: Temple Univ. Press), elaborates on the American-made characters of Fu Manchu and Charlie Chan, who have been emasculated in order to fulfill the White man's image of the Chinese male (179).

9. Kim, xv.

10. Amy Ling, *Between Worlds: Women Writers of Chinese Ancestry* (New York: Pergamon Press, 1990): 20.

11. bell hooks, "Reflections On Race and Sex," *Yearning: Race, Gender and Cultural Politics* (Boston: South End Press, 1990): 57-64.

12. Mary Crow Dog and Richard Erdoes, *Lakota Woman,* (New York: Harper Perennial, 1990). See specifically p. 38.

13. Deborah Woo, "The Gap Between Striving and Achieving: The Case of Asian American Women," *Making Waves: An Anthology of Writings By and About Asian American Women,* Asian Women United of California, ed. (Boston: Beacon Press, 1989): 185-194.

14. Woo, 186.

15. However, according to Woo, a gap exists between these perceived achievements and Asian Americans' subsequent occupational gains (186). For if one investigates the situation more closely, even though Asian American women, for example, possess college educations, they are consistently employed in what Woo calls the "usually less prestigious...rungs of the 'professional-managerial' class" (190).

16. Chira, 7.

17. Ibid.

18. This statement, however, could also provide the basis for constructing the stereotype that *all* Asians are hardworking. Contrary to this idea, I have met many unmotivated Asian and Asian American students.

19. See Ling, p. 20, where she briefly mentions this idea.

20 This notion of living on a border comes from both Guillermo Gómez-Peña, "Documented/Undocumented," in *The Graywolf Annual Five: Multicultural Literacy,* Rick Simonson and Scott Walker, eds. (Saint Paul: Graywolf Press, 1988): 127-134, and Gloria Anzaldúa, *Boderlands/La Frontera: The New Mestiza,* (San Francisco: Aunt Lute Books, 1987).

21. Ling, 20.

22. Kim, 146.

16

Support Groups in Higher Education

The Asian-American Experience

Alisa Jarin Gardiner, Harry W. Gardiner, Ormsin Sornmoopin Gardiner

Abstract

This chapter focuses on ethnic support groups in higher education designed to meet the unique needs and concerns of a growing number of college and university students of mixed cultural heritage. Particular attention is given to Asian-American groups and their efforts to deal with questions and problems of ethnic identity and acculturation resulting from the impact of two cultures on the psychological development of their members. Information is presented on the types and availability of support groups across the country as well as the design and implementation of a model group by the first author.

Introduction

Greater attention needs to be given to understanding and supporting students of mixed ethnic backgrounds whose needs have been inadequately addressed by the multicultural community on college and university campuses across the United States.

While we are aware of the controversy surrounding the term *Asian American* (with or without the hyphen), we do not intend to pursue that debate at this time. Instead, the purpose of this chapter is to highlight the normally unrecognized needs of a particular group within the Asian American community: individuals with one Asian and one non-Asian parent living in the United States. In the following discussion, we will focus on this group and define it as "Asian-American" with the hyphen.

Availability of Asian-American Support Groups

Three approaches were used to evaluate the current status of Asian-American support groups on college and university campuses. These included literature reviews, electronic mail contacts and telephone interviews.

The authors initially conducted an on-line review of the literature using a computer reference service called FirstSearch. Although several hundred periodical titles were reviewed, the search revealed a striking lack of material relating to ethnic support groups of any type. Not a single reference was found for groups designed specifically to meet the needs of students of mixed ethnic heritage. As a result, the second author sent an electronic mail request to several Special Interest Groups (SIGs) on the Internet e.g., XCULT-L (an electronic discussion group with an interest in cross-cultural topics) and ASIA-L (a discussion group focusing on topics related to Asia, Asian-Americans, and similar matters). While responses were received from fourteen list members, nine were writing to say they would like more information once the research was completed. The others provided a variety of suggestions, comments and materials.

The first author then conducted a series of telephone interviews with administrators of ten small, private, liberal arts colleges in Minnesota. The interviews revealed a clear absence of Asian-American support groups. On the other hand, each college had at least one administrative office for students of color, with names ranging from the Asian American Support Programs Office to the Office of Cultural Pluralism. Administrators at six of the ten colleges confirmed that an Asian American Student Group was active on their campus; one college had a separate program specifically for Southeast Asian students. None, however, spoke of an Asian-American support group. When asked their views on the need for Asian-American student support groups, administrators agreed that Asian-Americans experience needs and concerns which are distinctly different from other individuals.

Unfortunately, most of these research efforts led to the conclusion that either (1) there are few support groups of this type available to college students or (2) very few people are reporting information about such groups in the literature. This, coupled with the personal experiences of the authors, suggests that when students of mixed ethnic heritage want to join a campus cultural group they usually have to choose from among Asian, Hispanic, African American and similar groups or groups made up of Caucasians. Frequently, such a forced choice leads to feelings of isolation, personal doubt and questions and problems related to ethnic identity.

Ethnic identity of Asian-Americans

There is an extensive literature on ethnic identity and acculturation among Americans of Asian ancestry.[1]

Of particular interest to us here is the work that has been done with minority group adolescents. For example, Phinney in 1989 attempted to measure stages of ethnic identity development among several minority group adolescents (Asian-American, Black and Hispanic). Subjects were 10-grade students, all American-born, attending integrated urban high schools in the metropolitan Los Angeles area. Results of in-depth interviews revealed that almost half had not explored their ethnicity (diffusion/ foreclosure), nearly 25 percent were involved in some form of exploration (moratorium), and approximately 25 percent had explored, and were presently committed to, an ethnic identity (ethnic identity achieved). Subjects in the latter category also had the highest scores on an independent measure of ego identity and on psychological adjustment.[2]

While the process of identity development was similar for all three minority groups, the issues faced by each group were different. For example, among Asian-American students resolution of ethnic identity centered around pressures to achieve academically as well as concerns about quotas that make it more difficult to gain entrance into highly rated colleges.

In a more recent study, Phinney investigated attitudes toward acculturation and the factors related to these attitudes. A high school sample consisted of 134 Asians, 131 Blacks, 89 Hispanics, 41 of mixed background, 12 Whites and 10 "other." Among a college sample were 71 Asians, 17 Blacks, 75 Hispanics, 15 of mixed background, 43 Whites, and 2 "other."

Results indicate that students in culturally diverse settings strongly favor integration characterized by identification and association with one's traditional culture and that of the dominant society. In other words, students felt that minorities should learn to function in mainstream American society while maintaining their own cultural traditions. This attitude was endorsed by college students regardless of ethnic group, gender, social class, place of birth or self-identification. There was little support for the idea of separation with little or no interaction with the dominant society. Interestingly, assimilation, or identification solely with the culture of the dominant society and relinquishment of all ties to one's ethnic culture, was endorsed more by college students from Asian and mixed backgrounds than by those from Black or Hispanic backgrounds or by those who identified themselves as both ethnic and American. Phinney, et. al. concluded that multiculturalism may be a more appropriate model than assimilation for a diverse society like the United States that hopes to promote optimal development for members of all ethnic groups.[3]

Not only are adolescent Asian-Americans confronting the same identity problems as others their age but their search is increasingly complicated by the popular (and not entirely true) image of them as the "model minority"—a supernormal group that has achieved extraordinary academic and financial success in American society despite a long history of oppression.[4]

The number of American college students from Asian backgrounds tripled from 150,00 in 1976 to 448,000 in 1986 and is at an all-time high in 1994. With the increasing number of Asian-Americans attending colleges and universities in the United States, Toupin & Son designed a study to test the presumed universal validity of this model minority stereotype. They confirmed that Asian-American students were more likely to major in science or mathematics than non-Asian students—lending some support to the widely accepted stereotype. However, other findings contrasted sharply with this view. For example, significant numbers of Asian-Americans did not graduate, many had relatively low GPAs, and still others were more likely either to be placed on academic probation or to withdraw for medical reasons.

Based on their findings, Toupin & Son wondered why students like these were having such a difficult time in college. They offered several answers including the possibility that Asian-American students confront issues of identity which are made more complex by cultural heritage, e.g., Asian versus American identity. This presents a difficulty that needs to be faced in a less protected setting.[5]

In a recent paper, Gardiner & Mutter, present a model which addresses some of the issues related to the development of multicultural awareness and the successful establishment of ethnic identity. A developmental model, it consists of three hierarchical stages: (1) cultural dependence, where individuals identify with their own cultural heritage, (2) cultural independence, where individuals actively seek multicultural experiences, and (3) cultural interdependence where individuals share their multicultural experiences with their native culture.[6] This model shares some similarities with the typology for expanding ethnic identification found in the work of Banks.[7]

A major difference between these models is that while Banks' approach stresses more traditional Western individualistic values and ends with individuals experiencing a new culture, the Gardiner & Mutter model takes a more collectivist approach by taking individuals beyond independence and encouraging them to become multiculturally interdependent by sharing their experiences with others. The benefit of developing multicultural interdependence is that it results in positive changes in people's attitudes and the ways in which they view themselves and others.

The first author, an Asian-American herself, became acutely aware of the dilemma surrounding multicultural identity issues while attending a private undergraduate college. Since there were no clubs or support groups for students of mixed cultural backgrounds, she joined an Asian society. Keenly aware of the need for a different type of campus group, upon graduation, while working in the college's Multicultural Affairs Office, she designed and put into place a group that would meet the needs of students from bi-cultural families. It is this program that is described in the next section.

Design and implementation of a model support group

Carleton College is a small, private liberal arts college in Northfield, Minnesota. The student body is comprised of 1800 students, 288 of whom identify themselves as students of color. Of these, approximately 160 are of Asian descent. It is not entirely clear how many are Asian-American since a number of them chose only one ethnic heritage by which to identify themselves.

In 1991, the first author designed the framework for an interracial student support group at Carleton College. She began by interviewing interracial students who had identified themselves as "other" on their applications for college admission. The findings were unanimous: All students exhibited strong feelings about their mixed racial and cultural heritage and nearly all supported the idea of an interracial student group. The subject pool was then expanded to approximately 35 students, including interracial students who had identified with only one ethnic heritage on their applications.

The group has come to be known as "IRSO," an acronym for the Interracial Students' Organization. The group's stated purpose is to provide a support group for students of mixed cultural backgrounds in the multicultural community while promoting awareness of their unique needs and concerns. Membership is available to any student who has an interest in the concerns of mixed race students. Concerns are addressed in a variety of ways, including selecting and sharing literature on interracial issues with the Carleton community, sponsoring speakers who address interrracial concerns and ethnic relationships, and introducing films which explore the topic of interracial identity and relationships. IRSO receives support and funding from the Carleton Student Association. The consensus among members is that everyone contributes something positive to the group.

Some concluding comments and suggestions

All adolescents and young adults are confronted by identity issues that need to be successfully resolved if they are to become effective adults. The needs and concerns of Asian-Americans and others with mixed ethnic heritage present a unique situation.

The authors believe that all individuals with backgrounds of this type, at the elementary, secondary, or college level, should have support groups available to them, as do other ethnic groups, where issues of ethnic identity can be discussed and explored. The prototype for such a group, designed and implemented by the first author, has been described in this paper.

It is time to assess the activities of this group, analyze its successes and failures, and encourage others to develop similar groups at their educational institutions. It would also be useful to test the multicultural awareness model proposed by Gardiner and Mutter and the typology of ethnic identification put forth by Banks with members of the Asian-American student population.

Notes

1. Y. L. Espiritu, *Asian American Panethnicity: Bridging Institutions and Identities* (Philadelphia: Temple University Press, 1992); S. M. Furuto, *Social Work Practice with Asian Americans* (Newbury Park, CA: Sage, 1992); A. Marsella, G. DeVos, and F.L.K. Hsu, eds. (1985). *Culture and Self: Asian and Western Perspectives* (NY: Tavistock Publications, 1985); J. S. Phinney, V. Chavira and L. Williamson, "Acculturation Attitudes and Self-esteem Among High School and College Students." *Youth and Society* (1992): 23, 299-312; D. W. Sue and D. Sue, *Counseling the Culturally Different: Theory and Practice*, 2nd Edition. (NY: John Wiley & Sons, 1990).

2. J. S. Phinney, "Stages of Ethnic Identity Development in Minority Group Adolescents." *Journal of Early Adolescence*, 9, Feb-May,1989: 34-49.

3. Phinney (1992), 300, 309.

4. B. Suzuki, "Asian Americans As the 'Model Minority.'" *Change*, 21, Nov-Dec,1989: 13-19 and Sam Allis, "Education: Kicking the Nerd Syndrome," Time, March 25, 1991: 64, 66.

5. E. Toupin, and L. Son, "Preliminary Findings on Asian Americans: 'The Model Minority' in a Small Private East Coast College." *Journal of Cross-Cultural Psychology* (1991), 22: 403-417.

6. H. W. Gardiner and J. D. Mutter, "Becoming Multiculturally Sensitive." Paper presented at the 21st annual meeting of the Society for Cross-Cultural Research, Santa Fe, NM, 1993.

7. J. A. Banks, *Multicultural Education: Theory and Practice*, 2nd Edition. (Boston: Allyn & Bacon, 1988).

17

Asian American Faculty in U.S. Colleges and Universities

American Higher Education and the New Wave of Immigration[1]

Gabriel G. Manrique and Cecilia G. Manrique

Introduction

The authors conducted a survey of immigrant faculty of non-European origin in 1992. The purposes of conducting the survey were: to determine the characteristics of faculty in the U.S. who migrated from non-European countries; to study the factors affecting the decision of professionals to migrate; to examine the experiences of immigrant faculty with discrimination and prejudice; and to study their views on racial diversity on campuses. This paper presents our initial set of findings for one subset of respondents—immigrant faculty from Asia. This initial exposition of the information is intended as a prelude to further study of non-European immigrant faculty—an increasingly visible segment of the immigrant population but one that has been barely studied in the literature.

The new immigrants in U.S. colleges and universities

Although U.S. colleges and universities, in particular the research universities, have had a long tradition of attracting immigrant faculty, the large and continuing increase in the number of immigrant faculty in U.S. schools is a recent phenomenon that reflects major changes in U.S. immigration law passed in 1965.

The Immigration Act of 1965 removed national origins as the basis for immigration, thereby opening the doors for immigrants from non-European countries. In addition, preferences for immigrants were established that favored the migration of professionals and other persons whose skills were in high demand. With minor modifications, these principles of migration have been used in the recent immigration laws of 1986 and 1990.

As a result, a large majority of recent (post-1968) immigrants to the U.S. have come from non-European countries, particularly from Asia and the Indian Subcontinent. It is not surprising that many of the recent immigrant faculty in U.S. colleges and universities are also of non-European origin.[2]

The changes in U.S. immigration laws have allowed increasing numbers of Asians to come to the U.S. to study, earn their Ph.D.s, and then find jobs in U.S. colleges and universities. The laws have enabled foreign graduate students to acquire permanent resident status in the U.S. and to eventually acquire American citizenship.[3] The changes in immigration laws also coincided with the high demand for Ph.D.s as U.S. colleges expanded during the 1970s and 1980s. The Asian faculty that came with these changes comprise the group that we studied in this project.

Like most migration movements, the recent influx of Asian immigrants has been the source of both benefits and problems for the U.S. Their availability allowed colleges to fill faculty positions in fields which have had a shortage of native-born Ph.D.s. Immigrant faculty also gave schools a connection to the rest of the world at a time when the idea of "internationalizing the curriculum" was gaining acceptance. And for those who consider exposure to cultural diversity an important part of education, non-European immigrant faculty provided a beneficial dimension to U.S. schools as well as potential role models for minority students.[4] On the other hand, the presence of immigrant faculty can also generate problems for U.S. colleges and universities. When racism and prejudice surface on campus, some of these have been directed at immigrant faculty. In turn, these create tensions that disrupt learning. Other concerns include the speech of immigrant faculty and what effect this has on students, particularly those not used to different accents.[5]

The sample

To survey faculty who are non-European immigrants, the authors compiled a mailing list drawn from members of national professional organizations, such as the American Economics Association (AEA), the American Political Science Association (APSA), and from the faculty rosters in a random sample of school catalogs. The survey's cover letter specifically asked the recipients to respond only if they were first- or second-generation immigrants of non-European origin, regardless of their current citizenship or visa status.

The authors sent the survey to 1,380 faculty. The authors received 322 valid responses, giving us a survey response rate of 23.3percent. There were 210 respondents whose origin is either in Asia or the Indian Subcontinent. This paper is based on their responses.

The survey

The survey contained questions on the respondent's: 1) current institution, department, and personal information; 2) comparisons of professional opportunities between the U.S. and one's country of origin; 3) experiences with discrimination and racial prejudice; 4) perceptions of how one's race affects his/her work as a faculty member; and 5) views of his/her institution's efforts to increase the diversity of its faculty and students.

The survey results

The profile of the respondents

Of the 210 Asian respondents: 75 percent teach at state-supported institutions; 73 percent teach at comprehensive institutions; 43 percent work in Ph.D. granting institutions; 33 percent are in a college of business; 66 percent are tenured; 45 percent are full professors; and 88 percent are males. The average age of the respondents is 42 years and they have been with their current department an average of 14 years. The majority (85%) are married. There were respondents from 98 different schools.

Of the 210 respondents, 131 listed their origin as Asia/Pacific Islands and 79 listed the Indian Subcontinent. By country of birth, the greatest number of respondents come from India (71) and Korea (29). Although 91 percent are first generation immigrants, the majority now have U.S. citizenship (53%). Seventy-nine percent (79%) of the respondents reported that prior to assuming a full-time teaching position in the U.S., they came to the U.S. as graduate students, confirming how common it is for immigrant faculty to initially come to the U.S. for graduate studies, then find employment in a U.S. college or university, convert to immigrant or permanent resident status, and then apply for U.S. citizenship.

Migration as revealed preference

The decision to migrate is an extremely complex and personal one that involves economic, political, social and family considerations. One way of characterizing the factors affecting international migration is by distinguishing between push and pull factors. Certain factors push persons from the sending country while other factors pull persons to the receiving country.[6] We sought to determine what job-related push and pull factors affect immigrant faculty and found the following:

1. *The lack of job opportunities commensurate with one's training does not appear to be a factor pushing faculty to migrate from their country of origin.* Sixty-four percent responded that the probability of finding a job in their country of origin commensurate with their training was high, indicating that the perceived lack of suitable employment opportunities is not what pushes Asian faculty to migrate to the U.S.

2. *The chance to afford a higher standard of living can be a factor pulling faculty to migrate to the U.S.* Forty-two percent who replied said that if they were to work in their country of origin, the standard of living they would be able to afford would be "worse" or "much worse" than what they could currently afford in the U.S. Only 16 percent said their standard of living would be better. The other 42 percent said they would be able to afford the "same" standard of living. To the extent that economic considerations play a role in the decision to migrate, then, these perceived differences in the standard of living can help to explain why highly educated Asians migrate to the U.S.

3. *Access to better library and research facilities can be another factor pulling faculty to migrate to the U.S.* Seventy-three percent said that, compared to the U.S., their access to library and research facilities would be "worse." Only seven percent said it would be better.

4. *Increased academic freedom can be a factor pulling faculty to migrate to the U.S.* Forty-five percent said that, compared to the U.S., their academic freedom in their country of origin would be worse. Only six percent said that their academic freedom would be "better" in their country of origin. Because the activities of faculty revolve around the classroom and research, the authors chose to include these factors on the assumption that if academics view that the resources and atmosphere are such that they can perform their duties better in the U.S., then they may be pulled to migrate to the U.S. However, we are unable to assign relative weights to these factors.[7]

The decision to migrate is further complicated by the trade offs immigrants must make between benefits in their country of origin and benefits in the receiving country. For example, immigrants may trade off the familiarity of an extended family for potential economic gains. Immigration may also force persons to switch roles— from being part of the majority to being part of the minority in the U.S. This switch can be especially great for many Asian immigrants because: their cultures are distinctly different from the dominant culture in the U.S.; they look distinctly different from the majority in the U.S.; and they speak languages that are very different from English. Being placed with the minority may result in a loss of social standing relative to what they are accustomed to in their country of origin.

Becoming part of the minority may result in a loss of social standing relative to one's status in the country of origin. The respondents were asked to compare their social standing in the U.S. with what it would be in their country of origin. We found that:

5. *By migrating to the U.S., Asian faculty forego the higher social standing they would have in their country of origin.* Thirty-seven percent said that, compared to their social status in the U.S., their social status in their country of origin would be "much better," and another 33 percent said that it would be "better." Thus, a large majority felt they incurred some loss of social standing by choosing to migrate to the U.S. Only five percent said that their social status would be worse in their country of origin. This may indicate that academe tends to attract the elites from the LDCs (less developed countries) or that receiving a Ph.D. from a U.S. university elevates one to an elite position in LDCs.

6. *Asian immigrant faculty in the U.S. forego better opportunities for professional advancement in their country of origin.* Forty-one percent said that their opportunities for professional advancement would be better in their country of origin. However, 23 percent said that their opportunities for professional advancement would be worse in their country of origin.

The authors recognize that, in addition to those included in this study, there are other factors affecting the decision to migrate. However, if we treat the act of migrating to the U.S. as evidence of the revealed preference of individuals, then the conclusions from the findings in this section of the paper may be stated in either of the following ways: 1) Asian immigrant faculty attach a higher value to a higher standard of living, more academic freedom and better library and research facilities and less value to social standing and opportunities for professional advancement; or 2) (and we think this is the more appropriate conclusion) the loss of social standing and opportunities for professional advancement is not large enough to offset gains in standard of living, academic freedom and library facilities. These are consistent with our next finding:

7. *Asian faculty are not very likely to accept an offer of a permanent position in their country of origin.* Although 66 percent said that there was either a "very high" or "high" probability of receiving an offer of a teaching position in their country of origin, only 38 percent of the respondents said there was a "very high" or "high" probability that they would accept the offer.

Job discrimination against immigrant faculty

Unlike past waves of migration to the U.S., the latest and current wave has been dominated by people from non-European countries. These have created social tensions and problems, although it is not at all clear that these are any different from those that accompanied earlier waves of migration.[8]

Although immigrant faculty tend to be more highly educated than the typical immigrant, and although U.S. campuses may be more open than society in general, it is still possible for immigrant faculty to be subjected to discrimination and prejudice. Racism on campus is not unheard of and is not targeted solely at black Americans. Asians have increasingly become targets of racially motivated acts.[9] To learn more about the race-related experiences of immigrant faculty, we included questions about discrimination in the workplace. The authors defined discrimination in the work place as: an action taken towards a person based mainly on his/her race, which may involve promotion, salaries, or assignment of workload. Our results indicate that from the standpoint of Asian immigrant faculty, discrimination is alive and well on U.S. campuses.

1. One out of every five respondents said that they have been discriminated against by colleagues in their own department. A larger proportion, one out of every four, said that they had been discriminated against by colleagues outside their own department.

2. One out of every four respondents said that they have been discriminated against by administrators in their institution, and 18 percent did not think that their institution had policies and procedures to effectively handle cases of job discrimination.

3. More than half, 57 percent, said that they were aware of instances where foreign-born faculty had been discriminated against.

The reported extent of discrimination against Asian immigrant faculty is disturbing. However, it should also be noted that a substantial portion of the respondents, more than 40 percent, did not feel that they had been discriminated against by colleagues in their department, by colleagues outside the department or by administrators. The disparity in answers may be explained by other factors, such as one's rank, country of origin, type of institution, or length of stay in the U.S. which will be the subject of further analysis of this data and the next round of responses which the authors will pursue in the fall of 1993.

These survey results reveal, not surprisingly, that U.S. campuses are subject to the same tensions and problems that American society in general will continue to experience, for as long as the U.S. remains what it has always been—a nation of immigrants.[10]

Racial prejudice directed towards immigrant faculty

Racism is shown not only through workplace discrimination. On campuses, as in the rest of society, immigrants may be subjected to racial prejudice. The authors described acts of racial prejudice as adverse actions or hateful speech directed towards a person based largely on that person's race or ethnic origin. Faculty were asked questions regarding their experiences with overt acts of racial prejudice. The results provide evidence that even highly educated professors are victims of racial prejudice.

1. Only ten percent said that members of their own department had directed acts of racial prejudice towards them, but 20 percent said that colleagues from outside their department had done so.

2. Twenty-seven percent said students had directed acts of racial prejudice towards them.

3. Twenty-nine percent said that people in their community had directed acts of prejudice towards them or their families.

As with discrimination in the workplace, it should be noted that although there is evidence that Asian immigrant faculty experience acts of racism, 45 percent of the respondents said that they had not been subjected to acts of racism by their colleagues, students, or people in their community. These differences may be explained by factors such as the type of institution, location, and origin.

Racism on U.S. colleges and universities may merely reflect the trends in society. In addition, we should allow for the possibility that the extent of racism has been underreported in this study, since *racism and prejudice can be subtle or disguised* rather than overt. This may be especially true in campuses where blatant acts of racism and prejudice are proscribed by the tenets of collegiality and academic freedom.

Is race a handicap for Asian immigrant faculty?

Another purpose of our study was to examine how immigrant faculty perceive the impact their race, "foreignness," and accent have had on their work as academics. The authors also wanted to find out if immigrant faculty feel that, as minorities, they must work harder than other faculty to prove themselves professionally. The results show that significant portions of respondents do not think their race or accent adversely impact their performance.

1. Twenty-six percent strongly disagreed and another 33 percent disagreed with the statement, "My race is a barrier to my effectiveness as a teacher." Only 17 percent agreed with the statement.

2. Eighteen percent strongly disagreed and 25 percent disagreed with the statement, "My race has been a significant barrier to my professional advancement or promotion," and 25 percent agreed.

3. Twenty-four percent strongly disagreed and another 33 percent disagreed with the statement, "My speech accent is a barrier to my effectiveness as a teacher," and 22 percent agreed.

This generation of immigrants, which arrived and was hired in the 1970s and 1980s, would have been socialized into the principles of affirmative action. For this reason, immigrant faculty may think that their race was a factor in their getting hired. However, this was not supported by the survey results.

4. Forty-six percent strongly disagreed and another 32 percent disagreed with the statement, "My race was a factor in my getting hired for my current position."

Thus, most of the respondents did not think that they were hired because of their race. In a less than color blind society, it may even be asserted that Asian immigrants are hired in spite of their race. The negative response to this question can also be explained by the fact that, during the search process, the race of immigrant applicants is not directly addressed.

Our next finding below (5) is perhaps a better indicator that immigrant faculty are aware of the role that their race plays in their professional career. It reveals that, even if these Asian immigrant faculty do not regard their race as a significant handicap, a substantial majority agree that they have to work harder in order to prove themselves.

5. Twenty-eight percent strongly agreed and another 35 percent agreed with the statement, "Because of my race, I have to try harder to prove myself professionally."

The combination of findings 1 through 5 in this section enable us to draw a somewhat positive conclusion about how immigrant faculty view the role of their race. While Asian faculty recognize that they may face additional hurdles because of their race or "foreignness," they do not seem to view these as insurmountable.

Asian attitudes towards cultural diversity on campus

Many colleges and universities have been attempting to create a more racially and culturally diverse campus.[11] This may be a reaction to the changing demographics of the U.S., or a recognition of the inherent value of diversity, or both. The authors elicited the views of Asian faculty with regard to their respective institution's efforts at fostering diversity on campus, and we found that:

1. While 29 percent of the respondents said their institution was effective in recruiting faculty from diverse racial backgrounds, 24 percent thought that recruiting efforts were either ineffective or nonexistent in their institution.

2. The percentage of faculty who indicated that their institution was effective in retaining faculty from diverse backgrounds was equal to those who thought such retention efforts were ineffective or non-existent.

3. The respondents gave their institutions only slightly higher marks in rating the effectiveness of efforts to recruit and retain students from diverse racial backgrounds.

4. While 49 percent agreed with the statement, "My institution should recruit more faculty from diverse racial backgrounds," 40 percent neither agreed nor disagreed, and 11 percent disagreed.

5. While 56 percent agreed that their institution should recruit more students from diverse backgrounds, 35 percent neither agreed nor disagreed, and nine percent disagreed.

It is apparent from one through three, that there is no high degree of agreement on the effectiveness of university programs to recruit and retain racially diverse faculty and students. This most likely reflects the varying levels of commitment to racial diversity across campuses, the varying levels of sophistication and organization of such efforts, and the different lengths of time such efforts have been in place.

We also note, from four and five above, that as members of the minority, the respondents were not overwhelmingly in favor of recruiting more racially diverse faculty and students. A large number was non-committal about recruiting faculty and students from more racially diverse backgrounds. There are probably several explanations for this ambivalence. However, one view that was repeatedly expressed by respondents in the comments written on the survey was that the qualifications of job applicants should still take precedence over other considerations.

In spite of the ambivalence expressed about the recruitment of more racially diverse faculty and students, there appears to be strong support for multicultural programs on campus.

6. Sixty-nine percent agreed with the statement, "My present institution should do more to promote multi-racial awareness and sensitivity." Only seven percent disagreed with the statement.

That two-thirds of the respondents agreed with this statement can be a reflection of the following: respondents may feel that their institutions are simply not doing enough to promote racial awareness; respondents are reacting to incidents of discrimination or prejudice that they have witnessed or been subjected to; or respondents perceive that multi-cultural programs have inherent educational and social values which universities should encourage.

These initial findings can assist in understanding better the experiences and attitudes of immigrant faculty. In turn, this understanding may be used to increase their effectiveness, reduce some of the tensions created by an increasingly multi-racial mix on campuses, and formulate policies aimed at maximizing the contribution of immigrant faculty to U.S. higher education.

Notes

1. Support for this project was provided by the Bureau of Business and Economics Research of Winona State University, the Winona State University Foundation,

and by the Dean's Office, University of Wisconsin - LaCrosse. This paper is one in a series that the authors are writing based on the results of their survey of non-European immigrant faculty in U.S. colleges and universities.

2. David M. Reimers, *Still the Golden Door: The Third World Comes to America*. 2nd ed. (New York: Columbia University Press, 1992).

3. Ibid., 98.

4. In J.J. Siegfred, et al., "The Status and Prospects of the Economics Major," in *Journal of Economic Education*. 22 (Summer 1991): 197-224; J.K. Ehrhart, and B.R. Sandler. *Looking for More that a Few Good Women in Traditionally Male Fields*. Project on the Status and Education of Women. (Washington, DC: Association for American Colleges, 1987); and John Martha Tyler, "Academic Role Models Needed for Females in the Third World," in *Perspectives on Minority Women in Higher Education*, L. Welch, ed. 107-113 (New York: Praeger Publishers, 1992).

5. *Civil Rights Issues Facing Asian Americans in the 1990s*. (Washington, DC: United States Commission on Civil Rights, 1992).

6. Alejandro Portes and J. Borocz. "Contemporary Immigration: Theoretical Perspectives on Its Determinants and Modes of Incorporation," in *International Migration Review* (1991) 23 (3): 606-630.

7. Aristide Zolberg, "The Next Waves: Migration Theory for a Changing World," in *International Migration Review* (1991)28 (3): 403-430.

8. William Dudley, ed., *Immigration: Opposing Viewpoints* (San Diego: Greenhaven Press, 1991).

9. United States Commission on Civil Rights, op cit.

10. Nathan Glazer, *Clamor at the Gates* (San Francisco: Institute for Contemporary Studies, 1985); David Simcox, ed., *U.S. Immigration in the 1980s: Reappraisal and Reform*. (Boulder: Westview Press, 1988); Dudley, op. cit.

11. American Council on Education. *Minorities on Campus: A Handbook for Enhancing Diversity*. (Washington, DC: ACE, 1989).

Popular Culture

Popular culture reflects social knowledge and is a powerful medium for social change. It is a laboratory in which to highlight, explore and experiment with issues. The papers in this section show how drama, film, fiction, live performance, and television are used to articulate social reality and foreground issues of importance to Asian Americans. They discuss the implications of "the other" or alien and the role stereotypes play, for Asian Americans and non-Asian Americans. The papers address the under-representation, absence and negative images of Asian Americans so often seen in mass media which imply either lack of importance or social unacceptability. Currier and Bogstad discuss science fiction as a medium reflecting larger society which can foreground issues, show alternative viewpoints and allow readers to form positive affective ties to Asian American characters as the "human" versus the "other" or alien, thus serving as a powerful tool in the classroom. Du examines Chinese American drama. He discusses its transition from Chinese to Chinese American and the ways its depiction of Asian American counters the common negative characterizations as passive and feminine. Gerster looks at Asian American independent cinema. She contrasts its content and portrayal of Asian American cultural reality with the presentations by Hollywood. The many shorts and documentaries create a cinematic Asian American presence and present alternatives to Hollywood stereotypes. Lessick-Xiao discusses Wong Aoki and her attempts to "probe the past, live the present and shape the future" in live performances. Piehl and Ruppel's study looks at Asian American representation on prime-time television. They document the under-representation, the mostly derogatory depiction, the positioning of Asian American as "other" and emphasis on martial arts.

The papers in this section consider the "state" of Asian American presence and portrayal in popular culture, showing where we were in the past, where we are, and the possibilities for the future.

18

The Chinese American Drama

In Search of Gender and Identity— Focusing on David Henry Hwang

Wenwei Du

Until the 1970s, there had never been a Chinese American playwright of note in the American theatre. Chinese who were born in the United States began to write about their experience in this country in the 1940s but only in fiction and poetry. The authors were predominantly female. Dramatic accounts began to be known in the early 1970s when Frank Chin's path-breaking plays *The Chickencoop Chinaman* (1972), *The Year of the Dragon* (1974), and *Gee, Pop!* (1975) were produced.

To Chin and his fellow writers, the greater part of earlier Chinatown literature—written by white Americans and Chinese—was a stereotyped portrayal or distortion of Chinatown life and, in some cases, even insulted Chinese Americans. The same had been true on the American stage since Chinese began to be portrayed in the American domestic settings in the last quarter of the 19th century. Before 1900, there had been a number of plays—mostly melodramas about contemporary American society— using Chinese characters as comic figures.[1] The "Chinaman" became an American theatrical laughing stock. The birth of serious drama in the first two decades of the twentieth century lessened the demand for the stereo-typed Chinese fool. Yet this Chinese comic figure has continued to appear from time to time, especially in drawing-room comedies of the 1920s and 1930s. The tendency to stereotype Chinese characters on stage went along with other forms of popular literature such as fiction, movies, cartoons and television series to produce a series of pidgin-English speaking China Men, dutiful houseboys, submissive China Dolls, treacherous Dragon Ladies, inscrutable detectives and sinister Chinks. Portrayals of Chinese Americans on stage had been generally insensitive and negative.

A shift of view on the American stage appeared only after the Chinese fought with the Americans during World War II. During the 1950s the portrayal of the Chinese American underwent a process of "domestication": the Chinese Americans' dispositions and qualities were tamed to accord with American conventional values. This process was typified by *Flower Drum Song*, the only dramatic work exclusively about Chinese Americans on Broadway before the 1960s. The musical was adapted in 1958 by Richard Rodgers, Oscar Hammerstein II, and Joseph Fields from the popular novel of the same title by C. Y. Lee, a naturalized Chinese. With an altered thematic focus, the musical is set in Chinatown, San Francisco, and deals with the conflicts and compromises between the old and young generations in the form of a love story. Seemingly sympathetic, it shows the domestication of Chinese Americans into "admired" characters. First, the drama presents a model Chinese hero, Wang Ta, embraced with American traditional values and a model image of a docile Chinese woman, Mei Li. Secondly, the old generation is portrayed as possessing wisdom, and yet they are sterilized in that they all appear as either widows or widowers, implying that they are not masculine but feminine in terms of power and social potency. Thirdly, by using pseudo-Chinese spiritual purity to criticize the decadence caused by contemporary American materialistic culture, social commentary or satire is transformed into conventional wisdom for American audiences.

In contrast to the earlier comic Chinese figures on stage, the Chinese Americans in *Flower Drum Song* are "model" minority people. Although it seems to praise Chinese Americans from the white majority's point of view, the musical has been criticized as a pseudo-presentation of their life by the Chinese American playwrights. Chin and his fellow Asian authors identify the "model" minority "as a permanent inferior." "All that is required from him is that he accept his assigned status cheerfully and reject whatever aspects of his racial and cultural background prove offensive to the dominant white society. And of course he must never speak for himself."[2] To them, the castration of the Chinese "is also reflected ... in culture so that Chinese American males have not been permitted to speak in American literature."[3] Dissatisfied with the status quo, they realized that it was their task to express their own feelings and sensibilities as Chinese Americans, made possible only in the political atmosphere from the 1960s onward. From this historical context came the search for authentic Chinese American characters on the American stage.

In Chinese American drama, two themes in characterization have been dominant and interrelated: 1) most characters strive for a Chinese Americanness as their identity and 2) they appear as strong and assertive to batter the stereotyped image of the Chinese as "feminine." Both were initiated in Frank Chin's *The Chickencoop Chinaman*. This search for identity and gender is a cry from the heart of the yellow minority victimized in twentieth century America as faceless, identityless exotic cultural stereotypes, but individualized in Tam Lum, the play's Chinese American hero: he is a talented and suffering documentary filmmaker who, resplendent in cowboy shirt and cowboy boots, is fast-talking and aggressive, refuting while parodying stereotypes about Chinese Americans conveyed by the previous works of literature. Deeply rooted in the Chinatowns of America, the play's voice is bold, assertive, and vital in its confrontation of the issues of the self-contempt, passivity and femininity in the stereotyped Chinese American manhood.

Following Chin's example, there have appeared a series of plays in search of a Chinese American identity.[4] Chinese American playwrights have looked to history and their own lives for enlightenment. Though different in the treatment of their own Chinese American experiences, the search for an identity follows a pattern from being of Chinese descent to being a Chinese American and from being labelled as an alien to becoming a native. A primal version of this pattern can be seen in Genny Lim's *Paper Angels.* Based on her research on Angel Island, a detention station in San Francisco Bay for Chinese immigrants from 1910 to 1940, *Paper Angels* is a drama about the suffering lives and hopes of Chinese detainees set in 1915. It portrays the continuity and transition from Chinese to Chinese Americans. The leading character, Chin-gung, represents this transition in consciousness. He has lived in America for 40 years and worked on the transcontinental railroad. He returned to China for his wife but is coming back to America because his life is now part of this country. On the one hand, he is proud to be Chinese; on the other, he has given so much of his life, labor and soul to America that he wishes only to live out the rest of his days in this land. Yet when finally he is to be deported on the basis of a medical report, the blow is so severe that Chin-gung commits suicide.[5] All of the other characters present phases of the similar transition process. Lim's characterization presents the struggle, often painful, of changing outlooks. *Paper Angels* points to the overall framework of most Chinese American plays dealing with the identity issues: there has been a long and tortuous course taken by the Chinese in America to get themselves recognized in this country.

The process of transition from being Chinese to being Chinese American necessarily involves contradiction between the two. A number of plays focus on these conflicts between the old tradition and the new sensibility either in a relationship between Chinese parents and their American-born children or in a relationship between Chinese immigrants and Chinese Americans of the same generation. In Frank Chin's *Year of the Dragon*, the conflict is developed between the three cultures—Chinese, American, and Chinese American. Fred Eng, the main character who was born in China and raised in America, supports his family by running a Chinatown tour guide service. In his early forties, he still lives in the Chinatown apartment of his parents. The conflict between his duty as the oldest son and his hope of freeing himself from his bondage to Chinatown is externalized in the conflict between his Chinese father and him as Chinese American son. In Darrell Lum's *Oranges Are Lucky*, an old Chinese lady Ah Po struggles between her Chinese habits and her wish to be American; in Arthur Aw's *All Brand New Classic Chinese Theatre*, a much younger Michael is torn between his Caucasian girl friend, a metaphor for the new sensibility, and his Chinese mother, a reminder of the old tradition. What interests us is that *All Brand New Classical Chinese Theatre* provides two possible endings: one being the breakup between Michael and his girl friend through the mother's intervention, which stands for the incompatibility of the two cultures, and the other being the union of the two signifying the merging of the two cultures. The second ending is the goal to be achieved only with mutual acceptance of both cultures.

As continuity and conflicts coexist, the conflicts should be resolved in the continuity from being Chinese to becoming Chinese American. This theme is consciously and successfully treated in what David Henry Hwang called his "Chinese-American trilogy": *FOB* (—a coined acronym for "Fresh off the boat"), *The Dance and the Railroad*, and *Family Devotions*. According to the playwright himself, the concern with identity "is intimately related to my own desire to know myself" as "American-Chinese;" he wrote these plays to "explore racism and stereotyping" in American culture.[6]

Hwang's first play *FOB* is set in the back room of a small Chinese restaurant in California. The time is the present. The play intermingles the real in American society with the mystic in the Chinese heritage. It portrays three characters— Grace, Dale and Steve, all in their twenties— in a confrontational triangle dating game while each searches for a personal identity. Grace, a first-generation Chinese American is caught between Dale, an American of Chinese descent who considers himself "white" and Steve, a Chinese just fresh off the boat from "the Old Country"—each boy wants to have a date with Grace. Dale looks down upon Steve for being Chinese while Steve mocks Dale with the fact that no matter how "white" Dale feels or acts, on the outside he will always be "Chinese." To mediate between the two, Grace tells about her painful and rewarding experiences in her transition from Chinese to American— a personal struggle for identity. Along with the verbal fight, the characters surrealistically act out a physical fighting scene between "two figures from American literature" as the author calls them: Fa Mu Lan (Hua Mulan) from Maxine Hong Kingston's novel *The Woman Warrior* and Gwan Gung (Guan Gong) from Frank Chin's play *Gee, Pop!*[7] Steve associates himself with Gwan Gung, the god of warriors, and Grace relates herself to Fa Mu Lan, a woman warrior who disguises herself as a man to take her father's place in battle. As the result of the fighting game, Steve the Gwan Gung is struck down by Grace the Fa Mu Lan. After the symbolic battle ends, Steve says to Grace: "There are no gods that travel. Only warriors travel."[8] The message is that Gwan Gung as a god can only inspire warriors but can not fight for warriors and that the Chinese American needs Fa Mu Lan, a real human fighter, to fight for an identity in this society. Finally, Grace agrees to date Steve, leaving Dale alone. The symbolic union between Gwan Gung and Fa Mu Lan suggests the idea that striving for authentic identity is to fight against stereotyped image rather than to strive to be white as in the case of Dale.

The fighting spirit of the Chinese Americans is further reflected in Hwang's second play *The Dance and the Railroad*. The story focuses on the relationship of two Chinese railroad workers against the historical background of the 1867 strike launched by the Chinese Americans on the transcontinental railroad. On a mountain top, Lone is practicing his Chinese opera acrobatic skills. He had been trained to play the role of Gwan Gung in the "Old Country" and now, to escape famine at home, he has come to the New Country to work as a coolie on the railway. Ma, a newly arrived worker, comes to the mountain top to be a theatrical apprentice to Lone, enduring tremendous pains to learn the skills. Dreams of portraying Gwan Gung keep him in high spirits during the gloomy days of the strike. Finally, the strikers win. Ma goes down the mountain to resume the hardships of work. Agreeing to join the workers soon, Lone is left alone practicing his art again. From the beginning to the end, the play develops through the changes in attitude of the two men towards the strike. It starts with Lone's doubts about victory in the strike and Ma's blind optimism; it ends with Lone's belief in the strength of the China Men when united and Ma's understanding that the China Man's life in the New Land is hard. The significance of the drama lies in the symbolic role Gwan Gung played in the early history of the Chinese Americans. The practice of the skills of Chinese opera counters the dehumanizing effects of their hard labor in undignified circumstances; the symbol of Gwan Gung signifies the fighting spirit, if any, of the "dead" "China Men" in their forced isolation from the society.

The third play in the "trilogy" is *Family Devotions*, Hwang's most personal play. Its story of a rich Chinese American family's reception of its granduncle from China turns into a conflict that exposes the false "whiteness" of the Christian Chinese Americans. During the ceremony of Family Devotions, the family's two grandaunts force their brother Di-gou to convert to Christianity only to be faced with his revelation that the family story about See-goh-poh, who was believed to be the first Christian in the family and to have converted many Chinese into Christianity, was actually a fantasized illusion or an invented lie. The sudden deaths of the two Christian grandaunts caused by the revelation are poignant metaphors that total conversion to the white culture does not produce a real identity for Chinese Americans. Di-gou counsels Chester, the eldest grandson of the family, to remember the family's past: "Study your face and you will see— the shape of your face is the shape of faces back many generations—across an ocean, in another soil. You must become one with your family before you can hope to live away from it."[9] Only by forging a bond with one's original heritage can one find his or her own identity in this multi-cultured society.

Closely related to the identity of the Chinese American is the gender problem in which David Henry Hwang is most interested. One common theme Hwang traces through using combinations of reality and fantasy is, in his words, the "kind of fluidity of identity": "people become other people."[10] Like most Asian American authors, Hwang is very much concerned with the stereotype of Asians and Asian Americans as passive or "feminine." Some of his plays focus on the genders of protagonists. The true identity of Grace in *FOB* is realized in the combination of the surreal Fa Mu Lan and the living Chinese American girl. Hwang inserts a strong symbolism in the fighting spirit of Grace: like Fa Mu Lan, Grace possesses the masculine strength of a heroic fighter. The death of the female elders in *Family Devotions* signifies the death of the femininity forced upon the Chinese American by white majority culture. The suggestive linkage between the Chinese granduncle Di-gou and the young Chinese-American grandson Chester points to the birth of masculinity from the Chinese American.

The play that deals with the gender issue the most explicitly is Hwang's *M. Butterfly*. It is based on a 1986 *New York Times* news story about a spy trial in France concerning a French diplomat and a Chinese Peking Opera singer who were involved in a love affair. For 20 years, the diplomat did not know that the female-role performer whom he loved was actually a man. Borrowing the broad factual outline of the real spy case, Hwang transmutes the story into an amusing yet provocative drama. Hwang shortens the French word "Monsieur" into "M.," thus making the title of the play *M. Butterfly*. Hence, the author deliberately keeps the gender unclear in the English context until the play reaches the end.[11] It keeps the audience guessing: Miss Butterfly? Mrs. Butterfly? Ms. Butterfly? Mr. Butterfly? Or several of these possibilities simultaneously? To dispel the misconception that "Occidentals" are masculine while "Orientals" are feminine, the play's theme develops through the manipulation of gender in characterization. In the beginning, Song Liling, a female-role actor of the Peking Opera, disguises himself as a submissive and attractive woman in "her" romance with the French diplomat Rene Gallimard. Hoping to relive the love story of Puccini's famous opera *Madame Butterfly*, Gallimard sees himself as Pinkerton to "conquer" Song as Butterfly, a traditional version of the domination of the feminine East by the masculine West. As the plot progresses, Gallimard finds himself duped as Song reveals his true gender. The author creates a Western character in Gallimard who is sexually limp, impotent and futile. The very fact that Gallimard never discovered Song Liling's true sex is a strong indicator of his impotence. Even though he is a Western man, he does not possess the physical masculinity to realize his desire to dominate an Eastern "woman." In the play, he increasingly changes from male to female.

In contrast, Song Liling appears at first to be controlled by Gallimard because he knows his only chance to conquer is to become female: "You expect Oriental countries to submit to your guns, and you expect Oriental women to be submissive to your men. That's why you say they make the best wives…. I am an Oriental. And being an Oriental, I could never be completely a man."[12] It is his single performance of submissive Butterfly that wins Gallimard's heart. Once he successfully becomes Gallimard's fantasy "woman," Song begins to control Gallimard. Though always in female roles as a Peking Opera performer, Song plays the female fighting hero, a symbol of initiative and courage, which embodies the masculine spirit of Fa Mu Lan. It is Song who commands Gallimard to provide secret information. The final scenes, when Song Liling changes "her" Butterfly costume into his man's suit in the French courtroom and when Gallimard dons Butterfly's costume after Song's true sex is revealed, are highly symbolic in that the sex roles and the roles of dominance and submission have been completely reversed. The resultant effect is striking and poignant: the East is not always feminine, nor is the West always masculine; the West/male to East/female relationship is exposed as absurd.

Allegorically, *M. Butterfly* is also a search for the gender of the Chinese American. When a stereotyped perception is maintained long enough, it takes on a degree of reality which in turn tends to verify that stereotyped perception. It is Hwang's philosophical obsession to expose false identities as they have long been perceived in the mainstream literature. *M. Butterfly* is "a plea to all sides to cut through our respective layers of cultural and sexual misperception, to deal with one another truthfully for our mutual good, from the common and equal ground we share as human beings."[13]

As we have seen, from Frank Chin to David Henry Hwang there has been a continuous search for identity and gender: a struggle to rise from and above the heap of established stereotypes which had designated the Chinese Americans. The characters depicted by Chinese American playwrights speak their own speech. They are alive as real individuals. These characters are no longer conventional; each has a different personality yet all symbolize the different aspects of the Chinese American experience: suffering, anger, isolation, humiliation, self-contempt, joy, pride, aspiration, etc. Above all, a fighting spirit, expressive or innate, dominates all major characters as well as the playwriting— all aiming at a self-definition and socially-established identity. It is new drama, yet it is utterly American. David Henry Hwang's words ring true for all his fellow writers: "I write most confidently in the American idiom."[14] The works by Chinese American playwrights and theatre artists are now becoming an important element in attempts by the American theatre to come to grips with the multicultural character of American society and to portray it truthfully. The emergence of Chinese American plays, along with works by other ethnic writers, represents a political and social transformation of American drama and theatre.

Notes

1. For a discussion of these plays, see Stuart W. Hyde, "The Chinese Stereotype in American Melodrama," in *California Historical Society Quarterly*, 34 (1955): 357-365.

2. Elaine H. Kim, *Asian American Literature: An Introduction to the Writings and Their Social Context* (Philadelphia: Temple University Press, 1982): 18-9.

3. Ibid., 180.

4. Darrell H.Y. Lum, "My Home Is Down the Street," *Literary Arts Hawaii*, 78-79 (1986): 16-20; 80-81(1986): 20-22 and *Oranges Are Lucky*, in *Kumu Kahua Plays*, Dennis Carroll, ed. (Honolulu: University of Hawaii Press, 1983): 63-82.

5. The plot is based on Fred Wei-han Houn's discussion of the play. See Fred Wei-han Houn, "A Hell Called Angel," *Bridge*, 8.1 (1982): 43-44.

6. Words quoted in this paragraph are from Misha Berson, ed., *Between Worlds: Contemporary Asian-American Plays* (New York: Theatre Communication Group, 1990): 93, 94.

7. David Henry Hwang, playwright's note, *FOB and The House of Sleeping Beauties* (New York: Dramatists Play Service, Inc., 1983): 10.

8. Hwang, *FOB*, 49.

9. David Henry Hwang, *The Dance and the Railroad, Family Devotions* (New York: Dramatists Play Service, 1983): 77.

10. Berson, 94.

11. See David Henry Hwang, afterword, *M. Butterfly*, by Hwang (New York: New American Library, 1988): 96.

12. David Henry Hwang, *M. Butterfly* (New York: Dramatists Play Service, Inc., 1988): 62.

13. Hwang, afterword, *M. Butterfly*, 98.

14. Quoted from Patricia O'Haire, "Broadway 'Butterfly,'" *Daily News*, March 20, 1988: 5.

19

Fierce, Friendly Faction in Brenda Wong Aoki's *The Queen's Garden*

Anne E. Lessick-Xiao

It seems appropriate to be speaking about Brenda Wong Aoki at the National Asian American conference subtitled "Probing the Past, Living the Present, and Shaping the Future." Aoki, who has received numerous awards for her artistry including a Rockefeller Foundation grant in 1992, and who prefers the title of storyteller to that of performance artist has created *The Queen's Garden* which does exactly what this conference urges us to do, i.e. probe the past, live the present, and shape the future.

The vast majority of twentieth century Asian American writers have focused on their ancestral links to Asia, their daily, often frustrating, struggles living in the United States and speaking a second language, and their fears for the future. In *The Queen's Garden*, Aoki's autobiographical *nisei* character, Brenda, differs from characters of other Asian American writers in that she was born in southern California and, portrayed as a teenager in this work, made no pretense of knowing anything about Japan or China, or for that matter, Scotland or Spain, all lands of her ancestors. Additionally, Aoki clearly sympathizes with the wide variety of people (all of whom she "plays" in this one-person performance) who populate Brenda's freeway-bounded turf, which she defines as "between the 710, the 405, the oil fields and the water flood control," in Long Beach California in the mid-1960s. Whereas Jade Snow Wong, Amy Tan, Maxine Hong Kingston and Gish Jen all connect their plots to a specific ancestor or relative in Asia, Aoki interrogates existence on today's multiethnic America. Indeed, Brenda's friends are not only from various cultures but also represent the shadier economic side of Los Angeles County. Thus, while her stated borders are all on California soil, the implications of Aoki's current work while solidly linked to Asia, are more universal and therefore, more relevant to Midwesterners who rarely have the opportunity to see performance art or Asian American artists in general.

The Queen's Garden begins with the soft drumming, bass plucking and then mellow, but solemn saxophone moaning of Aoki's musical accompanists, Mark Izu and Joseph Perez.[1] This instrumental prelude is reminiscent of Japanese *noh* drama (which Aoki has studied extensively) where flutes and drums heighten the encounters that the troubled spirit (Brenda) has with the priest or bystander (the Queen). Similarly, *kyogen* theater, in which Aoki is also trained, has a role to play in *The Queen's Garden*. Dealing with everyday situations in a comical fashion, employing no special effects or masks, and using mime and vocalization, *kyogen* is, according to Don Kenny, "completely dependent for its dramatic effect upon the concentration skill of the actor,"[2] or actress in this case. With her words and actions and with lighting directed by Jose Lopez, Aoki has meshed the harsh street reality of Long Beach with the vitality and beauty of youth and music. In this way, Aoki has incorporated the Asian theatrical tradition with her own coming of age in the United States, a monumental tack which can not be accomplished without considerable difficulty.

The reasons for her difficulties are partially due to the complexity of her subject matter and partially due to the medium itself. By inviting the audience into the tough streets, Aoki must solve the problems of recreating this reality while maintaining artistic tension in the work. Furthermore, as she cross-examines the "model minority" role that the media would have us believe represents all Asians, Aoki simply has too much to say in an hour of stage time. In her attempt to show the "other" side of the model minority, Aoki sometimes loses her way.

Still another issue that Aoki tackles is the role of Asian American parents in the lives of their children. While most other Asian American writers focus on the parents, *The Queen's Garden* stresses the individual's struggle to grow in the United States. Nonetheless, the drive to do one's best to make one's parents proud surface when Brenda is chosen to attended the gifted class as a high school student in 1968. Even though she makes fun of the "f.o.b.—fresh off the boat" Vietnamese girl in her class, Aoki too applies herself and becomes the model student. Throughout her high school career she remains torn between doing well at school and hanging out with the Islanders, the local gang members who taught her how to be cool and who introduces her to the Queen, a stately Hawaiian of royal heritage, who is the aunt of Brenda's first love, Kali. While Brenda allows herself to be a weekend Westside warrior with the Islanders for a while, she finally admits to herself that she "will not be a fat mama in a mumu waiting for a welfare check" for the rest of her life.

Taking advantage of her academic success, Brenda uses the Ethnic Opportunity Program to leave the community and go to college. Upon her college graduation, she returns to teach at her high school alma mater. The American dream is complete! She now asks her students to call her by her first name, just as her high school teacher, Judy, had told her gifted class to do. Brenda's previously urban guerilla stance takes a beating here: whether Brenda has been co-opted or reformed by the system or whether this is an artist flaw in the performance depends on the observer's point of view.

Clearly, Aoki portrays Brenda as a young woman wooed by American society, which rewards those who succeed in understanding its game. As autobiography, this is acceptable and legitimate, but in a performance the confusion Aoki creates in the second half of the work is excessive. By playing all the characters herself, Aoki must reproduce the voices, actions, mannerisms and personalities of more than a dozen characters— Asian Americans, Hawaiians, Latinos and Caucasians. Due to the number of characters portrayed during her college and teaching years, some of the characters lose their distinctness and, thus, when Kali and Smoke, two Islander hoods from early days, reappear in Brenda's life after "four years, three months and twenty six days," the audience struggles to recall what Smoke had done to incur Kali's wrath. Thus, while the musical accompaniment at this point in the work subtly suggests that, as in *noh* drama, the ancestors and/or relatives are ill-at-ease with their progeny's current actions and foreshadows evil designs, Aoki's own performance is weak here.

Having tasted the American dream, Brenda leaves her family and friends and moves to San Francisco, renting an apartment in Haight Ashbury and teaching at a pre-school. Another five years of self-imposed exile pass; all that she has left of her own nuclear family is a "blue teacup—and then that broke." True, she has made her own identity, but she has also lost a lot so when her old pals ask her to come back down south for a visit, she goes but what she finds shatters what good memories or illusions she had. The Islander guys now have "bellies hanging over their belts" and AK-47s to protect their turf and drug deals. In the Queen's garden, on a dark moonless night, where "red, red roses, big as cabbages" grow, Brenda realizes that all the Islanders "find it easy to die but harder to live." In a senseless shoot-out, numerous gang members as well as the Queen, who was trying to reconcile the feuding gangs with her flowers, die. Nevertheless, Brenda does not become totally despondent. The performance ends with her return visit to the Queen's garden years later. She comments, "The garden was choked with weeds, and yet still some roses bloom every year."

For Brenda Wong Aoki, there is hope for the Asian American. She populates the stage with both male and female voices, songs and gesture of various ethnic groups who inhabit southern California, and has given us a prototype of that which will be developed on stage as more culturally sensitive performances renovate existing forms and frameworks of contemporary American literature, theater and performance art. While at least one critic has commented that Aoki's desire to entertain muddles her ability to send a message,[3] *The Queen's Garden* is a work of considerable depth and value. Aoki's background is *noh* and *kyogen* art, and her previous performance in both Los Angeles and the Bay area undoubtedly led her to develop issues from her personal experience in this work. We are in a renaissance of American literature, and it is the minority cultural artists whose works are the models that need to be studied and appreciated. As one of the Islanders states near the end of the performance, "Cut the source, destroy the self." *The Queen's Garden* demonstrates how separating oneself from one's heritage is detrimental to the individual as well as the community. As an adult, Aoki has probed into Asia's theatrical past, incorporating elements of *kyogen* and *noh* drama for her current work as well as investigating her personal history to present us with her understanding of the facts of life on the streets of contemporary urban America. Though not without weaknesses, *The Queen Garden*'s introspection gives us all hope for the future.

Notes

1. *The Queen's Garden* performance discussed in this article was performed at the University of Wisconsin-Madison on October 23, 1992.

2. Don Kenny, *Discover Japan: Words, Customs and Concepts* (New York: Kodansha International Ltd., 1983) Vol. 2, 155.

3. Amit Bhargava, "Brenda Wong Aoki: One Woman('s) Show," in *Bamboo Bridges,* Vol. V, n. 1, February 1993: 2.

20

Prime Time's Hidden Agenda

The Anti-Asian Bias of American Television, 1993

David Piehl and Richard Ruppel

Most American television viewers would agree that Asians and references to Asia are, at best, portrayed infrequently on the three national television networks. Consequently, we were not surprised when our study of one week of prime time television confirmed that Asians and Asian references were, indeed, grossly under-represented. What we did find surprising, however, and disturbing, was that virtually every reference to Asia and Asians, whether trivial or significant, drew upon derogatory stereotypes. We saw references to martial arts, ancient Asian traditions, Chinese food, and contemporary competition with Asian nations, and each was tendered in a formulaic way. Yet we saw no positive references to the truly contemporary culture and people of Asia.

Beginning January 10, 1993, we videotaped seven consecutive nights of prime time programming on CBS, NBC and ABC—(7-10 p.m., CST)—a total of 63 hours. We then viewed the tapes closely, looking for Asian (or Asian American) actors[1] and Asian references. We categorized roles of the Asian actors as either "primary" or "secondary," defining "primary characters" as those characters who had names, who had significant air time, and who were significant to the plot. We included as an "Asian reference" any audible or visual allusion to the people of the Far East or its location. These might have been geographical, linguistic, cultural, or tangible (food, clothing, products, etc.)

Quota appearances

Of the 26 programs broadcast by ABC during the week, no Asian actor appeared on 54 percent of the network's schedule. No Asians appeared on

179

61 percent of NBC's 23 programs, and none on 65 percent of CBS's offerings.

The flip side of those statistics, obviously, reveals that Asians did appear on forty percent of the networks' programs. This seems to suggest that they had a significant presence. But the vast majority of these actors made what we categorized as "quota appearances": appearances of Asians in crowds or as passers-by on streets which gave the viewer a sense of a heterogeneous society. Examples of Asians in Quota Appearances that were observed during the week included patrons in a restaurant, a member of the production crew working behind stage at a television station, and a man within a group of people being led by a realtor through a house that was for sale.

The median length of time these characters appeared on screen was three seconds, and we often had to review a tape several times to decide whether an actor making a quota appearance was in fact Asian. We believe that the average viewer would fail to notice the large majority of the Asians portrayed since most were unimportant to the plot, were seen only as members of group scenes, and were on the screen for such short amounts of time.

Major Asian or Asian American characters

During the week of programming we observed over five hundred major characters; only four were played by Asian or Asian American actors. Two were on what might be categorized, generally, as "real life" shows. The first was an heroic policeman on "Top Cops" (CBS). The story line of the program had a police officer interrupting a robbery in-progress. The policeman, an Asian American, was shot five times, yet he fought off his attacker, shot him, and pursued the other young men involved in the robbery. The real policeman narrated the action, but his part was played by an Asian actor. Oddly, the actor spoke accented English; the real policeman did not.

The second major Asian character appeared in "Date Line," a news-magazine show on CBS. One segment of the show—called "The Gift of a Smile"—involved American doctors who perform pro bono plastic surgery on indigent patients all over the world. A major portion of the show concerned their work in the Philippines.

A third character was Lucas, an Asian American[2] orphan, claiming to be the son of the title character of "Raven," a high-action (and high violence) drama on CBS. This episode did not provide much background information, so we never learned how Raven fathered an Amerasian child, but Lucas—about 14 years old—was spotted by a middle-man who attempted to sell him, literally, to Raven as his lost son. The middle-man was killed by thugs, the boy saw the murder, and the thugs attempted to track Lucas down and kill him. Raven's job was also unspecified in this episode, but he was a martial arts expert and a devotee of Eastern culture. He was shown meditating in a shrine within his house, and he attempted to teach Lucas using references to a traditional East; he told the boy that the house he worked on with him during the episode should grow "like a Japanese garden."

The last major Asian character was the most interesting. The actor Cary-Hiroyuki Tagawa played the alien "Zilon" on CBS's "Space Rangers." The show, which stole fairly blatantly from both the *Alien* and *Star Wars* films, was set, like *Alien*, in some gritty, technologically advanced but socially regressive future. The leading character was the handsome commander of a small group of soldier-technicians. Zilon was one of his men, but he did not live on the base with the others. Before the episode's mission, the commander visited Zilon to ask his help. Zilon was in some outdoor temple, adopting a worshipful position with his back turned. When he faced the commander, the viewer could see that he was not human. In fact, he was presented as a frightening and bestial figure throughout the episode. His voice was preternaturally resonant; he had telepathic powers, and even the other members of the crew feared him. When the commandos confronted the Banshees, monsters patterned after the Aliens in the *Alien* films, Zilon killed one with a ceremonial knife and then gave a wolfish howl of victory. At the end, he was shown growling, eating the severed arm of one of the monsters.

Zilon reveals the underside of American attitudes toward Asians. As a practitioner of a generic-Asian religion and generic-Asian martial arts, and as an Asian actor, his Far Easternness was heavily and pointedly stressed. At the same time, he was not human; he was the terrifying Other, half-man, half-monster. While the humans had a good deal of trouble killing the Banshees even with their advanced weaponry, Zilon killed one by himself, with only his ceremonial knife. The subtext of the entire episode was that it took a monster to kill a monster.

Because there were so few Asian and Asian American characters, the four characters that *were* represented, and especially the fictional characters, took on considerable significance, for they represent a glimpse of the American, imaginative vision of Asians. One, Lucas on the "Raven" episode, was an adolescent victim, a needy orphan who, understandably, hoped to pass himself off as the son of a relatively well-off, respected, and powerful American. The American became the boy's mentor, teaching him about life and about how to fight and defend himself, and then, at the show's conclusion, placing him with a wealthy American family for adoption. The white American was even in a position to teach the boy about his Asian past, from a quasi-Asian perspective. This relationship places Asians very clearly in a safe, dependent, and subordinate relationship with Americans.

The presentation of Lucas and Zilon appears to reflect a deep insecurity within American culture in its confrontation with the Far East. The boy represents a kind of fantasy wish fulfillment, where Americans can feel themselves to be in a dominating, paternalistic relationship with Asia. Zilon represents the other side of the same coin. The East is terrifyingly powerful, terrifyingly "Other" and strange. Superficially, of course, like Zilon, many Asians are our allies. But they remain fearful, potentially overwhelming foes. And their humanity is suspect.

Asian references

Along with the appearances of Asian actors we tabulated all references to Asia. Most fell into four categories: references to food, martial arts, a mysterious, traditional past, and contemporary competition.

Several of the shows we monitored contained relatively light-hearted references to economic competition with the nations of Asia. In two cases ("Evening Shade" on CBS and "Perry Mason" on NBC), groups of men joked about or simply noted Japanese American competition for the American car market. In a third, a foolish American senator on CBS's "Hearts' Afire" made jokes about other forms of competition, both in the production of consumer goods (hand woven toupees from Korea) that compete successfully within the American market, and in Olympic swimming. Speaking of their successes in swimming during the '92 Olympic Games, the senator wonders how the Chinese could have won so many medals: "There must be six pools in their entire country!" "Of course," he adds, "they are fairly tiny. Perhaps they can work out in wading pools."

According to the western stereotype, Asians are typically adept at martial arts, a belief television regularly reinforces. During our viewing week, the largest number of Asians that appeared together was on "America's Funniest Home Videos." The clip, twenty seconds long, showed a dozen Asian men preparing to begin a kick-boxing fight. The scene showed one of the fighters being accidentally kicked in the face by his own manager, who had been attempting to demonstrate a particular kick.

Chinese food is a very common Asian reference. A number of characters were shown eating Chinese food or contemplating ordering it. On ABC's "Jack's Place" a local newspaper sends its food editor to Jack's to do a restaurant review. After finishing her dinner, she invites Jack up to her apartment. When he arrived the following evening, he found that she had ordered her favorite food—Chinese, especially, she noted, "the spicy stuff" which "enhances digestion" and "increases memory." References to Asian food also occurred on "Coach" and "The Commish" on ABC, and on "Homicide" and "Law and Order" on NBC. On Friday night, the stars from ABC's "Step by Step" were shown, chopsticks in hand and sitting on the floor, eating and joking about Chinese food as they promoted the network's up-coming situation comedies.

The final and most frequent Asian reference was to a frozen past. Other than the references to competition, there were no references to a contemporary Far East, to a technologically advanced region that boasts, especially in Japan, of a high standard of living, social peace, and cohesion. Instead, the references depicted a "timeless" East, a place and people that are mystical—curiosities that need not be taken seriously. We saw statuettes of Buddha, ceramic Japanese temples as knickknacks, a number of Japanese gardens, and a Caucasian magician dressed in traditional Chinese garb. On "Colombo" (ABC), we saw the director of an American think-tank explain the ancient Chinese method of divining the future by reading sticks. The East, in these references, is both quaint and non-threatening.

The time frame of these representations of an East frozen in some unchanging past has an end-point, of course, and that end-point is World War II. The representation of Japan and the Japanese during that war was the most ominous reference we noted, ominous because, like so many stereotypes, it was presented without intentional vilification. During "20/20" (ABC), Hugh Downs presented the story concerning a new American pastime for the affluent. For $4,000, people play out their fantasies of being fighter pilots. But, instead of sitting in front of computer screens playing a simulation, a new California business allows them to fly actual fighter planes. These planes are equipped with laser light beams that can be aimed and shot at the "enemy"; smoke streams from the plane after a "hit." To enhance the fantasy for the television audience the ABC producer included footage from a John Wayne movie during which Japanese pilots were shot out of the sky. By skillfully editing together the tape of Hugh Downs piloting one of the planes with the film of John Wayne flying his, the producer made it appear that Downs was experiencing the thrill of the hunt. The hunted, in this case, were Japanese pilots.

In the "20/20" story, the Japanese were represented as both evil and ferocious, and the network's decision to resurrect this image as an appropriate target for wealthy, contemporary Americans in search of realistic fighter-pilot experiences reflects the view that Japan is still an enemy, still an adversary with which we are still in mortal combat. The field of competition, however, is obviously no longer the battlefields of a world war. The new competition occurs on the economic battlefield.

Conclusion

The most important conclusion we can gain from our study is that Asians and Asia are extraordinarily under-represented on American network television. Of the hundreds of major characters we saw during 63 hours of viewing, only one Asian was sure to be a continuing character in future weeks, and he was Zilon, the super subhuman on "Space Rangers." Other references were almost equally scarce, and they could be explained away as rather inconsequential examples of sloppy and careless thinking on the part of television's creators. For it is much easier to represent Asia in traditional and stereotypical ways than it is to try, in the superficial medium of network television, to come to grips with the complex, contemporary reality of the many nations and peoples of Asia. But we may also conclude that these references have a more subterranean source, one that should give us cause for concern. The Asian characters and references we saw may also be categorized as culturally subconscious attempts to control and dominate the Far East, or as direct references, either light-hearted or serious, to ferocious competition with a sometimes dangerous, even frightening foe.

Significance

The argument may be offered that the small number of Asians appearing on American network television simply reflects the relatively small number of Asian Americans within the American population.[3] We feel, however, the ramifications of television programming on the viewing public exceed a mere reflection of a perceived reality.[4] In fact, television's perceived reality, however misleading, too often becomes the viewers' actual reality. That is especially true now that the amount of television viewing is reaching unprecedented levels. Children spend more time attending to a mediated teacher of societal "reality" than they spend before a human one in the classroom. Virtually all social scientists have acknowledged that attitudes, values, and behavior may be developed, at least in part, through observational learning.[5] The observational learning concerning Asians and Asian Americans acquired by viewers watching prime time network television presents a distorted reality, at best, and, at worst, an incitement to bigotry. There is a large body of communication research, called Agenda-Setting research, that postulates that the media function as highly selective observers of the world's events. Such selective attention results in an incomplete, sometimes biased sense of reality on the part of the audience. The audience assumes that the media pay attention to things that make a difference in society, to things of consequence. Furthermore, the audience also believes the reverse is true: the subjects that are not covered by the media are of no consequence. Combining that view with the findings of our survey leads to the inevitable conclusion that Asia and Asian people make little difference in contemporary life, that they are of little consequence.

Since American children spend so much time in front of the television set accepting its content as reality, it is imperative that we understand the lesson they are receiving. We believe that lesson, as it concerns Asians and Asia, is inexorably negative.

Notes

1. For our log, we defined "Asian" as someone with ethnic origins in the Far East: China, Southeast Asia, Japan, Korea, Indonesia, or the Pacific Islands.

2. His mother was Asian, his father Anglo-American.

3. The 1990 census estimated that one in 33 Americans were of Asian descent, U.S. Census Bureau.

4. Television writers and producers invariably choose from the multitude of possibilities, only a small number of subjects with which to concern themselves. By doing so they create the medium's view of reality. Of course, it is not reality, it is a perceived reality.

5. See *Milestones in Mass Communications Research*, 2nd ed., Shearon A. Lowery and Melvin L. DeFleur, especially chapter 13: "The Agenda-Setting Function of the Press: Telling Us What to Think About," 327-352. (White Plains, NY: Longman, Inc. 1988).

21

The Asian American Renaissance in Independent Cinema and Valerie Soe's *New Year*

Carole Gerster

While Asian Americans have been independently producing films for some thirty years, the number and quality of short narratives and documentaries produced within the last decade merit recognition as an Asian American Renaissance in independent cinema. This renaissance is an extraordinary rebirth of learning—a re-visioning of history and of self. The films are various in subject matter and scope, ranging from Authur Dong's 1982 portrayal of his mother as one representative Chinese immigrant woman, in *Sewing Woman*, to Janice Tanaka's 1992 examination of the impact of internment secrecies on generations of Japanese Americans, in *Who's Going to Pay for These Donuts, Anyway?* Even in their variety these films share common ground: they reflect the experiences and concerns of specific Asian American communities and offer important counterpoints to mainstream Hollywood cinema. Understanding this renaissance provides a context with which to read uniquely individual films, such as Valerie Soe's *New Year*, even as reading this one film helps us to understand better the film renaissance of which it is a part.

Stressing the need for an autonomous Asian American cinema, film critic and filmmaker Renee Tajima explains important differences between Hollywood and independent films. "In recent years," she points out, Hollywood films "have undergone spectacular technical innovations. But whereas form has leaped toward the year 2000, it seems that content still straddles the turn of the last century… And the only real signs of life are stirring far away from Hollywood in the cutting rooms owned and operated by Asian America's independent producers."[1] As Tajima suggests, the content and form of Asian American cinema differs significantly from Hollywood films. In content, this independent cinema echoes the themes, concerns, and experiences reflected in Asian American literature. In form, the new film language of Asian American cinema is most often experimentally, rather than technically, innovative and consistently privileges a personal perspective, often juxtaposed against Hollywood's stereotypical images. In experimental film, the filmmaker is the inventor of the form and attempts to provide new ways of seeing, of knowing, to create a relationship between the spectator and the film different from mainstream Hollywood. Asian American cinema is designed to engage rather than to pacify passive viewers with stereotyped images and simple answers. With its experimental form and personal content, Asian American cinema seeks to avoid Hollywood imitation and assimilation and to create an Asian American identity—with voices and stories—of its own.

One common theme dramatically expressed in both literature and film is the need for an Asian American cinema that features Asian Americans. In Amy Tan's 1989 novel *The Joy Luck Club*, a the mother wants her nine-year-old daughter to become a Chinese Shirley Temple, to look and act like the blonde curly-top child movie star of the 1930s. Mother and daughter, Tan writes, would "watch Shirley's old movies on TV as though they were training films."[2] Sharon Jue's 1989 short (17 minute) film, with the revealing title *My Mother Thought She Was Audrey Hepburn*, also questions an older generation's reliance on Hollywood images for notions of the self. There has been, both Tan and Jue suggest, a lack of Asian Americans on film, and thus a lack of Asian American role models. As filmmaker Loni Ding points out, "the subtext of media absence is that the absent group 'doesn't count,' or is somehow unacceptable." Ding offers the solution adopted by both Tan and Jue: "For the problem of absence, the main work is to create presence" through "celebrations of ordinary people and celebrations of particular communities."[3] Celebrating ordinary people, and taking seriously the idea of featuring Asian Americans on film, Valerie Soe's 1986 short (1 and 1/2 minute) film, with the humorously ironic title *All Orientals Look the Same*, focuses on features. In just one and one-half minutes, dozens of faces appear on the screen to reveal dozens of distinct looks.

Other writers and filmmakers address the problems of Asian American women internalizing white standards of beauty and imitating the behavior and attitudes of cinematic stereotypes. Nellie Wong's poem "When I Was Growing Up" voices the perspective of a Chinese American woman looking back at her formative childhood years to recall that she "once longed to be white" and "began to wear imaginary pale skin," in part because when she went to the movies she saw "blonde movie stars

[and] white skin" presented as "desirable." Here Wong notes how exclusionary white standards of beauty have long dominated Hollywood films and have permeated the imaginations of Asian American viewers. As do a number of writers and filmmakers, Wong also criticizes the stereotype of the sexually exotic Asian American woman, prototypically characterized in *The World of Suzie Wong*, where Suzie is a Hong Kong prostitute with a white American lover. Wong's poem suggests that exotic Suzie Wong types in Hollywood cinema have offered only an unrealistic stereotype and portrayed white men as those most worth pleasing: "When I was growing up," her poem continues, "and a white man wanted/ to take me out, I thought I was special,/ an exotic gardenia anxious to fit/ the stereotype of an oriental chick."[4]

Independently made films rearticulate the sentiments in Wong's poem. Deborah Gee's 1988 documentary *Slaying the Dragon* includes clips from a dozen or more Hollywood films—including *The Thief of Bagdad* from 1924, *Dragon Seed* from 1944 (featuring Katherine Hepburn playing the Asian protagonist with adhesive tape over her eyes), *Sayonara* from 1957, *The World of Suzie Wong* from 1960, and *Year of the Dragon* from 1986 (featuring an American Suzie Wong as the love interest)—to document Hollywood's unreal standards of beauty and repeated stereotypes of Asian American women: the evil Dragon Lady, the subservient *geisha* girl and the seductively exotic Suzie Wong. Like Wong, Gee shows the detrimental effects these standards and stereotypes have on actual Asian American women, including newscaster Connie Chung, who are expected to replicate them. Helen Lee's 1990 short narrative film *Sally's Beauty Spot* also includes fragments from *The World of Suzie Wong*, to typify the lotus blossom (exotic love interest for a white man) stereotype her Chinese Canadian protagonist (played by Lee's real-life sister) must confront. In addition, Sally sees her dark-skin mole as emblematic of her color. She first tries to scrub it off, then sees it as a beauty spot. Reminiscent of the experience chronicled in Nellie Wong's poem, Sally must learn to see herself for herself, as counter example to Hollywood images of female worth and female beauty. In like manner, Pamela Tom's 1991 film *Two Lies* focuses on a recently divorced Chinese American who undergoes plastic surgery to make her eyes rounder. The action initiates intergenerational conflicts about beauty, conformity and Asian American identity. Each of these films takes on the formidable revisionary tasks of confronting western standards of beauty, of imagining Asian American women outside the mold of Hollywood stereotypes, and of depicting Asian American women in the process of redefining themselves. Wayne Wang's 1987 *Dim Sum Take-Out*, uses 12 minutes of out-takes from Wang's 1985 feature film *Dim Sum* to counter stereotypes about Asian American women. Here, five Chinese American women literally speak for themselves to reveal their personal feelings about independence, sexuality and ethnicity.

Still other writers and filmmakers advocate dismissing the stereotypes that Hollywood continues to feed the public imagination, by purposefully juxtaposing them against actual people and real families. Japanese American poet and author David Mura recognizes the power of Hollywood to define public images of Asian Americans, and stresses the need for films that undermine stereotypes. Mura quotes from Philip Kan Gotanda's play *Yankee Dawg You Die*: stereotypes can "kill the right of some Asian American child to be treated as a human being, to walk through the schoolyard and not be called a 'Chinaman gook' by some taunting kids who just saw the last Rambo film."[5]

Independent filmmakers agree. Unfortunately, Hollywood's portrayal of Asian as enemy, as other, or as scapegoat did not begin or end with Rambo as "all"-American hero, as Renee Tajima and Christine Choy's 1990 film *Yellow Tale Blues: Two American Families* demonstrates. *Yellow Tale Blues* includes clips from Hollywood movies—from a 1910 silent film to the 1961 *Breakfast at Tiffany's*—disclosing Hollywood's long history of creating disparaging images of Asians. But *Yellow Tale Blues* also juxtaposes these too familiar images with portraits of actual families: the Tajimas and the Choys. The uniquely personal replaces the stereotypical as we hear the differing histories and see the individual identities of the two filmmakers' own families. In a similar manner, Rea Tajiri's 1991 experimental documentary *History and Memory* juxtaposes Hollywood images of Japanese Americans and World War II propaganda with stories from the videomaker's own family, to remember the story and the people Hollywood chose to ignore. Arthur Dong's 1989 *Forbidden City*, about Asian American singing and dancing talents the equivalent of Frank Sinatra and Fred Astaire by supposed nonsinging and nondancing Asians, is yet another example of a film that takes film viewers behind the scenes and allows real people to speak (and perform) for themselves. The often revived Yellow Peril stereotype is effectively dismissed in Christine Choy and Renee Tajima's 1988 film *Who Killed Vincent Chin*, which confronts a Caucasian autoworker's confusion of Japanese and Chinese Americans, and the mistaken idea that Asian Americans in general are part of a Japanese threat to the car manufacturing industry in America. This film documents real anti-Asian scapegoating and violence, but it also includes interviews with Vincent Chin's mother, who discusses her son as her son. These filmmakers effectively follow the filmmaking method Loni

Ding describes as her "preferred approach," which is "to displace stereotypes by creating vital images of Asian Americans as real human beings, with individual faces, voices, and personal histories that we come to know and care about."[6]

Authors and filmmakers are also united in the task of constructing Asian American histories from multi-dimensional Asian American perspectives, to document the neglected or untold stories of the past as well as the realities of the present. Personal stories of Japanese internment alone offer a variety of perspectives. In Dwight Okita's poem "In Response to Executive Order 9066: ALL AMERICANS OF JAPANESE DESCENT MUST REPORT TO RELOCATION CENTERS," a fourteen-year-old school girl is confronted with the accusation "You're trying to start a war."[7] In John Okada's 1957 novel *No No Boy*, Ichiro refuses to leave his family in internment imprisonment to join the U. S. Army in battle against the Japanese and, after two years in prison, must try to reconstruct his life in a country still filled with anti-Japanese feelings. Jeanne Wakatsuki Houston's 1973 *Farewell to Manzanar*, a personal remembrance of evacuation, relocation, and return, became a film of the same title. What Wakatsuki Houston says of her novel is true of internment films in general: "It is a story, or a web of stories—my own, my father's, my family's—tracing a few paths, out of the multitude of paths that led up to and away from the experience of internment."[8] Loni Ding's 1984 film *Nisei Soldier: Standard Bearer for an Exiled People* tells the story of the moral dilemmas facing second generation (American born) Japanese American men who did enlist in the army during World War II even as their families were incarcerated in camps. Ding's film includes old newsreels and combat footage to document the battles these soldiers fought against fascism on foreign land and against prejudice at home. Immigration histories are also remembered and documented. Spencer Nakasako's 1984 film *Talking History* combines varying oral histories of immigration with historical footage of Japanese, Chinese, Korean, Filipino, and Laotian women. And the new immigrant experience is recorded in Rita LaDoux's 1983 film *Great Branches, New Roots: The Hmong Family*, which examines the lives of Hmong refugees trying to establish roots and facing such problems as lack of education, underemployment, shifting traditions, and changing cultural roles.

Family histories combining fiction and reality offer new avenues of self-discovery and cultural identity for both authors and filmmakers. Maxine Hong Kingston's 1976 novel *The Woman Warrior* is the narrator's (and Kingston's) attempt to locate the self as a Chinese American, within her mother's memories of a distant Chinese past and her own more immediate American experiences. Although diversity characterizes films by Asian Americans, one common thread is a self-conscious attempt to explore the tensions between hyphenated worlds and to forge viable Asian American identities. Mira Nair's 1982 *So Far From India* is the film portrait of a family literally split between the worlds of India and America, and of the immigrant husband's journey back to India to visit his wife and to confront their differing expectations for each other. Offering another journey of self-discovery, Loni Ding's 1987 *Island of Secret Memories* portrays an eleven-year-old boy's visit to Angel Island, where his grandfather was among those who were detained for years before being allowed to enter the country via the "Golden Gate." The boy imagines his grandfather's bed and personal items, including a pair of spectacles, which the boy tries on in order to "see" his history through his grandfather's eyes, a usable history of protest and resistance to unjust detention. Film spectators also see immigrant detention in a new way, as a personal story: the detention of a grandfather.

Asian American filmmaking is clearly experiencing a renaissance, evidenced by the number, variety, and quality of these recent films. One film in particular, however, might best serve to illustrate the larger renaissance of which it is a part. Valerie Soe's 1987 20-minute video *New Year: Part I and Part II* [9] is representative by virtue of its being unrepresentative. Asian American films are eclectic. It is also representative in that it is both a short narrative and a documentary, it addresses several concerns common to Asian American cinema, and it has an engaging experimental film style.

Rather than technically innovative (read "high production costs" here), Soe's film is experimentally innovative. It is obvious that it wasn't done by a large, impersonal production staff; instead, it has a home-made, personal quality. A film divided into two distinct parts, the first half is an autobiographical narrative presented in the form of storybook drawings. Soe's hand and arm visible on camera filling in the blank spaces of her story, and with Soe's off-camera voice-over delivers the narrative. Cinematic form helps create meaning, and we are visually invited to see this part of the film as a personal history, where the presence of the filmmaker is important. Rather than film someone else, or have someone else film her, Soe uses storybook drawings to signify that all media images are mediated, are images subjectively chosen and combined, rather than objectively recorded, to form a version of reality. A conventional film technique is to mask the subjectivity of the filmmaker, to offer the pretense of objectivity by making the filmmaker invisible. Conversely, Soe fills in the blanks of her story to let us know that she is the mediator here—visibly in charge of creating her own image. As she fills in and quite literally puts herself in the pictures, she exercises control of the creative process; as she narrates her own story in a first-person voice, hers is the undisguised controlling voice.

The personal perspective in Soe's film is important. Although it takes the unique form of storybook drawings, this personal point of view is representative of Asian American cinema at large, which most often takes the form of a personal history: a personal history of internment, of immigration, of seeking one's heritage. Unlike Hollywood films, which typically ignore or blur distinctions between Asian Americans, Soe's film does not attempt to represent *the* Asian American experience or point of view, or *the* Chinese American experience or point of view, or even *the* fourth-generation Chinese American experience or point of view. The first half of Soe's film is avowedly autobiographical. It is about her own childhood as a fourth-generation Chinese American living in one part of America, in one particular neighborhood, during one year in her life, told by herself, in her own voice, as she remembers it years later. Typical of Asian American cinema that attempts to record events ranging from the private to the historic, Soe's unique perspective on Chinese-American life purposefully leaves room for views other and different from her own and, in so doing, explicitly and effectively disavows and disallows stereotyping.

Soe also deconstructs specific stereotypes of various kinds. Stereotypical traits are dismissed when, Soe tells us she didn't particularly like Chinese food, and they are doubly dismissed when she tells us she didn't like it because her parents "made terrible rice." Stereotypical features are dismissed when, Soe tells us that the typical Valentine cards she got had faces drawn with buck teeth and slanty eyes, and the words "AH SO." Soe's drawing of this stereotyped Valentine-card face is very much unlike her drawings of herself. Soe also uses an experimental technique to dismiss stereotyped features. When, during the course of narrating her life through storybook drawings, the face of an actual Chinese American appears but is distorted because this person is pulling on her eyes and nose to make her features look like the Valentine-card face, we see how it is in fact a contorted and distorted idea of what a Chinese American really looks like, and we see what it is like to have one's life disrupted with a distorted image. Making a face at the camera allows Soe to re-present from her perspective all those distorted faces directed at her, and is a public gesture that allows her to make a face back. Soe's countering in-your-face humor contorts stereotyped ideas about straight-laced model minority Asian Americans.

Soe's narrative is twice interrupted with intertitles of child (and child-ish) nonsense rhymes: "Ching Chong Chinaman/ Sitting on a Fence/ Trying to Make a/ Dollar out of Five Cents" and "Chinese, Japanese, Dirty Knees/ Look at These." Like the distorted face, these intertitles allow us to see the discrimination Soe experienced as a child. Soe's storybook narrative is appropriate for the story of a child. It also suggests the need to go back to basics, to school ourselves on the fundamental, primary realities of Chinese American life. The childhood taunts remind us how nonsensical anti-Asian sentiments are, and that they begin very early in life.

In Soe's film the larger question of "What does it mean to be Asian American?" becomes the scaled-down, personal question "What did it mean to be a fourth-generation Chinese American in the San Francisco area of California in grade school?" The question is neither small nor trivial. In seeking her own cultural identity, Soe recognizes her links with tradition: Within her story she visits her grandmother, writes a card to her Ma-Ma (her grandmother) as a class assignment, and uses her grandmother's Lion Dance drum and dragon head for a Chinese New Year show-and-tell day at school. Outside the story proper, at film's end, in the place where cinematic convention places the film credits—the long lists of persons responsible for a film—Soe simply writes "To Ma-Ma © 1987." This 1987 memory of Soe's childhood is largely a memory of her grandmother.

Soe's film also takes account of her dual identity as a Chinese-hyphen-American. At her grandmother's, she likes to eat Bird's Nest and Wintermellon soup. In Chinatown, she enjoys eight-course Chinese dinners. At home she can't remember the Chinese words her parents try to teach her and she likes to eat spaghetti, fried chicken and tacos. At school, she writes "To Grandmother" on a card, but at home she changes it to read "To Ma-Ma." "I didn't want to be different," she says. She feels uncomfortable when her Caucasian teacher asks her to explain Chinese New Year during show and tell. But her apprehensions turn to self-pride when all her classmates want to pretend to be in the Chinatown parade, with her Ma-Ma's drum and dragon's head, and when they all enjoy the Chinese treats of candied coconut and melon slices that no one in the Soe family liked. What is "Chinese" and what is "American" become uniquely intertwined in Soe's memory.

The first part of Soe's film ends with another experimental technique. Soe's memory of herself, in the midst of celebrating Chinese New Year with her Caucasian schoolmates, comes to life as her black and white drawing of herself in her sequined red jacket and trousers becomes a color photograph. This moment of self-pride in being a Chinese American is realized in film, as Soe appears for the only time in a positive image created (photographed) by someone else. Her chosen image of herself on film depicts both her own pride in her cultural heritage and its recognition of worth by others. This image, like the rest of Soe's uniquely depicted personal memory, is filmed in opposition to mainstream Hollywood strategies and stereotypes. The first half of the film shows Soe in the process of imagining herself. It is first; it is primary; it is the most important, and it colors all that follows. Her memory serves as background against what we see in the second half of the film. The film as a whole moves from how Soe imagines herself to how Hollywood has imaged Asians and Asian Americans. The film juxtaposes imaging the complexity of one individual Chinese American child's identity with Hollywood's simplistic, cartoonish representations of all Asians.

The images that fill the screen in the Part II compilation documentary are not an extension of Soe's story; they are someone else's story. Beyond grade school, Soe's life has not yet been given media treatment; her story is unfinished. What has taken its place are the stereotyped images on TV and movie screens. Soe uses a series of five intertitles to label the stereotypes as she documents them. We read and see media images of "Japs, Slopes, and Gooks," "Fortune Cookie Philosophers," "The World Wide Empire of Evil," "Geisha Girls and Dragon Ladies," and "Masters of Kung Fu." Each of these segments about stereotypes shows caricatured Asians from a wide range of popular culture artifacts: from feature films, old newsreels seen in theatres before television, television shows, movie advertisements and comic books. The scenes and caricatures are shuffled, repeated, and run together without identification, indicating that they are recycled stereotypes with interchangeable parts. Like many Asian American films, Soe's includes numerous clips from Hollywood films, but rather than open her film with these misconceived images, or juxtapose them with real people throughout, Soe places them all at the end. She invites viewers to confront their own misconceptions, and to see where these misconceptions originated.

Soe's title *New Year* is purposely chosen. Part II re-presents Hollywood images in the context of a Chinese New Year, a new beginning in filmmaking that tells Chinese American stories from the perspectives of Chinese Americans and takes custody of Chinese American culture. Soe's title is well chosen not only in terms of describing the personal history this film records, but also in terms of the counter images to Hollywood cinema it presents, the Chinese American history it evokes, and even the form the end of the film takes. Although celebrated differently throughout the world, Chinese New Year is consistently used to settle "old accounts," is often viewed as "so sacred that whatever one thinks or does can cause serious consequences for the New Year and the future," and avoids words such as "finished" to avoid bad luck in the New Year.[10] While there is certainly a New Year—an Asian American Renaissance—in independent cinema, it has much unfinished work. As Soe demonstrates with the content and the form she has chosen, and with her telling title, both segments of this film— the part where she imagines herself and the part where she is falsely imagined—still represent the dual realities of being Asian American in America.

I would like to thank the Pacific Film Archive in Berkeley for assistance in researching this article.

Notes

1. Renee Tajima. "Lotus Blossoms Don't Bleed: Images of Asian Woman," in *Making Waves*, Asian Women of California, ed.(Boston: Beacon Press, 1989): 308.

2. Amy Tan, *The Joy Luck Club (*New York: Ivy Books by Ballantine Books, 1989).

3. Loni Ding, "Strategies of an Asian American Filmmaker," in *Moving the Image: Independent Asian Pacific American Media Arts*, Russell Leong, ed. (UCLA Asian American Studies Center, Visual Communications, Southern California Asian American Studies, 1991): 46-48.

4. Nellie Wong, "When I Was Growing Up," in *This Bridge Called My Back: Writings by Radical Women of Color,* Cherrie Moraga and Gloria Anzaldua, eds. (New York: Kitchen Table: Women of Color Press, 1981): 7-8.

5. David Mura, "Strangers in the Village," in *Multicultural Literary: Opening the American Mind,* Rick Simonson and Scott Walker, eds. (Saint Paul: Graywolf Press, 1988): 139-40.

6. Ding, 47.

7. Dwight Okita, "In Response to Executive Order 9066," in *Breaking Silence: An Anthology of contemporary Asian American Poets*, Joseph Bruchac, ed. (Greenfield, NY: Greenfield Review Press, 1983): 211.

8. Jeanne Wakatsuki Houston and James D. Houston, *Farewell to Manzanar* (Boston: Houghton Mifflin, 1973): x.

9. Valerie Soe, *New Year: Parts I and II.* Independent Film, 1987. (Distributor: Women Make Movies).

10. Charles Taylor, ed. *Handbook of Minority Student Services*, (Madison: Praxis Publications, 1986).

22

Asian American Themes and Issues in Science Fiction and Fantasy

Catherine M. Currier and Janice M. Bogstad

A number of science fiction and fantasy writers are currently using the genre to explore Asian and Asian American themes and issues. Using the traditional science fiction metaphors, such as the "alien," the authors can foreground issues which have surfaced in recent years as we struggle to incorporate diversity into the heretofore homogenized landscape of dominant American culture. Additionally, science fiction allows an exploration of the relationships between place and self, and can explode the idea that there is only one American culture. Rather, culture is articulated as a story we tell ourselves to ground our individual self-identity in a particular place and time, illuminating our strand in the tapestry of diverse cultures.

This paper shows how science fiction and fantasy have been employed as tools to distance the reader/student sufficiently from their immersion in a specific culture so that they can finally see it as one among many possible cultures. By describing some of the existing universe of science fiction and fantasy that deals with Asian themes and issues we are providing a reader's advisory function to facilitate their use as tools in the classroom.

The very presence of books with Asian American thematic content in the classroom, and the act of people reading these books, is important. Since mass market culture is often the only exposure that many people have to Asian history, myth, religion and other institutions of indigenous Asian society, it is doubly important that they are able to be critical/analytical about the representation these institutions take on in the mediated venue of mass culture. Additionally, fiction is able to affect a reader's response to an issue or concept, the Asian character, philosophy, religion, myth or other social institution can be so positioned so as to be both sympathetic and the reader's main link to the story, heightening the positive identification the reader makes with the character or concept. No book can satisfy all of a reader's demands but the titles discussed below serve as examples that focus on aspects of the ethnic experience from a variety of perspectives.

Since many academics are not familiar with the literatures of science fiction and fantasy let us ground the discussion by first talking about a potentially more common cultural referent, film. There have been a number of famous (or infamous) portrayals of Asians or Asian Americans on the screen. Among science fiction films, several recent examples can serve to frame the discussion.

The character, Sulu, in the "classic" "Star Trek" television series is a very important alternative to Hollywood stereotypes and Westernized reductions of the *samurai* ethic to a simple martial-arts practice. "Star Trek" was first aired from 1966-69, during the Vietnam era. At that time, Asian physical features and cultural referents were perceived negatively, a phenomenon arising from feelings of hostility towards all Asians which accompanied the conflict. This phenomenon was a repeat of the wholesale negativity towards ethnic Asians which characterized both the World War II era and the Korean conflict. While the hostility was generalized towards Asians by largely white citizens of the U.S., underlying it was an unacknowledged hostility to basic physical and cultural differences that made ethnic Asians clear targets regardless of their specific racial origins. Thus the character, Sulu, a bridge officer and a strong and positive figure within the context of the series, acted as a significant counterpoint to anti-Asian sentiments of the time. While his heritage is not a major focus of the show's content, it is presented in a positive manner. By portraying Sulu as one of the group (a human) and in contrast to other/outsiders (the aliens), his common humanity can be subtly foregrounded, allowing for closer viewer identification with the character, Sulu.

The Star Wars trilogy, *Star Wars*, *Return of the Jedi*, and *The Empire Strikes Back*, also incorporate images and concepts from Asian traditions. Popular encodings most often mix Daoism and Zen Buddhism with the martial arts of the Samurai as is seen in the Star Wars series. There the dark and light of Daoist philosophies are used in opposition, a Western concept, instead being portrayed as complementary and interdependent forces, a relationship they hold in the actual philosophy. Some of the forms and images from the "Empire" are modeled after Westernized interpretations of Asian culture, a variation on the theme of "the other" as alien and negative. The incorporation of reductionist, Westernized versions of Asian cultural institutions, whether in negative or positive contexts, is the most insidious use of Asian traditions, and is especially apparent in portrayals of philosophy, religion and martial arts. While consumers of mass culture vaguely recognized Asian content, they can remain happily ignorant of its true depths, thus having their way paved to a simplistic condemnation or valorization of what they are led to believe is "Asian." It is also the most pervasive representation in mass culture entertainment forms. The "dark side" as negative rather than interdependent with the "light side" is contrasted with the positive portrayal of "Jedi" philosophy. The techniques taught by Obi-wan, which is, incidentally, a name with Japanese phonemic structure, and his mentor, Yoda, are loosely based on Zen Buddhism, a fact which is never acknowledged, as is the religion of Spock, the Vulcan member of the "classic" Star Trek crew. These two examples are the most popular images where "alien" and "Asian" are conflated.

Modern Asian cultures are often represented as threats to the West, hence terms like Nixon's "Yellow Peril." An older novel that exemplifies this approach is Heinlein's *The Day After Tomorrow*. This is another use of Asian culture that is all too pervasive even in current science fiction that is otherwise interesting. For example, in the recent novel, *He, She and It* (1991), by Marge Piercy, the entire world is virtually controlled by Japanese-style businesses whose method of managing personal as well as public life for their workers is portrayed as invasive and monolithic. Opposed to it are the victims, de-skilled workers who are either out of work or hold precarious, short-term positions and members of "free towns" who battle the corporations to maintain their independence and the slight hope for a world in which self-determination is "once again possible." Similarly couched impressions of Japanese corporate culture as manipulative and alien to all Western concepts of freedom is all too easily a part of standard science fictional fare, as much as this attitude is part of our dominant culture. It is rarely acknowledged that in fact "Japanese" business methods are actually those of William Edward Deming, the inventor of Total Quality Management, who is American. The twenty-first century provides the primary narrative space of Piercy's novel, moving quickly from the Japanese-business environments, called Multi-enclaves, to one of the more Westernized, pastoral settings. The potential for a technological wonder or an oppressive horror either of which could result from the worldwide information net is the focus of this novel. Piercy, makes it clear that the way this "net" is institutionalized will be a significant factor in determining what kind of future our children have. The subtext of her novel is that a Japanese management model will result in the end of personal freedom. Will the technological promise of information access become a liberating or a disenfranchising mechanism for the vast number of individuals in our societies? Piercy presents a range of possibilities for different ethnic and social groups of her future society. Yet for our purposes, it is vital to note the unfavorable portrait of Japanese business which pervades this work. One could almost say she had borrowed this conception of Japanese culture from Philip K. Dick's *Man in a High Castle* (1965), a novel which postulated that the Japanese won World War II, thus suppressing all other ethnic cultures in the world.

This same set of assumptions that Asian models of business are oppressive to personal freedom is found in an otherwise fascinating novel by Maureen McHugh entitled *China Mountain Zhang* (1991). In this work, the near future of the world is dominated by the Chinese who insist on racial purity as a precursor to ultimate success in business. China and the Chinese have all the best housing, equipment and chances in life, and mixed race people as well as the non-Chinese are barred from advancement and, in many cases, education.

At the same time as the implicit and explicit condemnations of Asian cultures characterize one body of science fiction and fantasy novels, other novels show the effects of serious research into Asian institutions. In attempting to portray Asian cultural characteristics, rituals, customs and religion in a sympathetic manner, Asian and non-Asian authors focus on the culture rather than using it as a convenient, if inaccurate, stereotype. These other usages and presentation exist side by side with the more insidious acknowledged and unacknowledged uses of Asian cultures.

The novels of William John Watkins, *The Centrifugal Rickshaw Dancer* and *Going to See the End of the Sky*, both suggest that the martial arts training of mind and body that is associated with Zen will become significant in an environment where gravity is supplied by centrifugal forces and where there is a closed culture in the society of a space-colony, surely an innovative incorporation of Asian culture into the future.

Fantasy novels have an easier time integrating Asian cultures. Examples of these are Yep's Dragon series, as well as Roberta MacAvoy's *Tea With the Black Dragon* and *Twisting the Rope*, the novels of Barry Hughart, including *Eight Skilled Gentlemen*, *Bridge of Birds*, and *The Story of the Stone*, and Schwartz's *Silk Roads and Shadows*.

Yep and MacAvoy introduce the Asian rendition of the ever-popular dragon tale into Western fantasy fiction, Yep as young adult fiction and MacAvoy as a very adult version. They share a common thread in the Chinese dragon stories with a creature who appears as a human; Yep's is an old woman and MacAvoy's a late-middle-aged man. Both have already lived long lives. Yep's dragon is a totally fantastic creature in a totally fantastic setting which, nevertheless, has some characteristics of pre-nine-teenth century China. There is no evidence of Western contact in Yep's tale, and the features of his landscape and people resemble stories from Ming dynasty folktale collections. MacAvoy's dragon story occurs in an American setting and the dragon has many more human characteristics than Yep's. Especially, his interest in developing a lasting relationship with a middle-aged woman makes him endearing to Western readers but the fact remains that Yep's stories, while written for younger readers, incorporate more elements of Chinese culture and are therefore more use-ful in introducing that culture to outsiders. MacAvoy's dragon has more philosophical depth and can be seen as a device for introducing elements of Daoist thought to the Western reader.

By contrasting Hughart with Yep's Dragon series, we can create a frame for Hughart's "stories of an ancient China that never was," Hughart's *Bridge of Birds, Eight Skilled Gentlemen* and *Story of the Stone* are drawn from some of the same myths and legends and fictional works as Yep's Dragon series. While Hughart sets his fiction in a pre-Christian Era China, to correspond with the legends of Kungfuzi (Confucius), Mengzi (Mencius) and Laozi, his settings are drawn from Ming and Qing dynasty novels such as *Dream of the Red Chamber*, *Water Margin* and *Spring and Autumn Annals*. These are stories written down much later than they were created and, along with folk stories written down first in the Ming Dynasty such as are found in *Stories from a Ming Collection*. They make reference to fictional portraits of pre-eighteenth century China. In Yep, the characters come from a non-Christian frame of refer-ence where tales of dragons and other fantastic happenings are given the same level of credence as any biblical tale would be given in Western cul-ture whereas Hughart's stories are told as that, charming stories from another culture rather than the repositories of moral and cultural expecta-tions.

There are also fantastic stories where the history of Asians in America is integrated into the stories in an illuminating way. Karen Joy Fowler's *Sarah Canary* takes place in the late nineteenth-century Pacific North-west, and in Seattle and San Francisco. Laurence Yep's historic novels, *Serpent's Children* and *Mountain Light* narrate the same period of Chi-nese contact with America, but are set mostly in coastal China. Fowler's story is primarily told from the viewpoint of a young Chinese man, Chin, for whom omens and spirit visitations are a normal part of life. Side by side with this young railroad worker's knowledge of the fantastic is his understanding of his precarious place in the social climate of 1873. The text is punctuated with stories of Chinese who were hung, driven off cliffs, starved, beaten and, at best, separated from their families for many years by the "Laws of Exclusion" that kept wives in China and perpetuated some of the worst kinds of Chinese prostitution known in the country at that time.

Fowler demonstrates the actual similarities between Sarah Canary and Chin through many factual and analogical references to 1870s U.S. culture, with anecdotes about the treatment of Chinese. The story of oppressed classes in the late nineteenth century, this work of fiction is no mere catalog of mistreatment. Its juxtaposition of facts of the time with experiences of several Chinese men and women, White women, Indians, and blacks, immerse the reader in the atmosphere of a time when people could be denied basic rights because of their skin color or sex and when non-white groups could legally be singled out as sacrificial lambs for the frustrations of an uncertain economy and the exploitative side of a developing country.

We have tried to show the variety of approaches to Asian peoples and cultures are present in science fiction from the critical to the admiring. While the positive and knowledgeable portrayal is always preferable, any view can be the springboard to discussion and learning when framed by a concerned teacher. Further science fiction can help introduce the complexity and richness of various Asian cultures, thus providing a link to the cultural stories which help build self-identity.

Clash of Cultures

The writers in this section show cultural clashes in various forms to be primary to numerous aspects of Asian American life, from manners, to integration of language, to one's self-identity. In "Fictions of Witness: Relocations and Silence in Japanese American Narrative," John Streamas takes an innovative look at the term "Silence" to show how European and Asian Americans can operate under disparate assumptions concerning the use and emotional associations of a single word, noting that to assume silence as "bad" or breaking silence as "good" not only "betray[s] a prejudice of a Western criticism that recognizes only one kind of silence," but creates "a clash of imperatives within the Japanese American community itself." Melissa Littig Godoy's video script, compiled by high school students, based on oral interviews, illustrates the far-reaching effects when one's native and adapted tongues clash in daily life. Most dramatic among the clashes both within and between cultures that the Vietnam War brought about are the 30,000 Amerasian children abandoned in southeast Asia, "their G.I. fathers back in the U.S." In her "Reclamation of Historically Contextualized Identity *Even Though All I Asking For Is My Body,*" Lauri Sagle points out the clash between "fun-filled" tourist guide descriptions of Hawaii and the language of the Hawaiian's daily lives. Illustrating how this is reflected in contrasts between "tourist literature" and literature by writers such as Milton Murayama who let the people of the culture "speak for themselves," Sagle connects the ideologies involved to larger issues of colonization. Ronna C. Johnson's "John Okada's *No-No Boy*: Visions of Japanese Ethnic Identity and Revisions of 'Classic American' Literature" examines cultural conflicts in Okada's novel, not only of European American society against Japanese Americans, but of the internalization of White American racism among the Japanese Americans themselves—illustrated specifically in the clash between the "no-no boys" and "*nisei* patriots," and leading to the irony that the *issei* Japanese Americans were blamed for their own internment "because they are the biological source of the Otherness that enabled it." At the center of this piece is Johnson's suggestion that *No-No Boy* itself replicates and revises the traditional United States literary canon, thus clashing against works that have been termed "American literature"—and forcing us to reconsider that term.

23

Fictions of Witness

Relocation and Silence in Japanese American Narratives

John Streamas

In *Praises and Dispraises* Terrence Des Pres urges a role for writers in a nuclear age: "We still have poetry and fiction, the language of concrete perception, and the office of art isn't located in a government bunker but in the obligation to behold and witness, praise, denounce."[1] Silence appears to renounce this obligation and to refuse to praise and denounce, even to witness. When critics, historians, and editors apply the phrase "breaking silence" to recent literature of Japanese Americans' experience in American concentration camps during the Second World War, they must assume that for many years art either did not exist for camp inhabitants or did not fulfill its obligation. In his history *Strangers from a Different Shore* Ronald Takaki argues, "To confront the current problems of racism, Asian Americans know they must remember the past and break its silence…. Memories of the internment nightmare have haunted the older generation like ghosts. But the former prisoners have been unable to exorcise them by speaking out."[2] Silence is finally breaking because *sansei*, third-generation Japanese Americans, want to know the story and because hearings before the Commission on Wartime Relocation and Internment of Civilians have drawn out "scores of *issei* and *nisei*," first- and second-generation Japanese Americans, who lived in the camps. Yet *nisei* writer Yoshiko Uchida cautioned *sansei* against condemning her generation: "As they listen to our voices from the past… I ask that they remember they are listening in a totally different time; in a totally changed world."[4] Uchida herself wrote fictions of the camp experience: "I find it painful to continue remembering and writing about it. But I must."[5] To break silence in pain is to overcome what Michi Weglyn calls "an urge to invisibility."[6]

That silence and invisibility represent a menace in minority cultures cannot surprise us. But, in a culture whose silence is not only a reaction to political injustice but also an everyday negotiation with life, even a whisper of political engagement may echo and reverberate. In fact, aside from Uchida's work many fictions have broken silence. Examining four of them—John Okada's *No-No Boy*, Joy Kogawa's *Obasan*, Hisaye Yamamoto's "Las Vegas Charley" and "The Legend of Miss Sasagawara"—should establish an achievement in beholding and witnessing. But committed art, Des Pres insists, must also praise and denounce. These fictions, except for *No-No Boy*, refuse to shout in praise or denunciation. Rather, they challenge us to regard art's obligation, as Des Pres defines it, as relative: in a naturally silent people, praise and denunciation are subtle—implicit behind a whisper of witness.

This cautions us to make distinctions. Whereas for Western critics silence is usually bad, representing innate weakness or enforced submission, for Asians it assumes no inevitable moral cast. In fact Muriel Saville-Troike, positing "speech silences" whose meanings derive from "convention within particular speech communities," notes that the Japanese recognize a "wordless communication."[7] And D. T. Suzuki defines a silence:

> [I]n the working of the Eastern mind there is something calm, quiet, silent, undisturbable, which appears as if always looking into eternity.... It is the silence of an "eternal abyss" in which all contrasts and conditions are buried; it is the silence of God who, deeply absorbed in contemplation of his works past, present, and future, sits calmly on his throne of absolute oneness and allness. It is the "silence of thunder" obtained in the midst of the flash and uproar of opposing electric currents.[8]

A distinction between Eastern and Western silences is made in a poem, "Letters From Poston Relocation Camp," by David Mura. In his first letter to his wife Michiko, the speaker says that, in camp, "when the song ends, the silence / does not stop singing."[9] In his second letter he notes "many cries / clinging to the wind" to which "I wanted to answer: my lips / were cracked, dry."[10] In his last letter he writes Michiko that, without this chance to express his feelings, "I would be angry at you for not listening, / blaming you for what I haven't spoken."[11] During internment, then, silence has evolved from a vehicle for song to a condition of helplessness to, at last, an instrument of oppression and blame. Significantly, silence oppresses only at the end of internment, when the speaker feels alienated, disengaged from Japan and the United States; and silence soothes at the beginning, when he is most Japanese.

We should perceive at least two kinds of silence, an expressive kind that in Asian culture carries song and language and an oppressive kind that in both Eastern and Western cultures smothers and paralyzes. To assume that silence is necessarily bad, or that breaking silence is always and necessarily good—to assume, with activists today, that "silence equals death"—is to betray a prejudice of a Western criticism that recognizes only one kind of silence.

A clash of imperatives—to keep or to break silence—divides Japanese Americans, as Uchida and Takaki note, along generational lines, with *nisei* often caught in the middle. *Obasan* negotiates these imperatives, granting both "the ethic of strength in silence" to Obasan and Isamu and the need to "tell the unspeakable truths" to Emily.[12] Emily is of course an anomaly, an older Japanese Canadian who is politically active: her abundant records of the family's and the nation's wartime experience challenge Naomi to confront history. But the ultimate triumph is Naomi's: it is she who struggles with silence, resisting its petrifying force in Obasan but also resisting its complete breaking in the babbling of Aunt Emily. Though Emily's collection of documents evokes Naomi's memories, Emily herself is comical in her tireless ranting activism, whereas Obasan, for all her vexing obstinacy, is often noble. Moreover, the documents transform not Emily but Naomi, who overcomes her resistance to her own history, breaking silence without entirely condemning it.

The book's central metaphor is stone, which is "not only a metaphor for a hardship endured," writes Cheng Lok Chua, "but also a trope for the attitude of stoical, unspeaking silence."[13] Yet stone is never far from life-affirming qualities. Uncle's bread may be "like a lump of granite" that will "break your teeth," but it is edible and—sometimes with oatmeal and barley, carrots and potatoes, or "Alberta," Uncle's butter—it is eaten.[14] At book's end Naomi steps outside and sees the moon as "a pure white stone" whose reflection dances in the river's water "a quiet ballet, soundless as breath."[15] But Naomi knows throughout that silence can be powerfully expressive, can constitute a language. About Obasan, for example, she says, "The language of her grief is silence."[16] About teaching she notes that "it's the children who say nothing who are in trouble more than the ones who complain."[17] About the displaced Japanese Canadians she says, "We are the silences that speak from stone."[18] And near novel's end she dreams of a Grand Inquisitor torturing her mother: "What the Grand Inquisitor has never learned is that the avenues of speech are the avenues of silence. To hear my mother, to attend her speech, to attend the sound of stone, he must first become silent."[19] Silence then can provide a language by which we may understand fear and sorrow. Though its destructive force makes Obasan stonily inaccessible and Naomi weak, still its opposite—the murderous questioning of the Grand Inquisitor, the "spluttering" crusading of the "word warrior" Aunt Emily, and the "incessant and always so well-intentioned" remarks of such persons as Mr. Barker about "what we did to our Japanese"[20]—can be equally numbing, equally destructive. Naomi's triumph is that she extracts understanding from both silence and the breaking of silence. She compares her aunts— "One lives in sound, the other in stone"[21]—and separates from them. The language of Obasan's silence is for her too private; the box of Emily's papers is, for all its praise and denunciation, too public and coarse. In the brief monologue that frames the novel, Naomi says, "Unless the stone bursts with telling, there is in my life no living word."[22] But she adds, "The sound I hear is only sound. White sound. Words, when they fall, are pock marks on the earth."[23] What she wants is a silence that will speak a freeing word. What she offers is neither praise nor denunciation but her quiet witness. But of course this witness *is* the silence that speaks, the stone bursting with telling. In Kogawa's gentle irony, quiet Naomi accomplishes more than spluttering Emily.

The narrating voice in Yamamoto's "The Legend of Miss Sasagawara" is too colloquial to be as quiet as Naomi's: until the end its tone is comical. Kiku does not brood in metaphors: her concerns are the immediate, commonplace activities of camp life. She and her friend Elsie even dream of finishing college, finding good jobs, and securing "two nice, clean young men, preferably handsome, preferably rich, who would cherish us forever and a day."[24] But precisely because Kiku seems so normal, so indifferent to crusading or contemplation, Yamamoto is able to suffuse her story with an irony that is political. After all, camp life is not normal. The story's opening line describes the desert home as an "unlikely place of wind, sand, and heat."[25] The empty barracks of Block 33, when Miss Sasagawara and her father move in, are not "chopped up yet into the customary four apartments;" but later the Sasagawara apartment is "really only a cubicle because the once-empty barracks had soon been partitioned off into six units."[26] Moreover, medical care is not quite adequate, though Kiku, characteristically, names its deficiencies in parenthetical asides: Dr. Moritomo is not "technically" titled, for "evacuation had caught him with a few months to go on his degree," and "trembling old" Dr. Kawamoto "had retired several years before the war, but he had been drafted here."[27] And the block Christmas party is rich in comic irony, though Kiku grasps only enough of this to call the celebration "odd."

The greatest irony resides in Miss Sasagawara, who, in the already strange world of the camp, is considered strange. At first Elsie ascribes this strangeness to a life in ballet: "people like that are temperamental."[28] Others are less generous: the Sasakis and George call her crazy. Curiously, though, Kiku refrains from grand judgements. Her fascination with Miss Sasagawara reflects in her eagerness to tell her story and in her jealousy: she fantasizes about "the scintillating life Miss Sasagawara had led until now" in ballet, and she hopes for a body "as smooth and spare and well-turned" as Miss Sasagawara's.[29] But Kiku's affinity for Miss Sasagawara is much deeper than mere curiosity and jealousy. Miss Sasagawara's relationship to her Japanese American community is analogous to Japanese Americans' relationship to white America: a silent and exotic outsider, she is sent away—ironically, *to* California— "to a state institution."[30] Kiku may sense the analogy at the end of the story, for her tone changes: she apologizes for the "glibness" of her dismissal of Miss Sasagawara in the clichés of pop psychology. In fact her entire story has been glib. Now, however, the narrative is swallowed up in Miss Sasagawara's poem, a dark parable of her father's life in camp. Driven toward achieving wisdom and perfection, the man in the poem is "deaf and blind" to his companion's "passions rising, subsiding, and again rising"—passions felt "perhaps in anguished silence."[31] The qualifying "perhaps" suggests that Kiku does not fully appreciate the depth of Miss Sasagawara's silence. But the parable in the poem is analogous to Kiku's own story, or "legend," of Miss Sasagawara. Both poem and story concern a subject driven by a passionate perfectionism into isolation from a world in which injustice is casually accepted. Kiku herself may be too glib for praise and denunciation, though storytelling makes her, like her subject, an artist. Yamamoto's parable-within-a-legend witnesses for those who, in Miss Sasagawara's "anguished silence," are casualties of difference.

In this story Yamamoto refuses to subject silence to simple blunt praise or blame. In a brief passage in another story, "Las Vegas Charley," she announces her refusal. Charley recalls two life-threatening encounters with violent drunken men, a white American and a Mexican. The American holds Charley at knife-point, demanding to know whether he is Chinese or Japanese. Charley remains silent; and "after a few moments, possibly because he obtained no satisfaction, no argument, the man... closed his penknife" and goes away.[32] The Mexican, wanting to avenge his son's death in the Pacific war, threatens to kill Charley. "But somehow a Mexican had not been as intimidating as a white man," and Charley "talked his way out of that" situation.[33] In these scenes whether silence kills or saves depends on the antagonist. Equally significant is the fact that, for such a simple and unimaginative Japanese American as Charley, silence only kills or saves: it extends no alternatives, no prospects for transmutation into a language for art.

No subtler than "Las Vegas Charley," and much louder, is Okada's *No-No Boy*, which is set after the war but whose plot originates in its protagonist's negative responses to questions 27 and 28 of the government's "Application for Leave Clearance." The questionnaire aimed to recruit Japanese Americans into the army and to determine internees' loyalty. Question 28 in its original form was unanswerable for many internees: it asked them not only to "swear unqualified allegiance to the United States" and to "faithfully defend the United States from any or all attack by foreign or domestic forces" but also to "forswear any form of allegiance or obedience to the Japanese emperor." *Issei* "were by law ineligible because of race to become United States citizens," so question 28 asked them "voluntarily to assume stateless status."[34] But even a revised questionnaire posed a dilemma for *nisei*:

> Some contended that question 28 was a trap and that to forswear allegiance to Japan was to confess that such allegiance had once existed. Many answered question 27 conditionally, saying things like: "Yes, if my rights as citizen are restored," or "No, not unless the government recognizes my right to live anywhere in the United States." Some simply answered "No-No" out of understandable resentment over their treatment.... [35]

Okada's protagonist Ichiro, a no-no boy, spends two years in prison. When he comes home to Seattle he aims his bitterness not at America but at Japan—particularly at his mother, who embodies all that is for him most uselessly Japanese and alien. He blames her for making him neither wholly Japanese nor wholly American, and he regrets his no-no answers for betraying his American self.

We know so little of Ichiro's life in camp and in prison that we cannot know exactly why he spurned the loyalty oath. His most specific explanation suggests only that "I did not go because I was weak and could not do what I should have done."[36] But history suggests that his resistance must have demanded strength: Roger Daniels notes that "of the nearly 78,000 inmates who were eligible to register" an "overwhelming majority—more than 65,000—answered 'Yes' to question 28," and that only about 6700 answered "No."[37] Yoshiko Uchida said of the no-no boys, "It took courage for them to say no and to stand up for their civil rights."[38] But Ichiro's view of the past is necessarily warped by his present confusion and bitterness, so that he remembers none of the courage that might once have driven him. Training our attention on the rage and despair, Okada would seem to be validating Ichiro's repudiation of his past. Gayle K. Fujita Sato charges that the story "begins from the premise that saying 'No' was a mistake, and it affirms Ichiro's quest to return to a perceived prelapsarian condition of 'undivided,' 'unquestioned' loyalty."[39] In this view Okada would "affirm 'Japanese American' through a character who rejects everything 'Japanese'."[40] Certainly the brutal depiction of Ichiro's mother, the most unremittingly Japanese of Okada's characters, attests to this. But Ichiro himself is brutally depicted. He loathes himself no less than he loathes his mother's old-world ways. Moreover, the book's moral center resides first in Kenji and later in Gary. Kenji, Ichiro's apparent opposite, not only answers yes-yes but also fights in the war and incurs the disabling wound that eventually kills him. But though he assimilates easily into American culture, unlike Ichiro he refuses to target only Japanese culture for condemnation: he blames all ethnic and national communities for the bigotry that creates concentration camps. Gary, like Ichiro, spends years in prison; but he secures a comfortable self-definition that accepts his no-no answers and also, sympathetically, foresees hardships for *nisei* who submitted to the loyalty oath: "They'll find that they still can't buy a house in Broadmoor even with a million stones in the bank. They'll see themselves getting passed up for jobs by white fellows not quite so bright but white."[41] Gary's transformation into an artist is a function of his transformation from a talker into a thinker: "I've no one to talk to and no desire to talk," he says, "for I have nothing to say except what comes out of my paint tubes and brushes."[42] We never "see" Gary's paintings, and so we cannot know their quality. Yet we can suggest that, as he has known even more injustice than Ichiro, Gary may be the politically engaged artist whom Des Pres idealizes, committed surely to witness, perhaps even to praise and denunciation. Ironically, he earns a silence that Ichiro, desperate to be more American, would reject.

Irony is a device we do not often associate with Asian art. Yet Japanese American writers apply it to their narratives of internment, whether with Okada's blunt force or with Yamamoto's clever tone shifting. Irony, after all, names the very act of uprooting and imprisoning a racial group in a democracy boasting of its individual freedoms. In Gretel Ehrlich's novel *Heart Mountain* an old *issei*, asked for the cause of such racism, says, "No imagination."[43]

If indeed racism is informed by a lack of imagination, then one kind of silence—the kind that must be broken—is informed by a repression or a failure of imagination. Des Pres says, "The self that cannot speak, as the man or woman being tortured cannot, or the self that cannot find words to make its own, has not the means to join or withdraw from the world."[44]

But another kind of silence—a kind that speaks—is informed by endurance and calm. The fictions of Kogawa and Yamamoto break the first silence and, sometimes in irony, embrace the second. We should not be surprised when many characters in fictions of internment are artists: Naomi, Kiku, Miss Sasagawara, Gary. Kogawa implies that only art can interpret and transmit the language of a silence that speaks; and, further, that this is the language best equipped to break the silence that paralyzes.

Notes

1. Terrence Des Pres, *Praises and Dispraises: Poetry and Politics, the Twentieth Century* (New York: Viking, 1988): 231.

2. Ronald Takaki, *Strangers from a Different Shore: A History of Asian Americans* (New York: Penguin, 1990): 484.

3. Ibid., 485.

4. Roger Daniels, "Relocation, Redress, and the Report: A Historical Appraisal" in *Japanese Americans: From Relocation to Redress,* Roger Daniels, Sandra C. Taylor, and Harry H. L. Kitano, eds. (Seattle: University of Washington, 1991): 4.

5. Yoshiko Uchida, *The Invisible Thread* (Englewood Cliffs: Julian Messner, 1991): 133.

6. Michi Weglyn, *Years of Infamy: The Untold Story of America's Concentration Camps (*New York: Morrow, 1976): 270.

7. Muriel Saville-Troike, "The Place of Silence in an Integrated Theory of Communication" in *Perspectives on Silence*, Deborah Tannen and Muriel Saville-Troike, eds.(Norwood, NJ: Ablex, 1985): 10, 7.

8. D. T. Suzuki, *An Introduction to Zen Buddhism* (New York: Grove, 1964): 35-36.

9. David Mura, "Letters from Poston Relocation Camp (1942-45) " in *After We Lost Our Way* (New York: Dutton, 1989): 4-5.

10. Ibid., 36-37.

11. Ibid., 79-80.

12. Cheng Lok Chua, "Witnessing the Japanese Canadian Experience in World War II: Processual Structure, Symbolism, and Irony in Joy Kogawa's *Obasan*" in *Reading the Literatures of Asian America*, Shirley Geok-lin Lim and Amy Ling, eds. (Philadelphia: Temple University Press, 1992): 105.

13. Ibid., 104.

14. Joy Kogawa, *Obasan* (Boston: Godine, 1982) : 13.

15. Ibid., 247.

16. Ibid., 14.

17. Ibid., 34.

18. Ibid., 111.

19. Ibid., 228.

20. Ibid., 35, 32, 225.

21. Ibid., 32.

22. Ibid., iv.

23. Ibid.

24. Hisaye Yamamoto, "The Legend of Miss Sasagawara." in *Seventeen Syllables and Other Stories* (Latham, NY: Kitchen Table: Women of Color, 1988): 21.

25. Ibid., 20.

26. Ibid., 20, 22.

27. Ibid., 25, 26.

28. Ibid., 21.

29. Ibid., 21, 22.

30. Ibid., 30.

31. Ibid., 33.

32. Hisaye Yamamoto, "Las Vegas Charley." *Seventeen Syllables and Other Stories* (Latham, NY: Kitchen Table: Women of Color, 1988): 72.

33. Ibid.

34. Roger Daniels, *Concentration Camps North America: Japanese in the United States and Canada During World War II* (Malabar, FL: Krieger, 1981): 113.

35. Ibid., 114.

36. Ibid., 34.

37. Ibid., 114.

38. Ibid., 116.

39. Gayle K. Fujita Sato, "Momotaro's Exile: John Okada's No-No Boy" in *Reading the Literatures of Asian America*, Shirley Geok-lin Lim and Amy Ling, eds. (Philadelphia: Temple University Press, 1992): 241.

40. Ibid., 239.

41. Ibid., 227.

42. Ibid., 224.

43. Gretel Ehrlich, *Heart Mountain* (New York: Penguin, 1988): 179.

44. Op. cit., Des Pres, 230.

24

John Okada's *No-No Boy*

Visions of Japanese Ethnic Identity and Revisions of "Classic American" Literature

Ronna C. Johnson

> It is imperative to note that, above all, *No-No Boy* is a major novel of great depth and dimension and as such must be accorded the treatment it commands... the astute reader will recognize that the novel belongs to several major traditions, of its time and otherwise; the study of *No-No Boy* can contribute to any number of serious literary courses. – Lawson Fusao Inada

Published in 1957, John Okada's *No-No Boy*, is the first Japanese American novel.[1] It has been celebrated for its depiction of *nisei* resistance to civil rights violations of the wartime internment and for its reclamation of embattled Asian American masculinity.[2] Critics have generally dwelled on its cultural dimensions, while at the same time expressing disappointment that the novel's art and literary value have not been assessed.[3] I will take exception to the implication that its ethnicity and its artistry are separable. In my view, *No-No Boy*'s textualization of sociological, historical and ethnic interests in fictive narrative discourse demonstrates that such elements are integral to its literariness. *No-No Boy*, I shall suggest, self-consciously questions race and ethnicity, not simply as social categories, but in relation to an "American" literature which it seeks both to be counted in and to reconfigure.[4]

No-No Boy's ethnic and literary stance and status lie in its mode as an oscillating text, which its double negative title signifies. It is at once a "border" text which deessentializes, or shows the social construction of, assumptions about ethnicity, and a narrative which echoes and reproduces canonical tropes that are essentialist, or presented as natural, innate. Oscillation between these positions typifies its stance and grants its narrative complexity. The novel contends its era's biologically-based conclusions about race and identity, disputing assumptions of an ethnic monolith and the racial dyad of "classic" U.S. literature most familiarly represented by Huck and Jim. But it (re)inscribes essentialist interpretations with regard to women in its displacements onto the *issei* mother and objectification of the *nisei* female. Similarly, *No-No Boy* resolves questions of *nisei* identity through the male line, assimilating diverse views to a centrist position embodied by the protagonist. But in this, narrative resolution implies closures that are far more monolithic than its representations of ethnicity.

No-No Boy opens just after the close of the Japanese internment camps and the end of the Second World War, and explores the mood of *issei* (Japanese immigrants in America) and *nisei* (first generation, U.S. born Japanese Americans) through the charged figure of the no-no boy. A "no-no boy" is a term for interned *nisei* who answered "no" to two parts of a loyalty questionnaire administered by the U.S. government in 1943, and who refused induction when the draft was opened to them in January 1944.[5] Prosecuted and sentenced to three years in prison for violating the Selective Service Act, most were released after two years under a general pardon granted by President Truman in December 1947.[6] Taking place at a crucial historical moment, *No-No Boy* articulates varied community positions on draft evasion and service, and on Japanese and American identifications, refuting notions of an ethnic monolith by means of its emphasis on conflicting inter- and intragenerational perspectives.[7]

Set in Seattle, *No-No Boy* recounts the return of the titular protagonist, *nisei* draft resister Inchiro Yamada, after four years in camp and in prison. The plot devolves from Ichiro's belief that he cannot reclaim his birthright of American citizenship or reenter American life, even after serving prison time for his refusal.

> I…have made a mistake and… have served time, two years all told, and I have been granted a full pardon. Why is it then that I am unable to convince myself that I am no different from any other American? (82).

Ichiro's plea crystallizes the narrative's concern with the reestablishment of *nisei* self-respect after the internment and the war with Japan. Ichiro means "firstborn" in Japanese.[8] This name not only identifies the protagonist's familial place, but constitutes a signifier for his *nisei* generation, which is the first American born. A trope for the *nisei*, Ichiro the no-no boy may be termed a Japanese American "American Adam," a variant on the classic literary hero identified by R.W.B. Lewis, who posits that the American Adam's self-invention and solitary confrontation with "civilization" mark a quintessential New World character and experience.[9] Elaborating that paradigm, Okada's Japanese American "American Adam" embodies a point of new beginning, but one figured through reconciliation and restoration; synthesizing diverse community beliefs, his outlaw position is made the site of rebirth for the Adamic, American born *nisei*.

No-No Boy's claim to status as a work of "American" literature interrogates the category by, for one, redefining this "classic" narrative line. Its *nisei* double negative discourse expands traditional narrative models of individualistic Adamic defiance by characterizing *nisei* in terms which have been defined by critics as being neither Japanese nor American.[10] *No-No Boy* posits a fledgling, postwar American identity of full citizenship and tolerance of plurality that is also an expansion of narrative tradition to accommodate Other speaking subjects. As the no-no boy, an interned U.S. citizen and draft resister, complicates definitions of "American," the novel's accentuation of Japanese American Others challenges narrative conventions which are held to exemplify "American" literature.

No-No Boy frames its dispute with assumptions of an ethnic monolith by decrying the biologically-based racial essentialism which prevailed in contemporary notions of "American" identity. It suggests that Ichiro's decision is determined by history: for the traumatic event of Pearl Harbor restored biological determinism to democracy's definition of the citizen. After Pearl Harbor,

> the indignation, the hatred, the patriotism of the American people shifted into full-throated condemnation of the Japanese... who were born American and remained Japanese because biology does not know the meaning of patriotism (vii).

No-No Boy shows that biologically-based racial assumptions provide an always already existing marker of Otherness that is regarded as innate. This marker can be annexed to justify definitions of national identity that are simpler—and more politically expedient—than are the constructionist principles of citizenship prevailing by law in a democracy.[11] In the novel's view, discrimination results from racial essentialism, not non-conformity, for "fighting for his country... didn't do anything about his face to make [the *nisei* veteran] look more American" (159). *No-No Boy* specifies the "face" of the Other, demolishing white generalizations about *issei* and *nisei*, insisting that knowledge of patriotism, loyalty, or belief is not available in the look of a face. It contests the view that race is biologically inherent and opposes white racist assumptions of an ethnic monolith by inscribing widely divergent views among postwar *issei* and *nisei*. Though it acknowledges conservative assimilationist views held in the camps, *No-*

No Boy powerfully illustrates that the reestablishment of the *issei/nisei* community after the war requires an internal assimilation. Extremes of belief held by both *issei* and *nisei*, both no-no boy and veteran, are narratively examined, adjudicated, and reconciled in the figure of Ichiro Yamada, resulting in a centrist neither-nor *nisei* position on identity and citizenship.

No-No Boy insists that *nisei* are not born (American), they are made: produced by politics, history, culture. Complicating Japanese ethnic identity in this way, *No-No Boy* nevertheless also presents it as innate by making it familial, inscribing racial self-hatred as a generational legacy, and attributing biologically-based racial essentialism to genetic, familial inheritance. Inchiro's struggle with the competing claims of Japanese heritage and American citizenship charts the generational conflicts:

> When one is born in America… it is not an easy thing to discover suddenly that being American is a terribly incomplete thing if one's face is not white and one's parents are Japanese of the country Japan which attacked America (53-4).

No-No Boy shows the way politically instituted racial essentialism corrodes *nisei* self-esteem and engenders internalized racism. This intolerable condition is eased by being made in a sense biological; by projecting its source onto the *issei*, the text (re)inscribes a biological explanation for politically motivated prejudice. Then, the narrative further contains racial self-hatred in an essentializing way by making it a product of the female; Ichiro's mother, blamed for making him identify as Japanese and refuse induction, takes the fall for the U.S. government—for the camps and jail. In the following, mother and government are linked and conflated:

> Sometimes I think my mother is to blame. Sometimes I think it's bigger than her refusal to understand that I'm not like her. It didn't make sense. Not at all. First they jerked us off the Coast and put us in camps to prove to us that we weren't American enough to be trusted. Then they wanted to draft us into the army. I was bitter—mad and bitter (153).

The *issei* are blamed for the double bind created by the internment because they are the biological source of the Otherness that enabled it. They signify an impediment of origins, of biological and cultural materials that both constitute and complicate the *nisei* birthright. In this, the *issei* thus absorb *nisei* anger against government crimes and white racism.

No-No Boy further undermines its repudiation of race as an innate quality by absorbing the generational conflict into a gender conflict that is presented as natural. Let me mention two representative *issei* families, the Yamadas, parents of the no-no boy Ichiro, and the Kannos, parents of the decorated veteran Kenji. Although they appear to represent opposing poles of *issei* belief—loyalty to Japan versus American patriotism, ethnic segregation versus assimilation—both sets of *issei* parents figure a single theme: the reclamation of the intergenerational father-son bond, which has been sundered by the destructive *issei* mother and is restored by her death. In this, *No-No Boy* explains father-son relations with maternal enmity, much as it subsumes government crimes to *issei* family claims. The paranoid ethnicity of Ichiro's mother signifies a pathology of Japanese nationalism which is held responsible for Ichiro's decision. Further, the *issei* mother's emasculation of the father is correlated to her responsibility for *nisei* angst in Ichiro's bitter thoughts:

> Pa's okay, but he's a… goddamned fat grinning, spineless nobody. Ma is the rock… It was she who opened my mouth and made my lips move to sound the words that got me two years in prison and an emptiness that is more empty and frightening than the caverns of hell (12).

Nisei rage at unchecked maternal agency subsumes political motivations for draft resistance to familial power dynamics, which are deranged by the "fanatic" *issei* mother. Typifying the novel's unexamined and unrepentant sexism, Ichiro's mother is depicted as de-feminized, castrating, "a rock of hate… neither woman nor mother" (21). Her power upsets a naturalized gender order: "Ma's the one. Pa, he's just around. Still, his weakness is just as bad as Ma's strength…. He should have been a woman. He should have been Ma and Ma should have been Pa" (112). Unnatural sex roles account for the mother's pathological power to enforce her virulent, pro-Japan position; this inversion in parental roles is blamed for the son's alienation and existential paralysis.

The death of the *issei* mother cures the illness of unnaturally inverted gender roles. In the Kanno family, the morally conscientious father blames himself for his son's injurious participation in the war, an exoneration of the son which underwrites an idyllic father-son intimacy. Significantly, this positive figure of *issei* paternity is widowed: he can exemplify a laudable *issei* masculinity because there is no unnatural competition from an opinionated, paranoid pro-Japan mother. Just so, Ichiro's father is recuperated by the timely suicide of his "crazy" wife, whose death restores the father-son bond. Thus the *issei* are portrayed as victims, not of culture clash, but of a sex war. When men lose, the family is corrupted, maiming sons like Ichiro by exposing them to ruinous maternal demand. When the removal of wives permits men to win, *issei* fathers and their *nisei* sons can communicate and forgive, achieving intergenerational unity.

Nisei resolution of intragenerational division over the issue of service rests as well on a unifying centrist position. It is reached by the removal of obstacles to a resolution that recognizes both government culpability for the internment and *nisei* absolution for draft resistance. While dramatized in relations among *nisei* males, this centrist position is articulated as an ethos by Emi, the text's sole *nisei* woman. Emi exemplifies an ideal of available, nurturing femininity that expands the text's gender essentialism; that illuminates the text's patriarchal perspective, which also informs the blaming of the mother, and that demonstrates the text's affinity with predominating strains of "classic" U.S. narrative. Emi's pliancy and curative sexuality mitigate the unnatural dominance of the *issei* mother. Her sexual balm translates into a rhetoric for Ichiro's resumption of American life. She tells Ichiro:

> this country… made a mistake when they made you do what they did
> and they admit it by letting you run around loose. Try, if you can, to be
> equally big and forgive them…. (96).

Emi casts the crimes of the camps and of draft evasion as equal, mutually related, and equally in need of forgiveness. Her analysis restores Ichiro's masculine self-esteem by providing for his agency: he must forgive his country, for his "mistake was no bigger than the mistake [his] country made." She urges him to a patriotic "bigness that seems to want to bust out" (96)—a bigness that would bust out like ejaculation. This renewed potency depends on *nisei* recognition that the crime of the camps is as despicable and forgivable as that of draft evasion. The restoration of masculinity concretized in sex with Emi thus allows the least *nisei*, the outcast draft resister, to reclaim his American place and identity. Thus women in *No-No Boy* are bivalent tropes that signify what breaks *nisei* men, as in the *issei* mother's paranoid ethnicity, and what may heal them, as in Emi's sexual pliancy.

In a way that parallels its use of women, *No-No Boy*'s *nisei* drama of a generation of men sundered by the issue of service ultimately resorts to affirming the fundamental indivisibility and necessary unification of the *nisei* generation. In this, the novel's resolution in a single generational position also subverts its challenge to the ethnic monolith. *No-No Boy* presents Ichiro's homecoming as a circular odyssey among figures kaleidoscopically appearing, disappearing, and reappearing. Pairing Ichiro with a wide range of his peers, the novel sifts through their diverse positions to resolve his crisis, and depicts the recuperation of his divided generation by neutralizing the hostile patriotism of the veteran Eto, and killing off both the decorated war hero Kenji and the hedonistic no-no boy

Freddie Akimoto. This functional organization of plot constitutes *No-No Boy*'s renovation of a "classic" American narrative form, for its male pairs resemble but revise the dyadic buddy tale of canonical U.S. narrative. In Leslie Fiedler's description of the archetype, male narrative pairs like Huck and Jim form a dyad assembled by racialized designations—Light and Dark, rational European and intuitive African or Indian. These designations convey ideological implications for Americanness and moral worth based on skin color.[12] *No-No Boy* eliminates racial difference from the traditional dyad, destabilizing the trope's ideological valence. Further, it revises and reverses the partner-roles by making a hero of the pariah no-no boy Ichiro and killing off his "civilized" opposite, Kenji the veteran.

As the text works toward Ichiro's resolution of his "American" identity, it also purges *nisei* of certain problematic strands of belief. In effect, then, the narrative challenge to the ethnic monolith resolves in the collapsing of *nisei* into one position. Working through diverse *nisei* views in the fraternal pairs of the text's embedded buddy tales, dyads formed by veterans and no-no boys express extremes of *nisei* belief. In the novel's first pages, the veteran Eto spits on Ichiro for being a no-no boy: this act defines the historically produced *nisei* divisiveness that must be ameliorated. Eto betrays the *nisei* fear that veteran status is not enough to insure citizenship equal to that of whites; he blames no-no boys for white racism. On the other hand, no-no boy Freddie Akimoto defiantly refuses to accept either Eto's displaced anger or Ichiro's paralyzing guilt; just because "we picked the wrong side... Doesn't mean we gotta stop livin" (46). But, absorbing *nisei* rage against white racism, Freddie is assailed by Eto and another *nisei* patriot who believes that no-no boys poison *nisei* status in white America. The violence culminates in Freddie's accidental death, the event with which the novel ends.

In its refusal of linear, individualistic, autobiographic narrative conventions, and in its renovation of the "classic" buddy tale, *No-No Boy* stands as a countertext in one line of male-authored, male-centered U.S. narrative which it both revises and replicates. It destabilizes the individualistic narrative model by constructing its Adamic hero from multiple, mutually conflicting cultural positions. As the first Japanese American novel, *No-No Boy* thus enters U.S. literary history as a resister of simple cultural identifications and simple assimilationist models. It insists on the irreducible narrative complexity of ethnic positions which are traditionally tropified or elided in mainstream white texts, and yet it participates in a recognizable national literary continuum. Neither Japanese nor American, rejecting both split and dual constructions of identity, *No-No Boy* is at once document and art, both literate and literary, counter-text and classic text. Representing and produced by those historically designated Other, *No-No Boy* constitutes an important revision and expansion of the U.S. literary canon. Just as powerfully, it also insists on a reconsideration of what it means to be "American."

This paper is for Therese On and Anita Chang, former students who gave me No-No Boy, and graciously encouraged my learning.

Notes

1. For the publication history of *No-No Boy*, see "In Search of John Okada," reprinted as the "Afterword" to *No-No Boy* (Seattle: University of Washington Press, 1979): 256; a review of *No-No Boy* in the *Hokubei Mainchi* on June 2, 1957, cited in ed. by Jeffrey Paul Chan, Frank Chin, Lawson Fusao Inada, and Shawn H. Wong, *Aiiieeeee! An Anthology of Asian American Writers* (Washington D.C.: Howard University Press, 1974; rpt 1983): 128; a letter from Charles Tuttle, Chan et. al., "An Introduction to Chinese and Japanese American Literature," *Aiiieeeee!*, xxix, xxxvi-xxxvii; and Lawson Fusao Inada, "Introduction" to John Okada, *No-No Boy* (Seattle: University of Washington Press, 1979: rpt., originally published: Seattle: Combined Asian American Resources Project, 1977; rpt, original cloth edition published: Tokyo: Charles E. Tuttle, 1957): iii. Quotations from the novel are noted by page number and refer to the latest edition.

2. The editors of *Aiiieeeee!* bemoan "the lack of a recognized style of Asian American manhood" in U.S. culture and literary representations. "An Introduction to Chinese and Japanese American Literature," xxxviii.

3. See "An Introduction to Chinese and Japanese American Literature," xxxv. Also, Lawson Fusao Inada, "Of Place and Displacement: The Range of Japanese American Literature," in *Three American Literatures,* Houston A. Baker, ed.. (New York: MLA, 1982): 265. Inada's only reference to the artistry of *No-No Boy* in this article comes in a footnote, which forms the epigraph to this essay.

4. Okada's life and education suggest that *No-No Boy* is not autobiography and that it is informed by knowledge of literary history. See *Aiiieeeee!*, 128, and *The Big Aiiieeeee!* Jeffrey Paul Chan, Frank Chin, Lawson Fusao Inada, and Shawn Wong, eds. (New York: Penguin, 1991): 53-4.

5. In 1943, all internees were required to answer loyalty questionnaires. Question 27 asked draft-age males: "Are you willing to serve in the armed forces of the United States on combat duty, wherever ordered?" Question 28 asked all internees: "Will you swear unqualified allegiance to the United States of America and faithfully defend the United States from any or all attack by foreign or domestic forces, and forswear any form of allegiance or obedience to the Japanese emperor, or any other foreign government, power or organization?" "No-no boys" are those who answered "no" to both questions. Ronald Takaki, *Strangers from a Different Shore: A History of Asian Americans* (Boston: Little, Brown, 1989): 397-400.

6. "Come All Ye Asian American Writers," 81-2.

7. These conflicting perspectives also betray ethnic solidarity, a violation of community privacy which may have alienated *issei* and *nisei*, which perhaps accounts for their initial indifference to and/or rejection of the book. For further discussion of this problem, see Kimberle Crenshaw, "Whose Story Is It, Anyway? Feminist and Antiracist Appropriations of Anita Hill," in *Racing Justice, Engendering Power*, Toni Morrison, ed. (New York: Pantheon, 1992): 420. See also Gordon Hirabayashi, in *The Big Aiiieeeee!*, 479.

8. "Come All Ye Asian American Writers," 53.

9. R.W.B. Lewis theorizes the American Adam as the quintessential hero of "the" authentic American or New World narrative authored by such writers as Hawthorne, Melville, Twain, Hemingway, Bellow. *The American Adam: Innocence, Tragedy, and Tradition in the Nineteenth Century* (Chicago: University of Chicago Press: 1955). Problematizing the assumption of a white European identity for this canonical American Adam, *No-No Boy* appropriates the trope for Ichiro Yamada. The novel recounts this Adamic *nisei* hero's capacity to invent his own character, and author, if not his history, then his future. Extending self-invention to a whole generation (the *nisei*), the novel expands the canonical archetype to show that the "Other's" task of self-development is the same as that of the Adamic white man, in comparison to whom he is traditionally labelled "Other."

10. "An Introduction to Chinese and Japanese American Literature," xxxv.

11. This insight demonstrates Diana Fuss's recent argument that constructionist discourses —like the naturalization steps that produce U.S. citizens from immigrants —nevertheless preserve and depend on essentialism—like biological markers that rationalize discrimination against an Other to revoke citizenship. *Essentially Speaking: Feminism, Nature and Difference* (New York: Routledge, 1989).

12. Leslie Fiedler, *Love and Death in the American Novel* (New York: Stein and Day, 1974), 192. Fiedler's discussions, like R.W.B. Lewis's, describe texts in a white male-authored canon of U.S. literature, whose narrative conventions *No-No Boy* problematizes and participates in. In Okada's revision of canonical literature's "archetypal relation," the conformist veteran Kenji is positioned as the Light man, while the pariah Ichiro is positioned as the Dark, but the former dies and the latter survives to serve as the new postwar *nisei*—or, expanding Lewis's terms, as the Japanese American "American Adam."

25

Reclamation of Historically Contextualized Identity Even Though *All I Asking for Is My Body*

Lauri Sagle

Explore 120 tropical acres of Hawaii's famous fruits, crops and flowers in a Hawaiian Plantation setting. Take the scenic tram tour, a fun-filled narrated excursion through fields of sugarcane, macadamia, bananas, pineapples, papaya and more... Meet our people and hear about Maui's fascinating past... Share the experience of our real working plantation.[1]

Hawai'i, Hawai'i
Like a dream so I came
But my tears are flowing now
In the canefields.[2]

Which description might best evoke Hawai'i's plantation history? The first excerpt is an advertisement from an in-flight, tourist-oriented magazine published under the auspices of Aloha Airlines (circa May 1989), and the second is a plantation work song, or *hole hole bushi*, composed by early twentieth century plantation laborers. It is doubtful that contemporary tourists would be prepared to simulate "the experience of [a] real working plantation" if it were accurately reconstructed from "Maui's fascinating past." The tour guide's "fun-filled" narrative would have to include the fact that, prior to 1900, immigrant plantation workers were bound by the brutal contract labor system, worked 10-12 hours a day, six days a week, and were promptly arrested and punished if they attempted to "desert" before their contract was up.[3] The historical circumstances of eviction, imprisonment, fining, firing, and other creatively cruel practices for degrading plantation workers who demanded better working and living conditions (especially in the notable strikes of 1909 and 1920) would also need to be explored during our little plantation tram ride. "Hey!" a *malihini* shouts from back of the tram, "This is not entertaining!" Okay, then. Crank the illusion back up again, pipe the Hawaiian Muzak back into the system, and glide through those tranquil fields of sugarcane, macadamia, bananas, pineapples, papaya… whatever you wish. This illusion of Hawai'i is yours because you're paying for it. Or are you?

The flattening of history is integral to the tourist industry. It is much more convenient to believe that no one ever wept, sweated, or bled in the fields that helped sweeten coffee, frost cakes, or bake the All-American apple pie. But denying the historical struggles of Hawai'i's people creates a playground of images (smiling nubile images that perennially welcome the tourist with a fragrant lei), consequently suppressing such local issues as sovereignty for Native Hawaiians, a legacy of plantation paternalism, and serious current environmental concerns. Our live scenic tram ride through the sterile, meticulously arranged and maintained vegetative delights of a "real, working plantation" promotes a post-modern fantasy experience and tandem distortion of Hawai'i's culture and life-style. We must therefore look for starker shades of reality in Hawai'i's fiction, a wide genre whose practitioners have less to gain by presenting an uncomplicated facade of life in Hawai'i.

Fiction produced by Hawai'i writers is viable, diverse, real matter. It exists. But, as Eric Chock pointed out in his opening night introduction to the 1980 Writers of Hawai'i Conference, Hawai'i writers and Island literature in general have often been rendered invisible by dubious arbiters of literary merit. Chock observes that, "[i]n Hawai'i, which as John Dominis Holt said, 'gave the world the word *aloha*,' it is ironic that the most commonly held notion of our literature is that it is non-existent."[4] Except, of course, if it is propagandistic, airline or hotel sponsored "tourist literature." The following commentary on *All I Asking for Is My Body* is not refreshingly new or brilliant for those already familiar with the literature and history of Hawai'i. But for others, this overview may constitute a learning experience, an introduction, as the importance of supporting, respecting and proudly validating Hawai'i's literature should not be underestimated; images, stories, ideas, and perceptions about Hawai'i from Hawai'i's own people shape a more authentic understanding of the Islands—one that would not just benefit a tourist's perspective, but the perspectives of Islanders themselves. Experiencing literature this way, Chock says, "will lead to more pride among Hawai'i's people, and an awareness of Hawai'i's directions, past and present. And it will also provide more opportunities for people… who grew up here and want to be writers and need clear models for exactly what that is—a Hawai'i writer."[5]

Fortunately, the persistent quality of Hawai'i's writers has more markedly affected the literary landscape since 1980. But the struggle over control of our own identity as kama'aina is ongoing, and the tourist industry's caricature of Island culture is only one (albeit a significant one) aspect of this struggle. Milton Murayama captures another phase of this confrontation in *All I Asking For Is My Body*, a novel chronicling the experiences of the Oyama family in pre-World War II Maui, as related through the maturing consciousness of Kiyoshi Oyama. Murayama himself was born on Maui, "and grew up in Lahaina and on 'Pig Pen Avenue' in Puukolii,… a plantation camp, once home to over six hundred, [which now] no longer exists."[6] Murayama's literary contribution, informed by his own experiences growing up in a plantation camp, authenticates reality through fiction, and vice versa. Arnold Hiura is quoted in Franklin Odo's "Afterward" of *All I Asking* as stating, "we have… just histories and sociological studies on the plantation, but almost none that deal with it on a literary level… we have been denied, up to this work, an idea of what the real, human situation of the plantation has been."[7] Murayama's "real, human situation" resonates not only with those readers who are familiar with Hawai'i's plantations through lived experience, but also with those of us who grew up surrounded by the plantations' historical legacy. Encountering the cultural specificity of the Islands through Murayama's language, descriptions, and insights feels like coming home. Stephen Sumida, originally from Oahu and currently Professor of Asian American Studies at the University of Michigan, commented that *All I Asking For Is My Body* "allow[s] us to see, validated (insofar as might be necessary) in a published work of fiction, that Dick and Jane were not the only kids growing up in the world in our century… Murayama's story, his characters, and certainly his language were as familiar to me as if they were my own."[8] And, in a sense, they are.

At this meta-level of analysis, critics who are not from Hawai'i and who are encountering the novel for the first time should be aware of the cultural complexities informing its content while simultaneously practicing an awareness of their own socio-cultural position. One of the common "misreadings" (Sumida's term) of Murayama's novel flows out of the misinformation non-Islanders may possess about Hawai'i. Authoring and maintaining our own images and identities are imperative to our control over them, and part of this process includes re-possessing, contextualizing and historicizing these images when they are being misread. The central "misreading" Sumida focuses on is the "false issue" of "intercultural conflicts between generations," as embodied by the *issei* Mr. and Mrs. Oyama and their *nisei* children, particularly Tosh, their oldest son, and, to a less directly confrontational degree, Kiyo, the second oldest.[9] Sumida takes issue with critic Elaine H. Kim for "concentrat[ing] her discussion [of *All I Asking For Is My Body*] on the oppressiveness of the Japanese immigrant family and community."[10] Kim's observation that "[t]here is little of value in the Japanese family or community in *All I Asking For Is My Body*, except perhaps for the relationship between the two *nisei* brothers," Sumida finds to be a distortion of the novel's core conflicts.[11] "What," he asks, "if the novel... is a condemnation not of 'aspects' of 'the Japanese family or community' but of abuses against the family and community whether from inside or from outside the lives of the novel's three generations of Japanese Americans?"[12] As Sumida suggests, "the reading of satire [the genre he assigns to the novel] is usually set straight by values which readers are assumed to share," and critical misunderstandings may therefore proliferate in the space where culturally specific values don't intersect.[13]

Furthermore, the history of immigrant labor in the Hawaiian Islands is perfunctorily deflected in Kim's comment that "[t]he *issei*... have transplanted in Hawaii almost intact the feudal Japanese family, which constitutes a rigidly hierarchical pecking order that almost everyone in the Japanese American community supports."[14] We can hear the machinery of that smooth scenic tram gearing up again as the complex cultural and familial survival strategies are reduced to easily dismissed microcosms of feudalism. On the other hand, contextualized within a historical framework, those politicians, businessmen, and managers governing plantation operations comprised, as Ray Stannard Baker put it, "the last surviving vestige of feudalism in the United States," a more plausible analogy in terms of the vast amount of control plantations enacted over their workers' lives.[15] And this kind of racist, feudalistic plantation paternalism thrived in the Islands since "no white man would work in the fields for the wages the planters offered."[16] This ideology of paternalism, recounted by Ronald Takaki's *Pau Hana: Plantation Life and Labor in Hawaii*, and exemplified by the philosophy of the Hawaiian Sugar Planters' Association in the early twentieth century, held that "Caucasians were 'constitutionally and temperamentally unfitted for labor' in a tropical climate, while Asians and 'brown' men were 'peculiarly adapted to the exactions of tropical labor,' and could serve as satisfactory and 'permanent' field workers."[17] With racism, colonialism, and classism (if not caste-ism) intertwining in a macrocosm of feudalism, putative microcosms, even if they did exist as sharply characterized by Kim, could easily be subsumed under the larger system.

As it is, however, our literary heroes in *All I Asking* must gain this knowledge through their own personal experience. Toshio and Kiyoshi realize that something is *pilau* in paradise, but only incrementally can ascertain the source of it. The cultural values Elaine Kim construes as oppressive are the initial and natural target for Tosh, the rebellious older brother. Tosh's complaints directed at his mother and father are predicated on the Oyama family's stagnant status within the plantation social system. He criticizes his parents' value system, citing, among other things, "bear[ing] more children than [they] can send to school," and requiring of their children a type of filial piety which entails working off a $6,000 debt (a debt accumulated in part through their paternal grandfather's financial "bad luck," and in part through Mrs. Oyama's medical bills). Tosh wants exacting predictions from his parents on "How much?" and "How long?" he will be required to help in ameliorating the family debt, but Mrs. Oyama is evasive; plantation paternalism provides no neon exit signs pointing the way out, only a tenuous "opportunity" to survive on a quotidian basis. He is restless and enraged by his lack of opportunity and concomitant "place" in the system, and he literally and figuratively attempts to fight his way out by "practic[ing] all the parries and counters shown in Jimmy DeForest's *How to Box* pamphlets."[18]

A symbolically inevitable altercation ensues after Tosh accuses his father of being "really blind" in his denial of everything from the Japanese Army's incursion into Nanking to the chicanery of Mr. Oyama's father in leaving them a hefty debt. They come to blows, but Tosh, with his acquired boxing skills, derails his father with one "left hook." Hitting his father is an "unthinkable" transgression, the ultimate rebellion, but even though Tosh says afterwards that "it felt good," Tosh's position in the larger scheme of things—the plantation culture— is no different than it was before this confrontation. Despite the rage directed at his parents, whom he perceives as his immediate impediments to freedom, and his claims, post "left hook," to be the new "top man in the family," Tosh has some deeper recognition of the family's entrapment within the plantation framework: "All this bullshit about *chonan* (number one son) makes sense only if the old man is successful and got property. He leaves everything to the *chonan* and that way he no break up his property. But no father who's a plantation worker can call himself successful."[19] And with that, Tosh has identified the perpetuation of an oppressive caste system. The family values and the responsibility of the *chonan* are not harmful outside of the plantation system, as Tosh notes, but in conjunction with the exploitative plantation ideology they seem to form an entrapping symbiosis. As Stephen Sumida notes, "the parents become unwitting allies with the plantation in keeping the boys down,... [and thus] the plantation ends up accomplishing what it most desperately needs to: retain its stoop labor force," in other words, actualizing the original goal of the HSPA— "satisfactory and 'permanent' field workers."[20]

The "rigidly hierarchical pecking order" Kim ascribes to the "feudal Japanese family" aptly characterizes many early plantations' social constructs, not only as part of an abstract ideology, but also as a component of some of their working policies. Even if Tosh were able to finish school, historical evidence indicates that he may have been obstructed from doing so by agents of the plantation who were intent on crippling the second generation's ambitions. Takaki, in another fine work, *Strangers From a Different Shore*, reveals that "[a]t a conference of social workers in 1928, the governor of Hawaii urged them to direct the youth back to agriculture." Apparently, "[m]any planters did not want the children of plantation laborers to be educated beyond the sixth or eighth grade,... [preferring that] the schools... offer vocational training, not literature courses." One of the Grand Sugar Daddies himself, Richard Cooke, a president of C. Brewer and Company (which was "a major producer of sugar"), said that "the public-school teachers should not keep their students from working on the plantations, [and] [i]f the schools continued to give students high career aspirations, Cooke warned, 'we had better change our educational system here as soon as possible.'"[21] Another text, published originally in 1937, also bemoans the upward mobility of the younger generations, finding that "[t]he main source of present-day anxiety on the part of [Hawai'i's] leaders is [whether]... education may be lifting the children of the working classes so rapidly that they may be unwilling to follow their parents in the hard labor of the plantations." The author, Sidney Gulick, cheerfully goes on to report, however, that plantation managers have anticipated the friskiness of the second generation, thoughtfully intercepting their ambitions by implementing fun-to-use "labor saving machinery" and company policies which reflect "sympathetic understanding and treatment of the young people"[22]— as long as they stay in their place, that is.

Another hierarchically ordered system of relationships was facilitated through the promotion of ethnic rivalries by some of the plantations. The root of this type of "divide and rule strategy" was manifested as early as the 1850s, when planters determined that encouraging racial tensions may have a "stimulating effect" on production.[23]

Tosh begins to see through this manipulated social stratification, voicing his concern for striking Filipino workers, and suggesting that, "The Japanese should have joined them." "They can't win," Mr. Oyama responds, reminding Tosh that "[t]he Japanese went on strike in 1920 and 1922 and both times the others were the strikebreakers." "That's why," Tosh proclaims, "nobody can beat the plantation," but he also comments that, after all, "[w]e all fighting the same plantation." When his father says, "We should know our place and not anger them," Tosh counters with, "That's the trouble with the Japanese, they're yellow balls. You don't gain respect by *boto boto*. You gain respect by fighting. We have to fight them."[24] Tosh possesses an awareness of the plantation's "divide and conquer" agenda, but, given the historical precedents of factionalism, doesn't fully envision any alternative besides the vague notion of "fighting them." And the real trouble cannot be located within the Japanese value system since (as Mr. Oyama notes, contrary to Tosh's accusations) the Japanese immigrants had a history of striking, but within the methods of defusing strikes and strikers demands.

Kiyo, however, learns from Tosh's grumblings and propensity to "fight." Following Tosh's lead, he too initially tries physically fighting his way out of the system by practicing his boxing skills and eventually becoming good enough to fight in inter- Island "territorial finals." His progress closely parallels Tosh's: Tosh excels at boxing and gets promoted to a "truck driver's helper," then Kiyo makes his boxing debut, also getting promoted to a "truck driver's helper." But Kiyo ultimately recognizes that he must forge his own passage out of the system, and that "[b]oxing wasn't the way... But for a Japanese there were no jobs except the plantation... Even if you went to college, all you could be was a grammar school teacher, and if lucky, a high school teacher." After the bombing of Pearl Harbor, Kiyo's disorientation is exacerbated. He visits Mr. Takemoto, a Japanese school teacher and respected member of their community, hoping for enlightening instruction, but even Mr. Takemoto says that "it's hard to explain things rationally." As Kiyo walks out into the night, he feels that his ways of comprehending the world around him have collapsed and that, "[t]he once proud ground [he'd] been standing on had turned into soft shit."[25]

In a seemingly ironic move, Kiyo decides to volunteer for the "all-*nisei* regiment," perceiving this as "his chance delivered on a silver platter... to get out of [the] icky shit-hole [of Kahana]." And "[b]esides," he reasons, "once you fought, you earned the right to complain and participate, you earned the right to a future."[26] Between the family debt, the "prison term" of the plantation, and a world war, Kiyo has negligible control over the immediate possession of his body.

So on the eve of his participation in this final proving ground of war, Kiyo tests "fate" and the legacy of the Oyama luck, finally liberating himself through a calculated risk, perhaps the most democratic endeavor he has yet experienced. By "padrolling" in craps games, he emerges with enough winnings to nullify the family debt and with a philosophy that reorients the direction of his life. He literally "goes for broke," ultimately reclaiming his body and foreshadowing the real-life valor of the all Japanese American 442nd Regiment, termed, significantly, the "Go For Broke" Battalion. Also known as the "Purple Heart Battalion" for their high casualty rate, those who survived continued to break out after the war, utilizing "their G.I. Bill of Rights and disabled veterans' compensation to go on to college and to law school," eventually "acquir[ing] [significant] political power in Hawaii," and obviously, as Kiyo had hoped, the long overdue "right to a future."[27]

Perhaps the plantation system wasn't as monolithically oppressing as it appeared. Many immigrants and their families survived, settled, and prospered, and some, obviously, even wrote (and continue to write) about their experiences. Stephen Sumida comments, regarding Kiyo's maturation, that "[l]earning history and assuming responsibility are partners in one's growing up."[28] And as a third generation Island daughter, I think that applies to me too and to my responsibility, given the privilege of my education, to insist on the importance of cultural contextualization rather than a de-historicized "tropical plantation" joy ride. Listening to Hawai'i's stories and Hawai'i's people speak for themselves will reveal a fuller, truer sense of the Islands' *ohana*.

Glossary of Terms

aloha: word of greeting and farewell; love
issei: first-generation immigrant Japanese
kama'aina: native born, local Islanders
malihini: newcomer to the Islands
nisei: second generation Japanese-American
ohana: family
pau hana: quitting time; finished working
pilau: rotten, stinky, foul

Notes

1. *Spirit of Aloha* 14 (May 1989) 7.
2. Dennis M. Ogawa, *Kodomo No Tame Ni. For the Sake of the Children. The Japanese American Experience in Hawaii* (Honolulu: University of Hawaii Press, 1983): 11.
3. Ronald Takaki, *Pau Hana: Plantation Life and Labor in Hawaii* (Honolulu: University of Hawaii Press, 1983): 38.

4. Eric Chock, "On Local Literature," in *The Best of Bamboo Ridge*, Eric Chock and Darrell H.Y. Lum, eds., (Hawai'i: Bamboo Ridge Press, 1986): 7.

5. Ibid., 6.

6. Milton Murayama, *All I Asking For Is My Body*, (Honolulu: University of Hawaii Press, 1988): 111.

7. Ibid., 106.

8. Stephen H. Sumida, *Two Novels of Hawai'i* (Honolulu: Ku Pa'a Incorporated, 1989) 5.

9. Ibid., 5-6.

10. Ibid., 7.

11. Elaine Kim, *Asian American Literature: An Introduction to the Writings and Their Social Context* (Philadelphia: Temple University Press, 1982): 146.

12. Sumida, 12.

13. Ibid., 6.

14. Kim, 143.

15. Murayama, 33.

16. Gavan Daws, *Shoal of Time. A History of the Hawaiian Islands* (Honolulu: University of Hawaii Press, 1968): 307.

17. Takaki, *Pau Hana*, 66.

18. Murayama, 31.

19. Ibid., 44, 47, 49.

20. Sumida, 15; Takaki, *Pau Hana*, 66.

21. Ronald Takaki, *Strangers From a Different Shore. A History of Asian Americans* (New York: Penguin Books, 1989): 174, 172.

22. Sidney L. Gulick, *Mixing the Races in Hawaii. A Study of the Coming Neo-Hawaiian American Race* (Honolulu: Hawaiian Board Book Rooms, 1937): 58.

23. Takaki, 68.

24. Murayama, 36-37.

25. Ibid., 58, 68, 71, 82-83.

26. Murayama, 98.

27. Francine de Plessix Gray, *Hawaii: The Sugar Coated Fortress*, (New York: Vintage Books, 1973) 70-71.

28. Sumida, 17.

26

After the War: A Family Album[1]

Directed by Melissa Littig Godoy

Excerpt from an oral history television documentary about the Vietnam War as told by Hmong and Vietnamese refugees in Green Bay, Wisconsin.

FADE IN: Leaves fall through the early autumn sunlight at Fort Howard Cemetery in Green Bay. James McGlinn, Jr., a Green Bay West High School student sits cross-legged by the headstone of his father.

JIM: Hi. My name is James McGlinn. My father lies beneath me in the cemetery here in Green Bay. I never knew him. But I go to his high school and I have his name. The reason for this is the Vietnam War.

(Cut to the teenage producers of the video: Syda Xiong, Melody Xiong, Hue Yang, Pao Yang, and Jim McGlinn walking across a bridge.)

JIM: *(voice over)* My friends are Hmong people from Laos. They are here also because of the Vietnam War. We have come together to make a video about our families.

(SFX: Repeating camera shutter. The walk across the bridge becomes a series of stills. The stills of the producers become stills of the producers' families moving further into the past and ending with family photos shot in Laos.)
(MUSIC: Hmong folk song. Stills break into 1950s footage of Hmong people harvesting food and cooking. Cut to maps that depict the migration of the Hmong people.)

SYDA: *(voice over)* Hmong people originated in Mongolia and resettled in northern China about 4000 years ago. But these nomadic ancestors of ours continued to move every seven to ten years, eventually resettling in the mountains of Laos. We fought in the Lao army and participated in its economy. When we think of home, we think of Laos.

(Cut to Lou Vang, Syda's 62-year-old grandmother, speaking Hmong.)

LOU: In Laos we woke up with the roosters and started cooking breakfast, and before sunrise we were on our way to the farm in the dark. For the lazy ones, they waited until it was morning, then they would walk to their farm. Everybody was so energetic and hard-working, people who farmed wide farmlands, and we had no time to feel tired in our country Laos. Maybe our country was a very energetic country.

(Cut to Xeng Xiong, Syda's 44-year-old father, speaking English.)

XENG: Laos is a very small country, a freedom country. The people very good. Why I say very good? You can go from the north side to the south side, the east side to the west side, without money. No got a road. Just walk. You have food. You have a place to live, to sleep. No problem. Like I never know you, if you come to my house, I should be accept you like my guest, and give you food for you to eat. I got a place for you sleep.

(Cut to shelling in Saigon, 1954. SFX: War.)

JIM: *(voice over)* But in Vietnam, in 1954, war broke out between the Communist Viet Cong in the North and the U.S.-backed republic of South Vietnam.

(Cut to Loi Nguyen, a Vietnamese ex-POW, age 50.)

LOI: Before in the time 1954, the South Vietnam were peaceful. The president, Mr. Ngo Dinh Diem, he come back from America. He was a great man. *(Cut to archival footage to illustrate what Loi is saying.)*

By the help of America, the president, Mr. Ngo Din Diem, open many new schools, many hospitals, many new village, many new road. He was a kind man. He loved people and people loved him. But I am very sorry, because after that, many big officer of South Vietnam, they all went many of them took Vietnam. That means they good mind to make new government. In that time, the communists knew many of the organizations in South Vietnam, and the communists in the north of Vietnam enter the south of Vietnam.

SFX: *War rise and out. Cut to photo of Hmong Colonel Vang Pao.*

SYDA: *(voice over)* In 1958, the U.S. arranged for a Hmong tribesman, Colonel Vang Pao, to organize guerilla harassment of North Vietnamese troops occupying boarder areas east of the Plain de Jarres region of Laos.

(Fade out map of Plain de Jarres. Cut to Chao Yang, the 37-year-old father of Hue Yang. Then cut to photo of Hmong soldiers blocking the Ho Chi Minh Trail.)

CHAO: At that time, in 1960 to 1961, America had sent these people to Laos which were called CIA. We had to block the road so that the North Vietnamese could not send food and weapons to their people in South Vietnam.

(Cut to Xeng Xiong and then to map of the Ho Chi Minh Trail.)

XENG: Because Vietnam, he need Lao border to be they call the Ho Chi Minh Trail, come pass through the South.

(Cut to Xay Doua Xiong, Xeng's 80-year-old father.)

XAY DOUA: When the war started, I was scared and afraid, but they persuaded my son to go to war, and I didn't let them, but they took him anyway.

(Cut to Xeng, then to footage of Colonel Vang Pao leading Hmong troops in Laos in the 1960s.)

XENG: I start to go to war in 1967. My three brothers born before me, they go to the war.

(Cut to photos and archival footage of Hmong teenage soldiers.)

JIM: *(voice over)* The United States paid Hmong men approximately $20 a month to fight. Thirty thousand Hmong soldiers lost their lives in the Vietnam War. After the men were killed, the United States recruited boys as young as 10 to fight.

(Cut to Pa Chou Yang, Pao's father, age 52. Then cut to Hmong men digging trenches and helicopters dropping soldiers off to fight. SFX: Helicopters.)

PA CHOU: They had helicopters which took us to the mountains and battlefields since the communist base was close by. We had to dig our own fox holes and stay in and fight.

(Cut to helicopters then to Hiep.)

HIEP: During the Vietnam War, I was so young. I remember the helicopters blow on the sky in my village. I was so afraid about it.

(Cut to airplanes dropping bundles from the sky. Cut to ground shot of Hmong women with baskets on their backs running for food. A pair of hands scrapes rice out of dirt.)

SYDA: *(voice over)* The U.S. also provided rice and canned goods for the women left behind to support their families.

XENG: *(voice over)* Because they fight, go to fight, just the men. But the men dead. The wife, what are they going to do? They no got an idea, no got a power to find money, no food to support the kids. It's very terrible.

(Cut to Lou Vang.)

LOU: My husband was guarding the entrance to the village, and he was captured by the communists. We didn't hear anything from him for three years. That's why I married my second husband. Because of his disappearance, the U.S. helped support me with some money, but I cried for three years.

(Cut to a battle over the Plain de Jarres at night. Cut to airplanes dropping bombs during the day. Cut to men carrying a wounded Hmong woman on a stretcher. Cut to a Hmong funeral in Laos.)

PA CHOU: *(voice over)* During the battle, big airplanes called T-28 and F-14 flew over and dropped bombs all over the place while we fought below them. People were injured and killed all over, including us. We were lucky enough to survive.

(Cut to musical montage of Hmong soldiers fighting. Cut to moon. Cut to peaceful photo of Hiep's family's farm in Vietnam.)

HIEP: I grow up on farm until I got seven years old, then I go to big city. But without family. The reason is because we are poor, we are hungry and the war is so danger.

(Cut to portrait of James McGlinn, Sr., Captain, U.S. Army. Cut to candid of James McGlinn, Sr. with army buddies.)

HIEP: *(voice over)* When I met him I was 16 years old. I still going to school. Because he live across us, I saw him sometimes.

(Cut to Hiep in sync, then to candid of James, Sr. and Hiep together, very young.)

HIEP: It is hard to tell you that I loved him. It's because I was so young. He asked me to marry, but we didn't marry. We just stayed together.

(Cut to James, Jr. in sync, then to photo of himself as a baby in Hiep's arms.)

JIM: When he left Vietnam, I was, I didn't born yet. So when he came to America, when he go back to America, my mom she cannot stay in Saigon, capital, so she had to go back to my family. Then I was born in my family.

HIEP: After he left Vietnam, he went back to America. Then he start sending help until 1972. Then he quit it. I don't know what reason. I wrote some letters for him, but I didn't get any answer.

(Cut to photo of toddler Jim in Vietnam. Musical transition.)
(Cut to Loi. As he talks, cut to news footage of the fall of Saigon.)

LOI: We kill many V.C. in South Vietnam. But in the North Vietnam, they always enter South Vietnam with many people, many new soldiers, and many new weapons. You also know that after 1975, before that 1973, by the Paris Agreement, the U.S. army, Philippine, Thailand, Korea withdraw their armies' support. Only Vietnamese army in South Vietnam. In that time the north of communists of Vietnam by the helping of Russia, Red China, Hungary, Cuba, with all the new weapons, they enter the south of Vietnam. And they occupy Vietnam. South Vietnam.

(Cut to Vang Pao in an airplane. Cut to armed Hmong soldiers ducking into the thick jungle.)

PA CHOU: We were on the run since 1975 when our general Vang Pao left us. We had a hard time living since the communists took over Laos. We moved to the jungle and fought for four years until 1979.

(Cut to Lou, then to aerial shots of the jungle-covered mountains of Laos.)

LOU: During that time, we were chased by the communist soldiers. We moved from one place to another. We lived in the jungle, as well as the mountains. Whenever we hid the communist soldiers would always find us. When we were on the run, there was a lot of shooting and bombing so we threw all our goods and belongings away. When we were on the run we left a storage house full of rice behind.

(Cut to map of Laos and Thailand.)

JIM: *(voice over)* Beginning in May of 1975, almost half a million Hmong people began the long trip out of Laos to Thailand.

(Cut to Xeng in sync. Cut to photo of Syda as a baby, then back to Xeng.)

XENG: So at that time, I pushed my wife and my Syda, a little kid. At that time she's just no one year. She's just eleven months. Put inside airplane. Five days, five nights my head ache. I got a problem with my head. I worry too much, like a warstone in my head. I don't know what I'm going to do. I will go to the communist side... I will stay here to fight... or should we go with the boss? We go with the boss, they don't, they don't want you! They say only 2500 people go with the boss to the U.S.A. But the last minute, last three days, everybody run for survival.

(Cut to Hmong people leaving Laos by foot with the few belongings they can carry. Cut to Lou.)

LOU: During our run to Thailand, we were very scared. We didn't even have time to think about our lives. We only thought about what would happen if a gun went off on our heads, and that really scared us.

(Cut to 17-year-old producer Pao Yang.)

PAO: When my whole family, were traveling to Thailand, and we were ambushed on the way at this road. My dad was carrying me, and my mom was carrying my younger brother. And that's when my mom got shot. And as my dad was rushing to cross the street I noticed that there was a vine there, and it kind of like caught me in the neck. And I think my dad didn't have time to stop so he just pushed me, dragged me really hard right through the vine.

(Cut to Pao's mother, Chia Lor Yang, age 50.)

CHIA: On the way to Thailand, communist soldiers shot me in the arm. That's why I lost one of my arms. I couldn't run anywhere, so I lay there waiting for the communists to come and capture me. When I was captured, the communists took me back to their camp, and they cut off my arm.

(Cut to a pile of photographs of Hmong relatives. More photos fall onto the pile. The photo of a baby is dropped. SFX: Baby's cry.)

PA CHOU: Along the way many people died on top of each other. The elderly people who couldn't travel anymore were left behind to die. And for the children who cried a lot, they were drugged to death.

(Cut to Lou.)

LOU: It took us one month and seventeen days to reach Pajxoons, Thailand. When we arrived there, we were very skinny and bony. We slept all over the place like pigs that were about to die. There were no blankets, nothing for us to sleep on. We slept on banana leaves only.

(Cut to Ka.)

KA: We ate shrubs and twigs. That's how we got to Thailand. But not only that, when we got to Thailand, we were robbed and then we were put in a camp for three months.

(Cut to Lou.)

LOU: When we lived in Thailand we were kept in a camp and we could not get out to find logs or water, but you could get water from the camp. If you left the camp to find logs or other things, you were captured by the

Thai police and tortured or killed. Thai officers did not allow us to go out at all. Those who went out to buy food or cigarettes were tortured or beaten up badly.

(Cut to 17-year-old producer Hue Yang.)

HUE: I think spending my whole childhood life in the camp was fun and enjoyable, but when you're talking about the camp, the camp itself was very dirty. When it rained it was muddy, and it was hard to travel around the camp.

(Cut to Hue's father, Chao Yang. As he talks, cut to photo of him working in the camp.)

CHAO: I lived in Thailand from 1978 to 1988. The reason I stayed in the camp so long was because I distributed food and made sure everybody lived healthy lives. I also delivered letters.

(Cut to more camp photos. Musical transition.)

SYDA: *(voice over)* For those who stayed behind in Vietnam after the occupation, life was difficult.

(Cut to Loi. Cut to a North Vietnamese Communist meeting.)

LOI: When the communists occupy South Vietnam, many people were killed. And many members of their old government must enter the camp of communists.

JIM: Loi, who worked in intelligence for South Vietnam, was placed in communist re-education camps for nine years.

(Cut to Loi.)

LOI: They explain for us about the organization they call the political of Communists, but we don't hear it. We only eat vegetables and the rice of the India. That means the rice for the cow to eat. We eat the rice of cow! And at night, they put us in the dark room. We eat in room. We go to restroom in the room, only room. And many friends, many my friends died because no medicine. A great number of us died because of diarrhea.

(Cut to photograph of Jim as a child. Cut to communist soldier striding toward a tank in Saigon.)

JIM: When I was a child, I always scared. Y'know, I always scared, all the time, because the communist government, I afraid of them because, I think they gonna kill me because I am kinda Amerasian.

(Cut to Amerasian teenagers hanging out on the streets of Saigon.)

SYDA: By the end of the war, 30,000 Amerasian children, their GI fathers back in the United States, were left to survive, often on the streets.

(Cut to more Amerasian teenagers. Cut to Vietnamese woman picking up garbage at a market.)

JIM: They live outside. They don't have a house, even they don't have a father, like me, and they don't have mother either. And every morning they have to go, to the garbage, pick up the garbage and eat! *(Cut to Jim in sync. Cut to Amerasian teenager at school in Vietnam with younger students. Cut to obituary of James McGlinn, Sr.)*

When I finish high school, I cannot go to college because I were Amerasian. They not allow for the Amerasian to go to college. August 6, 1982, my mom she received the letter from my grandma, and the letter say that my father die because he was in an accident.

(Cut to Hiep in sync.)

HIEP: It's okay for me to live in Vietnam, but I think for my son's future. He is American. He go back to America.

(Cut to map depicting journey from Southeast Asia to America.)

JIM: Starting in 1975, 150,000 Southeast Asian war refugees began to emigrate to America.

(Map trip ends with zoom on Chicago. Cut to aerial of Chicago.)

XENG: The first time I come is very strange, especially I come in Chicago. Is a very big country. Has got an ambulance car, and a fireman car, truck. All night make noise. I think maybe something wrong. I wake up all the time. I scared. Because my country never heard of that.

(Cut to Pao in sync.)

PAO: When we first moved here it was pretty much challenging because then at that time, my sister she was still young, and she didn't know how to cook yet, so most of the time, my dad had to cook because my mom lost her arm. And we just had like to help each other a lot.

(Cut to Argyle Street, Chicago.)

PA CHOU: When we lived in Chicago, we were sworn at by people on the streets pointing at us, asking us why we were here in their country and that we were taking part of their income. They don't even know why we came here in the first place or that we were soldiers fighting with the Americans, and then we lost our country. That's why we're here.

(Cut to Syda in sync. Then cut to her somber kindergarten school photo. End with eighth grade graduation photo.)

SYDA: They would take paper, crumple it up and throw it at me. Y'know, call me "Chinese, Chinese. Go back, go back." And they always made fun of my eyes.

PA CHOU: For us elderly parents, we know that we have no hope for ourselves, but we took our children here to see if they'll have a better life in the future. For us parents, we can't do anything anymore. We can't even own a house or land. We always tell our children to study hard everyday because we want them to have a good future.

(Cut to younger Xiong daughters feeding a rooster in the Xiong's backyard.)
(Cut to a crowd of Hmong people at the New Year Celebration. Cut to Xeng Xiong thinking alone in his back yard.)

SYDA: *(voice over)* It has been almost 20 years since the Vietnam War ended. But its impact on families worldwide remains. Today 20,000 Southeast Asian refugees continue to resettle in the United States annually. This is the story of those who survived.

(Music. Credits.)

Notes

1. ©1992 by Melissa Littig Godoy. Written and produced by Melissa Littig Godoy, Peggy Kaiser, James McGlinn, Jr., Melody Xiong, Syda Xiong, Hue Yang, and Pao Yang. Additional research and editing by Por Choua Thao, Blia Vang, and Xang Yang. Produced at Northeastern Wisconsin In-School Telecommunications/CESA #7, IS-1110 University of Wisconsin-Green Bay, Green Bay, WI 54311. Videotape available by calling NEWIST at 1-800-633-7445. Project funded and administrated by the Job Training Partnership Act, Northeast Private Industry Council, Service Delivery Area #14 CESA #7 JTPA Director, Dan Konop.

After the War: A Family Album won first place in the Young Media Artist Division of the 1993 Utah Short Film and Video Festival.

Contributors

SUSAN MATOBA ADLER is presently an associate lecturer and Ph.D. dissertator in the Department of Curriculum and Instruction, School of Education, University of Wisconsin - Madison. Previously she was an assistant professor in the Department of Teaching, University of Wisconsin-Platteville, where she taught early childhood education and multicultural education courses.

VIDYUT AKLUJKAR writes poems, short stories, travelogues, and essays in English and Marathi. Her work is published in India, Canada, and the United States. She has taught courses in philosophy and Asian studies at Michigan State University, and the University of British Columbia, and her scholarly publications have appeared in several international journals.

JANICE BOGSTAD is an assistant professor in the McIntyre Library at the University of Wisconsin-Eau Claire. She has a B.A., M.A. and Ph.D. in comparative literature with a minor in the history of Chinese literature as well as an M.A. in library science and has taught courses in I Ching, history of the Chinese novel, Western classics to the Renaissance, library reference, and collection development. Her special interests are feminist theory; Anglo American, French and Chinese twentieth-century literature; and reader-response theory.

JANICE BOGSTAD is an associate professor of history at the University of Wisconsin - La Crosse, where she teaches Chinese, French, and world history. She is currently working with Annette White-Parks and Joyce Koskenmaki on an interdisciplinary course about the lives of Chinese and Chinese American women in history, literature and art.

MONICA CHIU holds a Master's degree in English from Binghamton University and is now working towards a Ph.D. at Emory University, specializing in Asian

American women writers. Her other interests include feminist theory, nineteenth- and twentieth-century American and British women writers, and the intersection between literature and medicine.

URSULA CHIU is a retired public school teacher who has extensive experience in working and living with Asian Americans.

ERIC CHOCK, a poet and teacher from Hawaii, co-founded *Bamboo Ridge, The Hawaii Writers Quarterly* with Darrell H. Lum, in 1978. He is the Hawaii Poets in the Schools Coordinator, where he has taught for the last 20 years. He has edited *Small Kid Time Hawaii,* an anthology of children's poems. A collection of Chock's own poems, *Last Days Here* (1991-1992) includes "Chinese Fireworks Banned in Hawaii," a Pushcart Prize-winning poem.

CATHERINE CURRIER is an assistant professor and automation manager at Murphy Library, University of Wisconsin-La Crosse. She has a B.A. in sociology, a B.A. and M.A. in library science, and is working on a Ph.D. in educational technology. She has done research and given presentations on gender-power-language and science fiction using feminist theory, critical theory and reader-response theory at library, women's studies, popular culture and science fiction literary conferences.

WENWEI DU has earned a Ph.D. in comparative literature and Chinese from Washington University in St. Louis. As an assistant professor, she teaches in the Department of Modern Languages and Literatures at Swarthmore College.

MICHAEL FERRIS is a non-traditional student, currently a sophomore majoring in political science at the University of Wisconsin-La Crosse. In the prior year he presented his paper on hunger in Russia at a conference on world hunger at Winona State University, in Winona, Minnesota, and he served as a panelist at the Wisconsin Political Science Association's annual meeting.

ALISA JARIN GARDINER, upon graduation from Carleton College, served as assistant to the director of multicultural affairs and founded the college's Interracial Student's Organization (IRSO). She is an independent diversity consultant specializing in Asian American and interracial issues. She is currently employed At Hewitt Associates in Chicago.

HARRY GARDINER is a cross-cultural psychologist and professor at the University of Wisconsin - La Crosse. His M.A. is from the University of Hawaii, and his Ph.D. is from the University of Manchester (England). He has been engaged in training, teaching, and research in Europe, Asia, and the United States. He is co-author of *Child and Adolescent Development*, chapters in several cross-cultural books, and he has written more than 60 articles in professional journals.

Contributors

ORMSIN SORNMOOPIN GARDINER is a native of Thailand and teaches mathematics at Winona State University. She works with international students as part of her teaching and as an advisor to her university's international studies program. She has presented papers on a variety of topics including "Attitudes toward the learning of mathematics: a cross-cultural study of Thai and American college women."

CAROLE GERSTER is an assistant professor of English at the University of Wisconsin - River Falls. She received her Ph.D. from the University of Minnesota, and has done post-doctoral work at Princeton University and at the University of California - Berkeley. She teaches a course on ethnic film and literature, and has published several articles on the topic of ethnic film and literature.

CHRISTIAN GHASARIAN is a French social anthropologist who has made his Ph.D. on the Tamil Diaspora in Reunion Island (French Department in the Indian Ocean). He has published a book entitled *Honneur, Chance et Destin. La culture indienne a Là Réunion.* Currently a research associate at the University of California-Berkeley, he is studying the cultural adaptation of immigrants from India in the San Francisco Bay Area.

MELISSA LITTIG GODOY graduated from Northwestern University with a degree in theater in 1985. She has since been developing original productions for theater and television, most recently training Southeast Asian teenagers in video production under a grant from the Job Training Partnership Act. Ms. Godoy writes and produces professional documentaries for Northeast Wisconsin In-School Telecommunications (NEWIST/CESA 7) and Wisconsin Public Television, producing as of late, "The Children of Divorce," "I Grow Old," and an anti-drug campaign "Getta Life" for the Wisconsin Department of Health and Social Services.

RAY HUTCHISON is associate professor of sociology and Chair, Urban and Regional Studies, at the University of Wisconsin - Green Bay. In 1990 he received the Faculty Research Scholar Award from the UW - System Institute on Race and Ethnicity for his research on the Hmong community in northeast Wisconsin. He has published research on the Hmong community in Wisconsin and on the Hispanic community in Chicago, and is the series editor of *Research in Urban Sociology* (JAI Press).

RONNA C. JOHNSON is a member of the English department and Director of Women's Studies at Tufts University. She writes on nineteenth- and twentieth-century American literature, and is completing a book about the Beat generation writer Jack Kerouac, titled "Gender and Narrative in Jack Kerouac: Anticipations of the Postmodern."

ANNE E. LESSICK-XIAO is the East Asian Studies Outreach Coordinator at the University of Wisconsin - Madison where she is completing her dissertation on contemporary Francophone Congolese literature in the Department of African Languages and Literature. She has been an English as a Second Language and Swahili instructor for 15 years.

AMY LING is associate professor of English and Director of the Asian American Studies program at the University of Wisconsin - Madison. She is the author of *Between Worlds: Women Writers of Chinese Ancestry* (Pergamon, 1991, now Teacher's College Press, Columbia University), a cultural history, and *Chinamerican Reflections*, a chapbook of her own poems and paintings. She has written numerous articles on Asian American literature, and co-edited half a dozen books.

DARRELL H.Y. LUM is a Chinese American writer born and raised in Hawaii. In 1978 he co-founded Bamboo Ridge Press, a non-profit literary small press, to publish work by and about Hawaii's people. He has published two collections of short stories, *Sun, Short Stories and Drama* (Bamboo Ridge Press, 1980) and *Pass On, No Pass Back* (Bamboo Ridge Press, 1990) which was named a National Book Award winner by the Association for Asian American Studies in 1992. He has had three plays produced by Kumu Kahua and the Honolulu Theater for Youth and received a National Endowment for the Arts fellowship in 1990.

CECILIA G. MANRIQUE is associate professor of political science at the University of Wisconsin - La Crosse and also serves on the faculty of the Women's Studies Department. She received her Ph.D. in political science from the University of Notre Dame, an M.A. in international affairs, and B.S. degrees in economics and computer science. She has published and done extensive work on integrating computers in courses, and in the field of international migration.

GABRIEL G. MANRIQUE is professor of economics at Winona State University, and also serves on the faculty of the international studies program. He received his Ph.D. in economics from the University of Notre Dame with a concentration on economic development, and in this regard, he has held fellowships at the U.S. Congress and the Overseas Development Council. His current research is on the relationship between third world economic development and international migration.

RORY J. ONG is an assistant professor at Washington State University where he teaches in the departments of English and Comparative American Cultures. He has published on the issue of the myth of the model minority, and is currently doing research on differences in Asian American discourses. His areas of interest include Asian American literature, cultural studies, and discourse theory.

DAVID PIEHL is an associate professor of mass communications at the University of Wisconsin - La Crosse. He earned his B.A. at the University of Illinois, Chicago (1968), an M.A. at Michigan State University (1969), and his Ph.D. at Northwestern University (1977). He has experience in both commercial radio and television. His research interest concerns the effects of the media on society.

MARSHA MOMOI PIEHL is director of personnel at Viterbo College, La Crosse, Wisconsin. She received her B.A. at the University of Illinois, Chicago. Her interests include minority studies, Asian culture and diversity issues.

RICHARD RUPPEL is an assistant professor of English at Viterbo College, LaCrosse - Wisconsin. He earned his A.B. at the University of Michigan (1976), his Masters in English at Duke University (1978), and his Ph.D. at the University of North Carolina (1988). Most of his research is in turn-of-the-century British colonial fiction, but he has recently turned his attention to contemporary popular culture.

LAURI SAGLE is from Hilo, Hawaii, on the rainy side of the Big Island. She is slowly getting her Ph.D. in American Studies at the University of New Mexico—a beautiful place, but with little rain, no ocean, and island-style sticky white rice in short supply. Lured into her field by Elvis Presley's siren song "Rock-a-Hula-Baby" from the movie *Blue Hawaii*, she is currently focusing on popular cultural portrayals of Hawaii.

MARIAN M. SCIACHITANO teaches composition at Washington State University. She is completing a Miami University dissertation on feminists of color and their relationship to the U.S. women's movement.

JOHN STREAMAS was born in Tokyo, and he is an instructor at Franklin University. He has published poems and has presented papers on closural epiphany and on Hisaye Yamamoto's stories.

QUN WANG is assistant professor of English at the University of Wisconsin - River Falls. He designed, implemented, and has been teaching "Asian American Literatures and Cultures" at River Falls. He has published several articles on the study of ethnic literature and culture. His articles on "Chinese American Literature" and "Japanese American Literature," and entries on "David Henry Hwang," "Chang-lin Tien," "Toshio Mori," and "David Mura" will be included in *The Asian American Encyclopedia*, which was published by Salem Press in Fall, 1993.

YUFENG WANG is currently an assistant professor of American history at Sinclair Community College, Dayton, Ohio. Ms. Wang is an A.B.D. at West Virginia University working toward completion of her Ph.D. degree. She received her undergraduate education at Nankai University, China, and completed her M.A. study at the College of William and Mary.

ANNETTE WHITE-PARKS, assistant professor of English at the University of Wisconsin - La Crosse, holds a Ph.D. in American studies and has authored various articles on Chinese American literature and culture. Her critical biography "Sui Sin Far: A Writer on the Chinese-Anglo Borders of North America," is forthcoming from the University of Illinois Press. Also forthcoming are: "Collected Writings by Sui Sin Far," co-edited with Amy Ling (University of Illinois Press); and "The Trickster in Turn-of-the-Century Literature," co-edited with Elizabeth Ammons (University of New England Press).

JUN XING is a Mellon Fellow in Asian American Studies at Emory University, Atlanta, Georgia. He received his Ph.D. in May, 1993 from the University of Minnesota. Currently, he is working on a book on Asian American independent cinema.

Index

2103